Demy 8vo, 514 pp. cloth, gilt lettered, 10/-; By Post, 10/6. Demy 4to, half Roxburgh, superior paper, gilt tops, Frontispiece and extra Plates, 30/-.

Nidderdale and th......

A YORKSH......

NUMEROUS I......

HARP......

Author of " The Craven and I......

A HAUNT OF THE NIGHTINGALE.

The work embraces an original and complete account, historical, scientific, and descriptive, of the whole valley of the Nidd from Nun Monkton to Whernside. Every town, village, and hamlet is graphically dilated upon; every notable building, every ancient monument, coat-of-arms, and heraldic bearing is noted and described in full detail.

The work also includes a complete record of the *Botany* of the Nidd Valley by Dr. F. Arnold Lees, F.L.S.; the *Mammalia, Birds, Fishes, &c.*, by Mr. Riley Fortune, F.Z.S., and the *Molluscan Fauna*, by Mr. W. Denison Roebuck, F.L.S.

Extended and highly favourable reviews have appeared in the *Times, Academy, Speaker, Daily Chronicle, Yorkshire Post, Leeds Mercury, Harrogate Advertiser, Nidderdale Herald, Craven Herald, Bradford Observer, Naturalist, &c.* In a three-page review of the book, the *Knaresborough Almanac* for 1895 observes that no writer, "Not even the renowned Hargrove, has sought out more original information than has Mr. Speight for his book. Everything in the valley of the slightest interest has been descriptively treated by a master hand."

LONDON: ELLIOT STOCK, 62, PATERNOSTER ROW, E.C.

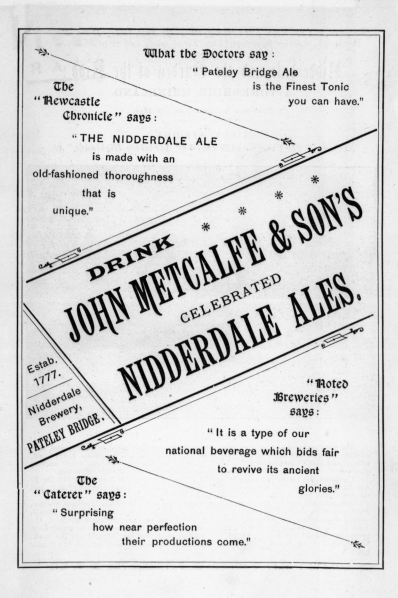

TRAMPS AND DRIVES

IN THE

CRAVEN HIGHLANDS.

ARRANGED FOR THE USE OF VISITORS,

BEING A NEW AND COMPLETE GUIDE TO THAT
ROMANTIC DISTRICT.

BY

HARRY SPEIGHT,

AUTHOR OF "THE CRAVEN AND NORTH-WEST YORKSHIRE HIGHLANDS;"
"NIDDERDALE AND THE GARDEN OF THE NIDD;"
"THROUGH AIREDALE FROM GOOLE TO MALHAM," ETC., ETC.

NUMEROUS ILLUSTRATIONS AND MAPS.

ENTERED AT STATIONERS' HALL.

LONDON : ELLIOT STOCK, 62, PATERNOSTER ROW, E.C.
1895.

PRINTED BY
G. F. SEWELL, 52, GODWIN STREET, BRADFORD, YORKS.

PREFACE.

SINCE the publication of my book, *The Craven and North-West Yorkshire Highlands*, three years ago, I have received many requests for a smaller and cheaper edition of the work, one more portable and usable for the purposes of a Guide. As the whole edition of the work named went rapidly out of print, I have met the suggestion by supplying in the present book a short, and in great measure a *new* history and descriptive account (interspersed with tradition and anecdote) of every town, village, and hamlet, with the surrounding country, between Skipton and Kirkby Lonsdale (inclusive),—following generally the picturesque escarpment of the Great Craven Fault, — and northwards as far as Wensleydale. This comprises the most interesting and romantic portion of Craven and bordering districts, and includes an area of little short of 500 square miles. It is a region of pure air and bracing breezes and of beauty and wonderment too,—abounding in crags and caves, and waterfalls, in grand sequestered glens and ample mountain scenery, where the naturalist of whatever creed, or lover of Nature, will find an abundance of good things.

Every object of interest along highway and byway and mountain track has been described, and the road to them and the distances have been given. While I may say that I am familiar with almost every yard of the ground comprised, and have visited every object mentioned, I must not forget to offer my best thanks to all who have in any way enabled me to make this little book, as I hope, trustworthy and complete.

H. SPEIGHT.

Bingley, Yorks., May, 1895.

From a Photograph by

A. Horner, Settle.

MALHAM TARN.

SKIPTON.

LEEDS, 24 m. BRADFORD, 17½ m. HARROGATE, 21 m. ILKLEY, 9 m.

TO picture Skipton at its most characteristic epoch we must go back a long stretch of time, when after the building of the Castle at the close of the Conqueror's reign, its feudal lords held almost regal power. Before the arrival of Robert de Romillé, its first Norman owner, the place was held by a few Saxon shepherds as its Domesday name *Sciptone* (A.S. *sceap*, a sheep) or *Town of Sheep*, implies. The Barons lived in great state at the Castle; they had a numerous train of attendants, and kept huntsmen, falconers, &c. ; they gave costly banquets, entertained royalty, formed royal alliances and otherwise intermarried with the best blood. The grant by King John, in 1204, of a weekly market and a bi-annual fair here promoted Skipton to a town of chief importance, and fit capital of Craven,—the *Craeg van*, or land of crags. It has always retained this distinctive title, and is the oldest chartered market town in Airedale, as well as one of the oldest in York-shire. About the time mentioned vast tracts of sheep walks began to be appropriated to the range of my lord's deer, and a long and blood-stained era of might against right set in. The hapless serf, with fear and trembling, stole beneath the castle walls, or made a detour believing he should lose his head if, meeting his mighty master, he should incur his displeasure, or mayhap be lynched for a frown ! Now, indeed, like the shadow of a cloud upon the rock this old sovereign glory has departed, and we stand in face of a mightier power, before the Castle portal looking up at its significant motto in stone,—
Desormais—*Hereafter !*

Even so it is now as in the days of Homer, when the great poet wrote,

> " Like leaves on trees the race of man is found,
> Now green in youth, now withering on the ground,
> Another race the following spring supplies,
> They fall successive, and successive rise,
> So generations in their course decay,
> So flourish these when those are passed away."

B

Of the Castle and Church (founded at the same period) we give a more particular account below. Skipton, now a busy extending town of some 12,000 inhabitants, and on the verge of incorporation, has several cotton spinning and weaving mills, the handsomest and largest, that of Messrs. John Dewhurst & Sons, Ld., employing about a thousand workpeople. The famous quarries of limestone at Hawbank employ also a large body of men, and there are besides two corn mills, tanneries, and important lead works. Among other principal buildings are the Town Hall, Temperance Hall, Grammar School, Christ Church, the Catholic Church of St. Stephen, the Convent, Presbytery, Mechanics' Institute (the old Tollbooth), several Nonconformist Chapels, &c. Dissent laid hold of Skipton at an early period. Fox, the Quaker founder, visited it in 1658. It was at Skipton and Carleton, about 1650, that the celebrated Rev. Oliver Heywood first preached in public, and no places suffered more severely than these during the religious persecutions that followed. Many took refuge in little accessible places where preaching houses were established, but where they were often found out and their adherents heavily fined or otherwise punished. A public Pillory stood opposite the Craven Bank in the High Street, until 1770, when it was taken down. All classes of criminals were put in this "wooden collar," which was not abolished by act of Parliament until the year of her present Majesty's accession. Near this Pillory in the High Street, — the principal thoroughfare in the town, leading to the church and castle,— was the old Market Cross, with its stone awning, and by it the Stocks. They were removed about the year 1840. Up to the end of last century sheep-stealers and others convicted of felony were publicly flogged at the Cross. This infliction was carried out almost within living recollection to the very letter of the Act, which ordained that the " bodie be beaten with whips until bloodie by reasone of such whipping." Whether the punishments of ear-cropping and slitting of nostrils existed here is doubtful, but there is evidence of an engine having been kept in the Tollbooth for branding felons. Another old-time punishment here was the Ducking Stool, once common in Airedale villages, for ' cooling ' female scolds. The custom of bull-baiting continued to the present century, and the ring that secured the bull-rope is kept at the *Bay Horse* Inn, opposite which is the flagstone to which the ring was fixed. According to the Court Leet accounts quoted by Mr. W. H. Dawson in his valuable History, the vendors of beef of bulls not previously baited were fined, an enactment that arose, we opine, from the belief that baiting, like game hunted, improved the flesh. Skipton has an old renown for its cattle fairs, and for the general excellent quality of the animals shewn. The celebrated 'Craven Heifer,' which has given name to many an inn, and whose bulky image (the animal weighed over 150 stones) figures on the notes of the Craven Bank, was reared on the rich sward of this parish, near Bolton Abbey.

Turning to the past history of Skipton, from the Romillés the barony, in 1152, came by marriage of Alice de Romillé to William Fitz Duncan, nephew of David, King of Scotland, and then through their daughter to the Earls of Albemarle, the last of whom, again a heiress, married in 1269, Edmund Plantagenet, second son of Henry III., surnamed Crutchback. Leaving no issue, the barony passed to the Crown,* and in 1311 was granted by Edward II. to Robert de Clifford, a descendant of a warlike family that joined the Conqueror, and was ultimately established at Clifford Castle, in Herefordshire. That frail beauty, the 'Fair Rosamond,' paramour of Henry II., and who is supposed to have been poisoned by his Queen at Woodstock, in 1177, was daughter of Walter de Clifford, whose son, Walter, was attainted for enforcing an officer who waited upon him, to "eate the King's Writ, waxe and all," for which offence he narrowly escaped confiscation of his whole patrimony. With the exception of two short intervals the lordship of Skipton has remained continuously with this

---

* That the castle and manor were Crown property early in the reign of Edward I. is evidenced by the following Royal grant made A.D. 1281. " Pro Hospitale Sanctæ Mariæ extra Bishopsgate London. Rex concessit Alienoræ matri suæ pro vita *Castrum et Manerium de Skipton*, Manerium de Pokelington in Com Ebor, Maneria de Middleton et de Dertforde in Com Kanciæ ac alia." *Vide Calendarium Rotul. Patent.* (Vol. 4, Record Office.)

family for over five hundred years. It is now vested in Baron Hothfield, and consists of some 13,000 acres.

The Castle. Of the original building erected by Robert de Romillé after the accession of William I. in 1066, nothing is believed to remain but the western doorway of the inner castle, (consisting of a treble semi-circular arch resting upon square piers), and possibly the north tower of the gateway and the dungeon. In the 12th century it appears to have been overthrown by the Scots, and remained in a semi-ruinous state until the installation of the first Lord Clifford in 1311. He set about the building of an impregnable fortress, as now existing, and which consists of seven massive round towers, connected by rectilinear apartments enclosing a spacious irregular quadrangle, and an inner one, known as the Conduit Court, in the centre of which is a large old yew tree. Upon foundations of solid rock, the thick, firmly-built walls on the north side are raised above a lofty natural precipice, whilst on the opposite side the great gateway with portcullis was protected by a deep moat, over which a draw-bridge was thrown. This Lord Clifford fell with many another English noble at the battle of Bannockburn in 1314. During the rule of his successor, Roger Lord Clifford, King Edward II. visited the castle in Oct. 1323, and again in 1324. In 1367 a royal license to enclose 500 acres of land for a park was obtained. John, ninth Lord Clifford, and a conspicuous character in Shakespeare's *Henry VI.*, lost his estates for the part he played on the side of the Lancastrians during the Wars of the Roses. His son Henry, the 'Shepherd Lord,' regained the Skipton lands on the accession of Henry VII. He took a principal command at the battle of Flodden, in 1513, and died at Barden Tower ten years later. Henry, eleventh Lord of Skipton, was created Earl of Cumberland. He made a fortunate alliance with the Lady Margaret Percy, and his son Henry, at the age of twenty, (1537) married the Lady Eleanor Brandon, daughter of the Duke of Suffolk, by Mary, Queen Dowager of France, and granddaughter of Henry VII. The ceremony took place in the Royal presence in the magnificent gallery of Skipton Castle, built specially with the Octagon Tower by the young knight's father for their reception. This august Lady Clifford during her residence at Skipton was made co-heir-presumptive to the Throne of England. Her son George, third Earl of Cumberland, (1558-1605), won the admiration and favour of Queen Elizabeth for his gallantry against the Spanish Armada. He had a strong love of adventure and made many voyages to the West Indies. He was one of the peers who sat in judgment on the ill-starred Mary Queen of Scots, whose Room in Skipton Castle is pointed out as the traditional place of her temporary incarceration. This Earl was father of Lady Anne, the celebrated Countess of Dorset, Pembroke, and Montgomery, who was born in the castle on Jan. 30th, 1590, and died at Brougham at the age of 85. It was she who repaired the castle after the siege in the Civil Wars. She was a noble-minded woman, of great Christian piety, and high accomplishments. She restored Barden Tower, and the tower, &c. of Skipton church, and she has left some interesting literary *Memorials*. The large family painting, now at Appleby Castle, contains her portrait with a biography.* By the hand of her daughter the estate descended to the present noble family of Tufton.

Skipton Castle has sustained two important sieges, first during the insurrection of 1536 known as the Pilgrimage of Grace, when it was the only stronghold in the West Riding that held out for the King ; and again a long three years' siege during the Civil War, which terminated in its surrender to the Parliamentary army on Dec. 21st, 1645. The story of the Siege has been often told, but the Terms of Surrender of the Castle to Col. Richard Thorneton, Commander-in-chief of the opposing forces, have only recently come to light.

Appended are the ARTICLES agreed upon :—

1. That Sir John Mallory with all the rest of the Officers, Gentlemen, and Souldiers, shall march out betwixt this and Tuesday next before twelve of the clocke, surrendering the Castle, with all the Armes, Ordnance, and Ammunition, without any prejudice done to them, with all the goods and provisions whatsoever in the said Castle, not to be purloyned or imbezzled, and whosoever shall be found offending after the sealing of these Articles for the misdisposing of goods, shall be given up to Justice and treble satisfaction to be given for the goods so conveyed by the said party, if he be worth it, if not, then to be made good by the Governour.

2. That all prisoners now in the Castle, of what quality or condition soever, shall be set at liberty upon the sealing of these Articles.

3. That after the signing of these Articles two such Officers as Col. Thorneton shall appoint shall be admitted to go into the Castle, and see the evidence houses lockt up and sealed, and have an accompt of all spare Armes and Ammunition, and such a guard at such a time as Col. Thorneton shall appoint to goe in.

4. That the Governour, Officers, and Souldiers of Horse and Foot with their Horses and proper Arms as to horse and foot, that march out accordingley to the Honour of a Souldier, (viz.) with Colours flying, Trumpets sounding, Drums beating, Matches lighted at both ends, and Bullets in their mouthes, every Trooper and every Foot Souldier three charges of powder, and the Officers of Commission to march with their wearing apparell that is properly their owne in their Port-mantles, and not have anything taken from them, and that the Common Souldiers shall not march away with any Bag and Baggage.

5. That all Gentlemen not in the condition of a Souldier have their horses and swords, and be allowed to march to the King or his Garrisons, or their own homes, and be protected in either condition as they shall make choyce of.

---

* For an admirably penned story of her life *see* Hartley Coleridge's *Northern Worthies*.

6. That all Officers and Souldiers of Horse and Foot, Gentlemen, Townesmen, or other persons whatever belonging to this Garrison, shall have liberty, conduct and protection to go to his Majesty, or such of his Garrisons as shall be agreed of.

7. That all Officers, Souldiers, Gentlemen, Townesmen or others desiring to goe and live at home, shall have free leave there to remain under the protection of the Parliament.

8. That all Souldiers or other persons that are sick or hurt, and not able to goe to their homes or other places where they desire, shall have leave to stay here at Skipton, and shall be allowed necessary accomodation untill it please God they shall recover, and then to have Passes upon their desires to goe to their home or to such of his Majestie's next Garrisons they shall make choyce of.

9. That all women and Children within this Garrison be suffered to go with or to such as they shall desire to their own habitations.

10. That all the hangings and other goods given in by Inventory to be the Countess of Pembroke's shall be there secured by themselves and not made sale of untill the Lady of Pembroke bee made acquainted therewith, but to be prized with the rest.

11. That all the evidences and writings whatever belonging to the Countess of Pembroke or to the Countess of Corke in any of the Evidence Houses of this Castle, shall not be looked into by any, untill both the Countesses be acquainted therewith, and for that end that two Moneths time for notice to be given them, and the Kayes to be delivered to Col. Thorneton, who is interested with them in the meantime.

12. That all possible care be taken to preserve the Woods and Parks belonging to both the Ladies.

13. That those that intend to march to his Majesty or any of his Garrisons march but six miles a day, and free Quarter during all their March, and that a sufficient Convoy be allowed them, and may conduct them to Nottingham, and from thence to one of these foure Garrisons as shall be there named by them to the Commander in Chiefe of the Convoy, viz., Banbury, Worcester, Hereford, or Litchfield.

14. That if any persons belonging to this Garrison shall misdemean themselves in the march, it shall not extend further than the parties offending, upon whom Justice shall be done according to the fault committed.

15. That if any Officers or Souldiers shall be necessitated to buy horses, or anything else in their march, shall have liberty for that purpose, and after payment enjoyment thereof during the protection of the Convoy.

These Articles are agreed of us who were appointed to treate for the rendition of Skipton Castle, in the behalf of Sir John Mallory, Govenour of Skipton.

FERDINANDO LEIGH.   FRAN. COBB.
JOHN TEMPEST.   MICAH TOMPSON.

The Castle walls are in some places ten to eleven feet thick. A peculiar feature of its interior arrangements, is that no two rooms in it are on the same level, whilst each is provided with two doors for egress in case of danger. On the left of the court yard is the castle dungeon, a gloomy apartment 16 ft. by 8 ft., and 9 ft. high, in which it may be guessed that many a luckless prisoner has grown pale within its damp and cheerless environment. Many of the lower apartments of the castle were used for storage of provisions and for cattle lairs in times of siege. The Banqueting Hall, facing the court-

SKIPTON CASTLE.

yard, is lighted by three windows, and is a fine apartment about 50 ft. in length. Adjoining it are the Drawing Room, Muniment Room, and Mary Queen of Scots room. On the right of the archway is the Shell House, so called from one of its rooms being decorated with sea shells, trophies of the buccaneering Earl of Cumberland. On the west side a narrow staircase conducts to 'Fair Rosamond's Chamber.' This is in the oldest part of the castle, and her visit or birth here (as is traditionally reported) must have taken place long before the Cliffords came into possession, as already stated, in 1311. In several of the rooms, and notably in the State Chamber, are preserved many specimens of antique furniture and curious old tapestry. Many relics, including paintings, have, however, been transferred to Appleby. Visitors, we may add, are shewn through the Castle after 9 a.m. on application at the Custodian's Office.

The Parish Church. Founded probably towards the end of the Conqueror's reign. From the foundation of their monastery at Embsay to the Dissolution it formed an endowment of the Canons of

Bolton. The present building, of different periods, comprises nave with clerestory, chancel, side aisles, and gallery at west end. The only portion left of the original Norman church is the sedilia of four stone seats, with pointed arches and cylindrical columns, in the south wall of the nave. From appearances in the stonework the whole chancel of three aisles has been added to the original building eastward, probably about 1483, for in that year Richard III., who, when Duke of Gloucester, occasionally resided at the castle, decreed a payment for the repair of this church. The handsome flat oak roof is also referable to this period. In 1655 the church was beautifully restored by the able Countess of Pembroke, whose initials A.P. appear on many of the windows. The elegant oak screen, originally surmounted by a rood-loft, is said to have been the gift of the monks of Bolton. Over the gallery is a curious 'poker painting,' burnt on sycamore wood, representing the "Angel and Shepherds of Bethlehem." It is the work of a native artist named George Smith, who also executed in 1798 the painting of the Royal Arms hung above the sedilia. The church contains many monuments and inscriptions of interest, a splendid reredos, and some admirable illuminated windows by Capronnier, of Brussels. There are three tombs of the Cliffords, Earls of Cumberland, with brasses, restored by the Duke of Devonshire in 1867 at a cost of £1000. The vault was opened in 1803 for inspection by Dr. Whitaker, who describes the appearance of the bodies in his "History of Craven."* In 1854 the floor of the church, beneath which hundreds of interments have been made, was covered with nine inches of concrete. From the tower, 'curfew' bell is tolled nightly at eight o'clock, and the mediæval custom of burial by torchlight was only discontinued early in the present century.

Castle Woods. This beautiful domain that once formed part of the private grounds of the early Cliffords, is now generously open to the public. The woods clothe the sides of a deep and picturesque dell, with a stream in the bottom, and paths in various directions. The trees are more remarkable for their altitude than for their girth, being closely planted on the steep acclivities, amongst them the pine tribe, which have a peculiarly vitalizing influence on the air, and thereby enhance the salubrity of a place, do very well here. A nice round (1½-2 hrs.) through the woods is to follow the Embsay road (½ m.) to the Bailey Cottage on *l.* A fine old rosemary tree 8 ft. high is a noteworthy object in the garden here. Follow the path along the top about ¾ m., descending over the footbridge, where the stream is seen foaming over low rocks, and ascend *l.* along the opposite side of glen (a way hardly practicable in wet weather), emerging over a step-style into the lane, whence *l.* 20 yds. and over style on *l.* up fields to the top when a splendid **View,** the best of any around Skipton, is had. Below the spectator lies the whole town, with its two

---

* Similarly, in 1813, the vault and body of the unfortunate monarch, Charles I., whose cause the Cliffords ever heroically upheld, were examined by Sir Henry Halford and other gentlemen. The remains were tolerably entire, and in good condition, amidst the gums and resins used for their preservation.

churches at opposite extremites, forming from this point an irregular crescent. Southwards we see Farnhill Crag, Rumbalds Moor, Cononley Moor, &c. ; westwards the ascending roads to Colne, over Elslack and Carleton moors, whilst north of these Pendle Hill, with Easington Fell beyond Clitheroe, rear their majestic elevated lines on the horizon. North again is all the range of Flasby Fell, and to the east we see Hawe Bank (Skipton Rock), Embsay Crag, and the road to Barden, with Beamsley Beacon beyond. As this beautiful panorama can be viewed by a walk of 5-7 mins. from Skipton church it is worth seeking on its own account. Opposite the *Royal Oak* ascend the hill to the gas lamp above the Wesleyan Chapel, whence turn *l.* to the field top.

As affording some idea of the natural vegetable productions of this part of Airedale we here furnish, by the help of Messrs. T. W. Edmondson and L. Rotheray, members of the Craven Naturalists' Society, a list of the more interesting species occurring in these woods. The soil is calcareous.

Trees. Oak, ash, elm, sycamore, birch, beech, hornbeam, alder, horse-chestnut, hawthorn, bird-cherry, holly, elder, mt.-ash, goat-willow, crack-willow, black poplar, yew, Scotch fir, and four or five other species of pine.

Shrubs. Blackthorn, guelder-rose, dog-rose, honeysuckle, ivy, wayfaring-tree, hazel, raspberry, dewberry, bramble, broom, woody-nightshade, &c.

Flowers. Wood anemone, crowfoot (*R. auricomus* and *bulbosus*), winter-cress, rock-cress, bitter-cress (*C. amara*), whitlow-grass, stitchwort (*S. Graminea*), St. John's wort (*H. perforatum* and *hirsutum*), wood-sorrel, bitter-vetch (*L. macrorrhizus*), water-avens, alternate and opposite-leaved golden-saxifrage, gt. hairy willow-herb, enchanter's nightshade, wood-sanicle, moschatel, cross-wort, sweet wood-ruff, burdock (*A. minus*), wall-lettuce, hawk-weed (*H. boreale*), hawk's-beard (*C. paludosa*), yellow goat's beard, cowslip, comfrey, giant bell-flower, sweet marjoram, bugle, yellow pimpernel, wood-rush, early purple and spotted orchis, herb-paris or true-love, wild basil, cuckoo-pint or wake robin, yellow flag, tway-blade, greater toothwort, scorpion-grass (*M. Sylvatica* and *cæspitosa*), wood-betony, blue-bell, &c.

Ferns. *Lastreæ filix-mas, Athyrium filix fœmina,* var. *rhœticum, Polypodium vulgare* and *robertianum, Scolopendrium vulgare, Polystichium aculeatum,* &c.

Skipton-Rock Quarry. This is one of the 'sights' of Craven, and especially to the geologist, as shewing the extraordinary stratification on the north side of the great Skipton anticlinal. The quarry is reached by entering a stile about ¼ m. on the Harrogate road, and thence by a cottage at its west end. This portion is not now worked, and has recently been planted by the Castle authorities. The quarry, which is leased by the Leeds and Liverpool Canal Co., extends for about 1000 yds., and at its greatest elevation is about 260 ft. high. The limestone is largely used for the repair of roads, and for the smelting of iron, &c. The beds at the west end have a dip W.N.W. of 40° to 50°, increasing almost vertically eastwards. As much as 20,000 tons of rock, we are told, have been dislodged by one blast. The stone is conveyed in waggons from the quarry by an inclined tram, worked by steel-wire ropes from the engine-house at Embsay, down to a branch of the canal behind Skipton Castle to the boats. As much as 40 tons (in 8 waggons) can thus be lowered at once ; but before 1836 the stone was carted through the town to the canal.

Craven Baths and Sulphur Wells. There is nothing of much visual interest here now, but the spot was formerly a noted and favourite resort. Pass the Devonshire Hotel and across Draughton beck by the old Grammar School, and then along the Addingham old road about ¼ m. to first house on *l.* The sulphur spring rises at the dip of the hill, where is a pleasantly-wooded dingle through which a stream runs that formerly supplied the baths. These consisted of plunge, shower, and swimming baths, and were organised by the late Dr. Dodgson about fifty years ago. Around the Well House opposite were pleasure grounds maintained by subscription. Two or three years ago the well fell into disuse, and is now flagged over. In dry seasons it was said to have a very disagreeable smell. Its constituent gases are sulphuretted hydrogen and carbonic acid, and solid contents, carbonate of iron, sulphate of magnesia, muriate of soda, and muriate of lime and iodine. A little higher up the road are three reservoirs that supply Skipton with water.

The visitor will find Skipton a capital centre for many delightful walking and driving tours, and there is excellent accommodation at the various hotels in the town.

'BUSES PLY BETWEEN

Skipton and Grassington, (10 m.) **and Buckden,** (18½ m.) *Daily,* (Mail). Leaves S. (Post Off.) 6-0 a.m., arr. B. 9-20 a.m. On Sunday leaves S., 8-45 a.m., arr. B. 12-5 p.m. On *Mon.. Wed.,* and *Sat.* leaves S. at 3-0 p.m. for Buckden, and 4-50 p.m. for Grassington only. **Return** (Mail) from B., 3-40 p.m., arr. S. 6-40 p.m. On Sunday leaves 2-0 p.m., arr. 5-0 p.m. On *Mon., Wed.,* and *Sat.* leaves B. 6-15 a.m., arr. S. 9-15 a.m. From Grassington, 7-30 a.m. daily. Single fares : Grassington, 1s. 6d. ; Buckden, 3s.

Skipton and Broughton (3½ m.) **East Marton** (5½ m.) **Horton Lane Ends** (9 m.) **Gisburn** (11 m.) Daily, (Mail). Leaves S. 6-0 a.m., arr. G. 7-45 a.m. On Sunday leaves S. 8-45 a.m., arr. G. 10-30 a.m. **Return** (Mail) from G. 4-15 p.m., arr. S. 6-0 p.m. Sunday leaves 3-10 p.m., arr. 4-50 p.m. Single fares : Broughton, 6d. ; East Marton, 9d. ; Horton Lane Ends, 1s. 2d. ; Gisburn, 1s. 6d.

Skipton and Bolton Abbey P.O. (6 m.) (Mail) week-days only. Leaves S. 6-0 a.m., arr. B. 7-15 a.m. **Return** from B. 5-0 p.m., arr. S. 6-20 p.m. *From Nov. 1st to March 31st, leaves B. at 4-0 p.m.* Single fare, 1s.

In the season (on week-days) Messrs. Cook & Son issue day-tickets from **Leeds and Bradford** by rail to **Skipton,** and thence by conveyance by any of the following routes : (1) **To Barden Tower,** Appletreewick, Burnsall, and return by Grassington and Rylstone. (2) **To Malham** and back by Eshton and Airton. (3) **To Kilnsey Crag** by Threshfield, returning through Grass Woods and Grassington. Return fare for any route 5s.

EXCURSIONS FROM SKIPTON.

Skipton to Broughton, 3½ m., **Elslack,** 5 m. Crossing the Aire bridge two miles out of Skipton, through a rich open country, just after passing the old *Bull* inn (3 m.), a fine view of **Broughton Hall,** occupying a low warm situation is bad. The present building dates from 1597, and was anciently called Gilliot's Place. The knightly family of Gilliot were settled at Broughton at an early period, and their name occurs in the oldest charters. In A.D. 1300 we find John Gyliot (*milit*) witness to a deed relating to lands at Glusburn, and again in 1340 Peter Gilliott occurs in a quit-claim dated from the same place. In the reign of Edward II. the Broughton estate was granted to John Tempest, of Bracewell, and since 1406, when Roger Tempest married Katherine, sole heiress of Peter Gilliott, Broughton has been their property and residence. The late Sir Chas. Robt. Tempest, who was High Sheriff in 1839, was created Baronet in 1841, and died unmarried in 1865. He devised his estates at Broughton in Yorkshire and Coleby in Lincolnshire to his great-nephew, Henry A. J. Tempest, who was born in 1863, and died in April, 1891, and whose father, Sir Chas. Hy. Tempest, Bart., is the present occupant. The Hall was some time the residence of the late Chas. Semon, Esq., founder of the Semon Convalescent Home at Ilkley, in 1874. Immediately on passing the Hall, a road on *l.* crosses the bridge before the lodge gates, which may be followed up a shady lane on to the fields direct to **Broughton Church.** This is a Norman foundation, but nothing of the original structure is believed to remain but the doorway and font. Whitaker gives a list of the vicars from A.D. 1247. On the south side of the present building is an old stone with a rude cross enclosing two minor crosses. The tombs of the Moorhouses, of Elslack, Englands of Bingley, and Ayrtons of Rylstone, who were of one family, lie close together on the left of the path before the church porch. Near here are several very old dated gravestones, and one (dateless) bears the device of a sword. The interior of the church contains several lengthy monumental inscriptions, in Latin, to the Tempest family.

The tourist may follow the rural church lane (the old Roman road to Ribchester) past the White House to **Elslack,** or leave the lane by a path through the fields by the railway side to the station. Hereabouts he will see traces of the furrows made when the now green pastures once smiled with corn. The manor of *Eleslac* (as it is written in Domesday) was in Henry III.'s time a possession of the

Norman family of De Altaripa, and afterwards of the Malhams,
Royalist officers in the Civil Wars. **Elslack Hall,** their seat
(now the property of Mr. Lane Fox), had, in Dodsworth's time, a
dungeon, which he describes as having a "hole in the top to let
folks down, and no door." There are two stones on different parts
of the building inscribed R B 1672, doubtless meant to commemorate
the restoration of the hall by its then proprietor, Robt. Benson,
father of the first Lord Bingley, who had acquired it from the
Malhams. At the east end are two old mullions of six lights, and on
the west side are the perfect remains of a moat. Some years ago a
human skeleton was found behind one of the panels in the interior,
but how or why it came there is not known. The house is now
occupied as a farm by Mr. R. Horner. The **White House,** already
mentioned, was the home of the Moorhouse family from about the
period of the Rebellion of 1745 until 1876, when old Mr. John
Moorhouse, having no issue, retired with his wife to Cowling. They
farmed about 100 acres, including the wood, and glebe lands at
Broughton. The family came from Skibeden, where they were
settled at the time of the Civil Wars, in which they took an active
part. For fully six centuries they have resided in the liberty of
Skipton ; three of this family being enrolled in the Poll Tax of
Richard II., A.D. 1379. There are several memorials of them in
Skipton Church. Adjoining the beck close by is the **School-house,**
for many years tenanted by a worthy veteran, Mr. Enoch Hall. He
served in the Peninsular wars, and was also one of the guards of
Napoleon at St. Helena. Ultimately he came to Elslack, where for
many long years he taught the village school, giving plums and
delicious gooseberries from his well-kept garden as prizes to his apt
scholars. He died in June, 1883, in his 90th year. Often during our
many weeks' stay at this place have we chatted with the old man,
who was full of racy anecdote and stories of his early soldier life
abroad. When newspapers were scarce the late Mr. Ed. Baines (Sir
Edward's father) used to come over here occasionally, and bring
with him a copy of the *Leeds Mercury* for an old Chartist named
Cooper, living up on the moor side, and who was a particularly
intelligent man, and the only one who took a paper in these parts.
During the French wars people came to him for many miles round
to hear the news. On one occasion an anxious wiseacre from Cracoe
passed a night at his house, and on the following day, when Mr.
Baines arrived with the newspaper, it was reported that Napoleon
had reached Cracoe, at which the old man was in a terrible plight.
He threw up his arms, exclaiming, "Oh ! my dear wife and bairnies,
they will all be murdered when I get hame !" But when he did get
'hame,' his delight knew no bounds when, seeing his family all right,
it was explained that Cracow in Russia, was meant ! But he vowed
he would never leave home again. At that time the guards were
stationed on Elslack Moor (*see Airedale*). Near the station is a hill
(cut through by the railway) called Burwins, on which there was
a castle, conjectured by Dodsworth to be Danish, but which Whitaker
believes may have been Roman. Not a vestige of the building now

remains. But the name is certainly indicative of a Saxon structure, from A. S. *Bur*, a strong house or dwelling, and *win*, a victory, from which it may be inferred that it was a fortified outpost or castle erected by a conquering army as a defence to the surrounding communities ; the populous Saxon settlement at Carleton, and likewise Skipton, being at no great distance. *Apropos*, it may be observed that there is a street in Norwich leading up to the ancient Castle, called Ber Street, and in Leeds (with its traditional castle) there is Boar Lane, anciently Bur Lane.

Skipton to Marton, 5½ m. ; **Gisburn,** 11 m. By road past Broughton Hall (3 m.) as last route, and Crickle Ho. (5 m.). In a field below this house is a large sulphur spring, which is mentioned in *Bray's Tour*, 1783. The spot was considered dangerous, and is now covered in. The water upon analysis was found deficient in saline matter, and consequently little benefitting to the human subject, but by bathing it is said to have been very efficacious for the cure of mange in dogs. There is a similar spring at Broughton, near a row of dwellings called after it Sulphur Well Houses. About **East Marton** (inn) the land is nicely wooded and undulating, and the canal intersecting the east end of the village, winds under the picturesque old church. On the village green is a large plane tree, encircled with a good seat. From the rising ground the Weets, above Barnoldswick, and Pendle Hill form an attractive view. On the south side of the church are the remains of a moat that once surrounded the manor house of the Martons, now represented by the family at Capon Wray, near Lancaster. Pedigrees of these mesne lords, and of the Hebers, to whom the estates came by purchase, are given by Whitaker in the *History of Craven.* The church is a venerable edifice of Norman date, built upon a foundation probably destroyed by the Danes.* It has a low embattled tower, with sundial inscribed " Dono Ant. Hartley, 1714." On the north and east walls there is some evident Norman stonework of the 'herring-bone' type. The interior consists of nave, divided by a row of octagonal pillars supporting pointed arches, and chancel, with flat plaster roof. It is fitted entirely with oak, and contains interesting memorials to the families of Roundell, Heber, Stockdale, and Currer, of Gledstone, as well as tablets of arms. In the belfry is a rude stone font (believed to be Saxon) placed upon three short cylindrical supports of later date. The coloured windows are by Taylor (late O'Connor), of London. Proceeding hence to **West Marton** (1 m.), at the turn of the road (11 m. to Settle) a pleasing view is had of the white

---

* On this supposition the church, like many others known to have existed before the Conquest, is not mentioned in *Domesday*. Moreover, no official injunction was laid on the jurors at this Survey to return the churches. Ellis, in his Introduction to Domesday Book, says the mention of them, if made at all, was likely to be irregular. "The whole number returned," he observes, "only amounts to a few more than 1700 ; one only can be found in Cambridgeshire, and none in Lancashire (between the Ribble and the Mersey), Cornwall, or even Middlesex, the seat of the metropolis. It is acknowledged that the Conqueror destroyed 36 churches to make the New Forest, and therefore churches must have been plentiful."

gleaming front of Malham Cove, with Ryeloaf and Kirkby Fell, and
N.N.W. the top of Giggleswick Scars and half the height of Ingleborough. There is a neat well-to-do look about this picturesque
little place. It possesses a capital village Institute, with a spacious
lecture or ball-room, library, &c. By the road side is an admirably
arranged fountain, 'for man, horse, and dog,' a Jubilee gift of
Mrs. Roundell. Marton was anciently much more populous and
important than it is now. In the Poll Tax of A.D. 1379, among the
76 towns and villages comprised in the wapentake of Staincliffe,
Marton ranks *second* in the amount (35s. 4d.) contributed. Bolton
coming first with 48s. 4d., and Skipton third with 35s. Some of the
houses are of old date. One we notice is inscribed   B
another   S   and another G— Yew Tree House, AM 1703
so called IM 1711, from a large 1690, old yew in its garden, was
the family seat of the Hartleys, and afterwards of the Roundells
before the erection of Gledstone Hall about a century ago. In 1739
by the marriage of Danson Roundell, Esq., D.L., of Marton, with
Ellen, heiress of Christopher Hartley, Esq., the Marton estate of the
latter was thus transmitted. Marton Hall, the seat of the Hebers for
upwards of two centuries, lies pleasantly sheltered amid wood. It
had once a fine deer park attached. The building is 'rough cast,'
and has a spacious gateway and ponderous oak door that opens into a
porch and court-yard, which give the place a very strong and castle-
like look. " No house," observes Whitaker in the *History of Craven*,
" mentioned within the compass of this work, and in the present
generation, has been connected with greater virtues or equal talents."
Of this family was the celebrated Bishop Heber, " the Christian, the
scholar, and the poet," born at Malpas in 1783, and died in India in
1826. The hall here was bought by Thomas Heber, of Elslack,
about 1535.

Passing Yew Tree Ho. the tourist may now proceed by way of
Gledstone, a delightful walk, and shortly regain the Gisburn road.
In descending the hollow, and overlooking the Mere House,* Malham
Cove, and Gt. Whernside are well seen. The rich gardens and glass-
houses of **Gledstone Hall** (C. S. Roundell, Esq., J.P.) are now
passed, with their choice stock of fruit and flowers. A speciality
among the latter is a splendid assortment of chrysanthemums, which
have taken many prizes. In the year 1890 a remarkably fine pumpkin
weighing 84 lbs. was grown here. Taking the first road on *l.* in view
of the hall, a pleasant country walk brings us on to the main roa l
again by Crook Ho. and over Monk Bridge, probably so called from
the monks of Kirkstall (who owned Bracewell church, &c.) having
been the original builders of it. Here a road diverges to Bracewell
(1 m.) and opposite is Horton Bridge (Lane Ends). **Horton** is
mentioned in *Domesday*, but the old hall and manor-house are now
both tenanted as farms, and possess nothing of special interest. 2 m
hence is **Gisburn**, (pop. 530), a pleasant, old-fashioned market

* Marton is supposed to be *Mere town*, from the low grounds having once been
covered with water.

town on the old coach-road from York to Liverpool, (and now noted for its sheep and cattle fairs). In monkish days it was the property of the Abbots of Sallay. The manor was purchased, 13th Elizabeth, by the family of Lister, afterwards Lords Ribblesdale, who now own some 5-6000 acres here. Gisburn Park, their seat, was formerly noted for its fine herd of wild cattle, descendants of the indigenous race which once ranged the Lancashire forests. The animals were hornless and of a creamy white, with the exception of the tips of their noses, ears, and feet. The race died out about thirty years ago. The house, situated upon an eminence near the confluence of the Ribble and Stockbeck, contains, amongst other things, some notable paintings, and an ancient drinking-horn (of buffalo) supported by three silver feet, and inscribed in Latin : "He that fights against three shall lose two." The park-lodge is a handsome piece of Gothic architecture, ornamented with figures, &c., designed by the late Lord Ribblesdale. The church here is probably not older than the time of Henry VII., although of Norman origin, and given in the reign of Henry II. to the Nunnery of Stainfield, co. Lincoln. It contains some good stain-glass, &c., and is well worth inspection.

Skipton to Flasby over the Fell, 5½ m. A trip for dry weather only. Take the Rylstone road to the 2-mile stone from Skipton (4 m. to Cracoe). Just above is Crookrise Ho., where permission should be obtained to cross the fell. Make then for the depression between the north hill and Sharper, whence the view in every direction is grand. There is little doubt that when sufficiently clear, the white scar of Malham Cove might be seen from this depression from the hills about Sawood, Wadsworth, and Haworth, as well as from Pendle Hill. Looking N., we have Gt. Whernside, Fountains Fell, Ingleborough, &c. ; to the S., Denholme, Haworth, and Boulsworth moors, and S.W., Pendle Hill. To the S E. Culling-worth and Bingley moors, with the Druids' Altar, and a grand sweep of Airedale from Farnhill Crag up towards Hellifield. E. is Embsay Crag, and N.E. Norton Tower, Rylstone Fell, and the little limestone town of Grassington, with the white road over Grassington Moor backed by the great Wham. Follow the wall down through a gateway, and straight away down Black Lane (a narrow miry way) to the beck at Flasby. The beck may be crossed and an ascent made to an old house inscribed RMO 1685, whence a charming walk may be had by way of Hetton to Rylstone (2 m.), or a return can be made to Gargrave by Eshton Bridge, (an ancient structure mentioned in A.D. 1314) 2 m. From Flasby there is also a path over Scarnber Fell by the new reservoir on to the Hetton and Winterburn road for Malham, &c. Flasby Hall (Capt. J. N. Preston) lies quietly and charmingly embosomed in deep woods. A chapel oratory and burial-ground appear anciently to have existed here, from the number of human bones that have been dug up. Possibly it was one of the 'Seven Churches' of Gargrave traditionally destroyed by the Scots.

Skipton to Bolton Abbey, 6 m. Follow the Knaresborough (24 m.) road past the Castle, which gradually ascends to High Skibeden (2 m.), where the hard, blackish limestone on the south side of the long anticlinal ridge is well observed in a quarry north of

the highway. Here the rocks dip sharply to the south-east, or in a precisely contrary direction to those described at Haw Bank (*see* p. 13). The farm here has been in the occupation of Mr. Robt. Birtwhistle for about half a century past. The Birtwhistles are descendants of the old yeomanry class, and have been settled in Craven for ages. In 1478 we find W. Britwysall installed vicar of Kildwick and Skipton. Kildwick being the mother church, Skipton was then, and up to 1843, served by a curate. The tourist now descends to the railway, which here attains, between Skipton and Ilkley, its highest level (513 ft.) On this side the bridge is a 'Holy Well,' a common resort of pilgrims in monkish days, and the brook issuing from it is now called Helliwell beck. At the four lane ends a turn *l.* is made, when soon the Wharfedale hills appear, with Beamsley Beacon occuping the centre of vision. The little village of Draughton is seen away up on *r.*, and a descent is made past Bolton Abbey sta., near which, at the Hambleton Quarry, is a grand exposure of the carboniferous or mountain limestone, traversed by veins of calcite, and contorted, as is often the case along this remarkable anticlinal, in the most curious fashion. On the east side the beds dip north-west at an angle of about 40 degrees, and at this end form one of the finest examples of a trough, or synclinal, that is to be found anywhere. To the west the beds appear vertical, showing the immense lateral pressure they sustained during formation. The well-known walk hence to Bolton Woods needs no description.

Skipton to Draughton, 3¼ m., **(for Bolton Abbey).** From the High Street, on Otley Street, and along the Otley road, 2 m., where Skibeden quarry and farm (above) are seen, and up on *r.* Close House, for more than a century from the time of Queen Elizabeth the home of the Moorhouse family (*see* p. 15), above which, under Rumbalds Moor, at an altitude of 1000 ft., runs the old Roman road and former coach road from Skipton to Addingham. Between our road and Close House is a line of thorns which marks the old and rather narrow thoroughfare constructed in 1802 from Skipton to Bolton, which crossed the present highway at the 'Half-way Ash' (near the 2 m. to Skipton mile-stone) and continued through the fields to Draughton, and by the school-house under Haw Pike to Bolton Bridge. We emerge at Draughton opposite the wonderful Quarry and small Wesleyan Chapel. Views of this famous Draughton Quarry have frequently been engraved for illustrating the phenomena of contorted strata in geological text-books, &c. The section here worked occupies a basin-like cavity open to the north, and at the east end forms a double anticlinal ; the limestone dipping sharp N. and S. at an angle of 80°, resembling the pointed arch of some majestic fane. It is a site of extraordinary geological interest, which as we have remarked, has often been described. Formerly the stone was burned for lime on the spot and used by local farmers for the land. Just above is the *Matchless* Inn, a name that will readily be conjectured to be derived from the natural aspect of the above quarry. This, however, is not the case; it was so-called from a splendid entire horse, which earned in a single season (now about a century ago), sufficient for its owner to purchase the property and build the inn which has since stood here. The old whitewashed Manor House at the low end of the village was built by the

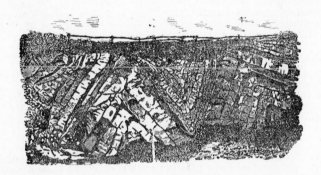

DRAUGHTON QUARRY,—CONTORTED LIMESTONE.

Wainmans of Carr Head. Over the door appear the initials and date R M W 1669. There is a thoroughly rustic charm about this little country place. It is partly wooded, undulating, and tolerably well sheltered ; on the mossy walls we have noticed the pretty toad-flax continue in flower until the snows of a November day have extinguishd the tiny blossoms.

Skipton to Embsay, 2 m., **Barden,** 7 m. By the Bailey road past the Castle and forward between Flasby Fell and Haw Bank (*see* p. 13), From the *Cavendish Arms* the road ascends through **Embsay,** and at the *Elm Tree* Inn diverges *r.* up to the church. Opposite the church a field path shortens the road to Eastby (3 m.) Embsay (in Domesday, *Embesie*) formed part of the ancient Saxon Cure of Earl Edwin, whose seat was at Bolton. The Augustinian Priory founded here 21st Henry I. by William de Meschines, lord of Egremond, &c., and Cecily, daughter of Robert de Romillé, his wife, was endowed with the village of Embsay and the churches of Skipton and Carleton. To these original benefactions were added by Cecily de Romillé (only daughter of the above), who adopted her mother's name, the "village of Kildewic, with the mill, and soc, or

C

suit thereof, and the Hagh* (of Crookeris), and all the premises of Aspsiche from the boundaries of Fern-Hill to those of Silesden to Aspsiche, and following Aspsiche to the river Ayre."† The Priory was translated to Bolton about A.D. 1154, according to the well-known tradition of that "endless sorrow" to Cecily de Romillé caused by the loss of her only son, the "Boy of Egremond," in the Strid, a story which is in the main a fiction, as he was a witness to the charter of translation. A charter for the holding of a fair at Embsay was granted by Edward I., A.D. 1305, when the Canons of Bolton had a rent of the mill here with the tolls. In 1318, during a most unsparing raid by the Scots, their grange was destroyed. For some centuries after the removal of the Priory to Bolton, a church was continued at Embsay, but after the Dissolution of the monastery in 1540, it appears to have lapsed into ruins. Interments, however, continued to be made here until a late date. Embsay Kirk (Capt. John Hodgson), which occupies the site, was built about 1780 by Wm. Baynes, a lawyer, and a relative of John Baynes Garforth, of Steeton Hall, and doubtless much of the material of the old priory was utilized in its erection. Possibly some of the under portions and out-buildings may have been restored upon the original structure. The outer wall of the vaulted cellar is about a yard thick, and the arched roofs of several out-houses contain stones, which appear from the masons' marks, to have occupied different positions to what they do at present. No plan of the Abbey has yet been made, nor have the foundations been fully excavated. In 1889, whilst cutting a walk at the east end of the house portions of three walls were discovered, all running east and west; the two north ones coming to an angle at their eastern extremities, and the south and middle walls forming a passage about two yards wide. Just below this south wall were found several human skeletons, one entire, uncoffined, lay between two long blocks of stone, covered by a slab ornamented with a cross, which from its design cannot be older than Edward II., when the Knights of Malta arose in England. It is well known that none of the Priors of Bolton were buried here after the translation in 1154, excepting perhaps Prior Grene, who retired to Embsay about 1417. The stone is preserved in the arbour, near which are several ancient yew trees. Behind the house is an old disused spring, said to have been enclosed by the monks. It is called St. Cuthbert's Well, after the patron saint of the original priory. The present church was built shortly before Embsay was constituted a separate parish in 1855.

Ascending through Eastby by the ruined mill, built for a cotton-mill about middle of last century by the family of Chamberlain, memorials of whom are to be seen in Skipton church, the tourist

---

* HAGA: Every lesser estate, indeed even a single field, was called *haga*, since every particular property with the Anglo-Saxons was enclosed. The strong masculine inflection *hege* (gen. *heges* or *heages*) signifies a hedge or fence; and *haga*, a plot of ground fenced in and surrounded by hedges." Leo's *Local Nomenclature of the Anglo-Saxons.*

† Burton's *Monasticon Ebor.*

arrives at a fragrant fir plantation, and continues along the elevation, with an expansive and enjoyable panorama before him. Westward are Pendle Hill and the Lancashire moors with Bolland Fells. On the opposite side of the valley is Draughton Height, with its solitary farm, and below it Chelker reservoir. Beyond the dip of the moor above Seamoor House is the small gap leading to the Double Stones and Gill Grange. At the foot of the hill is Addingham, and S.E. Rumbalds Moor, with Otley Chevin, Yeadon Haw, &c. About 2 m. from Barden a descent is made in view of the far-extending lake-like reservoir ; the upper (53¾ acres) having an elevation of 1170 ft., and the lower reservoir (56 acres) being 697 ft. above sea level. Before us are the beautiful woods of Bolton, with the wild heathery moors of upper Wharfedale beyond. There is the rocky knoll of Simon Seat, and away on our left the craggy top of Cracoe Fell, whilst northwards stretch the long boundary line of Grassington Moor, crowned by the Gt. Wham (1900 ft.) The tourist leaves the moor road near Scale House, within a few minutes walk of Barden Tower.

Skipton to Rylstone, 5 m., **Grassington,** 10 m. The road skirts Flasby Fell with Embsay Crag on *r.*, and at 2 m. passes a substantial residence known from remote times as *None-go-by*, which

in the days of the early Cliffords was the lodge or keep of their Foresters. At that period, we may observe, matrimony was subject to a singular toll in the Forest of Skipton, which explains the origin of the name *None-go-by*. "Ev'rie bryde," says this ancient edict, "cumynge this waye shulde eyther gyve her lefte shoo or iiis. ivd. to the Forester of Crookrise by way of custome or gaytcloys."

About half-a-mile further on and the old Bar-house is passed. The pedestrian who wishes to escape the heat and dust of the highroad may leave it here and follow the path up to Norton Tower, (whence there is a grand view), descending on to the road again near Rylstone. The direction of the former coach-road (now grass grown) can be traced west of the present highway, which was made in 1853. **Norton Tower** is a conspicuous and impressive object seen from the road, particularly when the old sombre ruin is observed against a clear evening sky. Says the late poet-laureate, Wordsworth,

> " High on a point of rugged ground,
>   Among the wastes of Rylstone Fell,
>   Above the loftiest ridge or mound
>   Where foresters or shepherds dwell,
>   An edifice of warlike frame
>   Stands single,—Norton Tower its name ! "

The Protestant Cliffords and the Catholic Nortons, whose estates joined here, long continued in deadly feud, and many bitter quarrels arose as to the right of one or the other to impound the deer and hunt in the other's domain. The fortalice erected on Crookrise by the Cliffords, almost within bow-shot of the watch-tower of their opponents, has long ago disappeared. After the attainture of Richard Norton for his share in the 'Rising in the North' (A.D. 1569) in favour of Mary Stuart and the Catholic succession, the manors of Rylstone, Threshfield, Cracoe, Linton and other lands belonging to the Nortons in Craven were granted to their great territorial foemen, the Cliffords, Earls of Cumberland. The tourist now passes the turretted **Scale House**, one of the stateliest and most compact old mansions in Craven, associated with the troublous times of Craven Quakerism, where the Friends had a meeting-house and a burial-ground as early as 1650. The late Capt. Blake, who died in 1870, and from whom the property was acquired by its present owner, Capt. Henderson, J.P., added two wings to the house, and otherwise improved it. The Blakes are an old Derbyshire family who settled at Rylstone about a century ago. Mr. Blake was for nearly forty years steward to the Earl of Burlington, and his daughter married a Mr. Moorhouse, a gentleman farmer at Gargrave, and a captain in Lord Ribblesdale's yeomanry. His relative, Nancy Moorhouse, sister of Thomas Moorhouse, who died at Elslack in 1863, married a Mr. Ayrton, who for some time resided at Scale House (*see* p. 15). The only representative of the Blakes now at Rylstone is Miss Blake, who formerly lived at the Manor House, and who now occupies a pretty little mansion near the ornamental lake in the village. Descending a rich avenue we come upon this beautiful and sequestered little place ; the old walls decked with herb-robert and dainty saxifrage ; the whole embowered with flowering thorns, red and white, tall chestnuts, limes, elms, copper-beeches, laburnums, and towering larches, &c., surrounding the bird-haunted little mere, and from whose water-reflected boughs the throstle and blackbird pipe their sweet matin and evening lays ! **Rylstone** gave name to the ancient family of Rilleston, who were settled here probably at the time of the Conquest. A chapel of their foundation is known to have existed here as early as A.D. 1160. About 1434 they became matrimonially allied with the Radcliffes, a family that expired in an heiress (*temp.* Henry VIII.) who was married to John Norton, father of Richard, attainted as before stated after the Rebellion of 1569. The Norton woods here are still called by many of the aged inhabitants in the vicinity *John's Wood*, after this old John Norton. The ancient Manor House, with its Elizabethan *Vivery*, or pleasure-grounds, with fish-ponds, &c., disappeared many years since, and all that remains of the latter are a few mounds that once formed the ground-work of the rockeries, &c., adjoining the present building. A very old (undated) sun-dial on the south gable is said to have been preserved from the original building, and there is also a carved stone taken from it now set up in the clerestory of the church. The present Manor Hall (J. Proctor, Esq.) is a large modern mansion, whose front windows frame an exquisite picture of Norton Tower surrounded by an extent of native wood and fell. The church at Rylstone was wholly rebuilt in 1854. It contains some choice stain-glass and several memorial brasses, and outside are some ancient stones recovered from the old church, and bearing sculptured devices. The ancient bells, re-cast by Mears, bore a co-eval inscription, " In God is all." This, engraved in Gothic letters, was misread by antiquaries, and oft quoted, for ' *I.N.* (John Norton) *God us ayde,*' and is so alluded to by Wordsworth, in the 7th canto of the *White Doe of Ry'stone.* The story of Emily, the last of the Nortons, and of the milk-white doe and its weekly pilgrimage to the grave of the Nortons at Bolton Priory need not be repeated here. The traditional track of the mysterious animal is still pointed out in the depression below the old stone cross on Rylstone Fell and the lower Norton Tower. The reader should consult Wordsworth's beautiful poem on the subject.

Continuing through a pleasant and invigorating country we reach **Cracoe** (6 m.) with its two inns, and **Linton** (8½ m.), when the road ascends to Grassington, which is nearly 200 ft. above the Wharfe. Just before the road diverges to Linton there is a quarry of fossiliferous limestone, of passing interest to the geologist. Linton is picturesquely placed, and it possesses a conspicuous charity hospital, founded in 1751. Its ancient Norman church has been largely rebuilt, and in 1862 was thoroughly restored. The Rev. Benj. Smith, B.D., an eccentric nephew of the celebrated Sir Isaac Newton, was for many years, until his death in 1776, rector of this parish. He regarded the parishioners as " baptised brutes," and they denounced him equally unceremoniously as a " perfect ass." Their admiration was evidently mutual. Stories of the parson's peculiarities and habits have been often recounted.

Cracoe to Thorpe by Elbolton Cave, 2½ m. Visitors to Cracoe may conveniently explore **Threapland Gill,** a picturesque ravine a little east of the village. To Elbolton, soon after leaving Cracoe a lane on *l.* (2 m. to Thorpe) continues for about a mile to the first farmhouse, opposite which a path leads up through fields about ¾ m., until the crest of the hill is reached, when just over top on *l.* the fossiliferous *debris* of the famous bone cave will be seen. In the fields *en route* abundance of the mountain violet (*V. lutea*) and pretty pink-eyed primrose (*P. farinosa*) may be seen in flower about June, whilst growing on the slopes about the cave are the beautiful rock-rose, sand-wort, and several saxifrages. **Elbolton Cave,** or Knave Knoll Hole (as anciently known) is remarkable for the discovery of pre-historic animal remains made in it in 1888, otherwise there is little to attract the visitor within its gloomy cells. The cave has a narrow pit-like entrance descended by ladders to a (total) vertical depth of about 70 ft. The first chamber is about 20 ft. deep, the second 32 ft., and a third 15 ft., the latter terminating in a pool of water reduced by excavating to a depth of 4 ft. From this point a passage runs to what looks like an old lead-working. The entire length of the cave from the summit mouth to the pool may be taken as 140 ft. At the base of the first chamber were found, mingled with loose angular pieces of limestone and a little brown earth, four entire human skeletons, *in situ,* as buried (in the usual sitting postures) and the remains of at least eight others, together with bone implements, fragments of pot, and remains of wild-boar, horse, dog, wolf.

wild-cat, red-deer, and Celtic short-horn, all of Neolithic age (2-4000 years old). Below this upper cave earth was a layer of clay containing more loose stones and much stalagmitic breccia, and in this deposit have been found quantities of well-preserved bones of bears (amongst them the huge grizzly, now extinct in the Old World), and Alpine foxes, hares, and reindeer. The complete absence of iron, bronze, or even flint implements would appear to indicate either a remarkable poverty of these humble cave-dwellers, or the extreme antiquity of the race inhabiting the cave,—before metal was generally wrought or the traffic in flint commenced. Only bone implements have been found. The worn and polished footholds in the upper chamber shew that the present entrance was also that used by the cave-men. The excavations have been conducted by the Rev. E. Jones, F.G.S., late of Embsay, and last year a grant was made by the British Association for the further exploration of the cave. The visitor, after enjoying the ample prospect that is to be obtained from the summit of this knoll may descend to the path by which he came, which soon developes to a cart track and crosses the stream to the hidden little hamlet of Thorpe. There is no inn here. To Grassington or Burnsall it is 1½ m.

Rylstone to Hetton, ½ m.; **Malham,** 6 m. This is a fine but rather rough cross-country trip. A lane by the lake drops to a stone foot-bridge, when a narrow lane and field are ascended to **Hetton.** Much of the land in this township once belonged to the monks of Furness, and after the deposition of the Nortons in 1569, the manor was granted by the Crown to the Earl of Cumberland, and is now held by the Duke of Devonshire. Hetton is a quiet, retired place, upon an elevated plateau commanding a pleasing view of the opposite fells. It has a neat Wesleyan chapel, built in 1859, whilst church folks go to Rylstone. It has a small way-side inn, and if a *name* can presage comfort and fair treatment, the traveller ought to obtain it here. Hetton Rushbearing, as the annual Feast was called, is now hardly remembered, and has been substituted by annual sports, held about the middle of July, when wrestling matches, races, &c., take place, but these, however, have now almost died out. The population is decreasing.

At the low end of the village (opposite a green-gabled house) a broad grassy lane leads over Hetton Common, commanding a picturesque view of the round, green knolls of Elbolton, Skelterton, and Cale, with the high, rocky summit of Cracoe Fell. At the top of the road cross a (temporary) tram-line laid down by the Leeds and Liverpool Canal Company for the conveyance of gritstone from the summit of Boss Moor (1100 ft.) to their new reservoir now being constructed in the Winterburn valley. This reservoir, we may here remark, is a gigantic undertaking on which the Company has been engaged some years. It is calculated to hold, when full, 285,000,000 gallons, the area of the top water being about 40 acres. The approximate cost, when complete, is estimated at £85,000 to £90,000.

Descend the fell-side into the lonely Hetton Beck dale,—one of the most solitary valleys in all Yorkshire, and crossing the handsome little bridge, lately built by the Canal Company of the excellent Boss Moor stone, a gate is opened opposite, and the fell ascended by a well-defined track. Continuing through a number of gateways, with fine retrospective views of Flasby and Cracoe Fells, &c., the head of Whetstone Gill is passed a short distance to *l.* of an old quarry ; when, after crossing a small gill, the depression between the Weets on *r.* and Hanlith Moor on *l.* is traversed, whence are seen the Kirkby Fells and Ryeloaf with the village of Malham below. [Coming *from Malham to Hetton*, a good guide for the direction to be taken is the white quarried summit of Boss Moor looking east from the Weets ; a little south of the quarry the path runs over Hetton Common from the Beck bridge (as above), or the tourist may pass down the valley to Winterburn, 2 m.] From the Weets (1380 ft.), a plain, peaty, gritstone height, which can be ascended in a few minutes from here, a magnificent view over Lancashire, West Craven, and eastward as far as Gt. Whernside and the Wharfedale hills, is obtainable. Our track now goes down sharp, keeping Hanlith Gill on *l.*, and when in the bottom the stream is crossed by a footbridge near a barn, and the path followed up fields on to the Gordale road, ½ m. above Malham.

SKIPTON TO GARGRAVE.

E have now reached the very interesting upper region of the Aire, where our river waters some of the richest of pastures in the heart of Craven. Twenty to thirty years ago there were hundreds of acres under the plough, but now there is hardly an acre of corn land to be seen. It is the practice of the present generation of farmers to buy lean stock and fatten it for the local markets, and on some of the best grazing it is possible to turn out two lots of cattle in a season, by giving the land only a fortnight's rest in mid season. But quality rather than quantity is the farmers' chief aim, and in this respect Craven fed beef is admittedly highly nutritious, and is unsurpassed in grain and flavour. It is worth noting that five to six centuries ago, under the feudal system, land in this district was let at about 9d an acre; in 1612 we find it fetched 6s., and latterly £4 to £5 !

To Gargrave there are several routes; by the highroad, (4 m.), or along the south side of the canal (4½ m.), or through Stirton and Thorlby (4½ m.), all nice walks. Another route (4½ m.) which we will describe, is from Skipton station to ascend to the far bank of the canal and continue as far as Mr. Dewhurst's boat-house, about half-a-mile. Before the canal was made rather over a century ago, there stood at its junction with the road to Broughton, a stately old residence of the Republican Lamberts, (afterwards of Calton), called Winterwell Hall. It is described as having in Henry VIII.'s time a tower, great parlour, and chamber over it, with study under it. A large and very cold well near the house was swallowed up by the canal. Observing from the bank the beautiful Elizabethan mansion of Aireville (J. B. Dewhurst, Esq., J.P., C.C.), occupying a warm and sheltered situation, though standing, perhaps, somewhat low for effect, we come to the private boat-house, and here enter a gate-way, and turning into the field sharp to the right, keep the bed of the stream on our right all the way up. Some lofty and luxuriant thorn trees are passed on the way, as well as some maples and ash trees, and we observe also one large oak. The oak, however, is ill-suited to the limestone of Craven, but it agrees well with the ash, which in some places where the oak is of stunted growth, spreads her roots over the rich, shallow soil, and attains the stateliest proportions. An old flowery lane is presently entered, which veers left on to the high road, 3 m. from Gargrave. From this point the northern slope of Pendle Hill stands out grandly, but it is seen even to better advantage when opposite Thorlby, a half-mile further on.

Having Bracewell's Cotton Mills,* and the huge glacial mounds referred to elsewhere, about Gargrave before us, we reach the summit of the road (420 ft.), and look down on to the low ground on the far side of the river under Butter Haw. There in the days of Roman sovereignty in Britain some wealthy Roman magister had his stately seat. Of this once splendid villa, however, no traces now remain, but in the middle of last century, when it was first opened, extensive foundations, along with coloured tiles, &c., were discovered. Dr. Whitaker assumes the building to have occupied a parallelogram about 300 feet long and 180 feet wide. The site is now known as Kirk Sink, from a tradition that a great ecclesiastical edifice once stood there and somehow mysteriously disappeared !

We now proceed under the rugged and picturesque Flasby Fell, once wholly clad with native wood, which two

* The chimneys of these mills are seen a long way off (*see* p. 217). But it is a fact worth recording that chimneys are no modern innovation at Gargrave, for at a time when such objects were exceedingly rare in England, there was a chimney at Gargrave as appears by the following entry in the *Compotus* of Bolton Abbey for A.D. 1311. " *Pro camino rect. de Gayrgrave faciendo, et dato eidem, IXs.*" This we should think is the earliest extant reference to a chimney in Yorkshire. Beckman, an authoritative writer on this subject, observes " The oldest certain account of chimneys with which I am acquainted occurs in the year 1347 ; for an inscription, which is still existing, or did exist at Venice, relates that at the above period, a great many chimneys were thrown down by an earthquake." It is, however, tolerably certain that there was a form of flue for the conveyance of smoke in some of our castles and abbeys before this time.

or three centuries ago gave cover to antlered and other kinds of game, but now looking stiff and formal with a recent plantation of fir along its upper slope. Hares are the only game hunted in the locality now. Crossing the canal at the first "lock" upon it from Bingley, we go over Holme Bridge, and pass the kennels of the Craven Harriers, where a subscription pack of hounds is kept. A few foxes, however, are found, and occasionally reynard descends on 'my neighbour's farm' and runs off with a prime-fed duck or goose.

GARGRAVE.

Gargrave, Ghergrave, Gayregraf, or Gerigraph, as it is variously spelled in old charters, is very delightfully situated, and round about it is trim, rich, and park-like, having a semi-private aspect even about the public ways. There is indeed a real look of country pride and unbusied retirement about the place, truly refreshing to the town dweller. Picturesque old lanes, lined with noble ash trees and sycamores, converge upon the village, and hereabouts we see, too, in this warm, wooded vale, well-kept gardens mantled with sweet-smelling roses, clematis, and scarlet-runners, and peaches even ripening their fruit under sheltered walls— pictures of luxuriant beauty! Dr. Whitaker supposes Gargrave to mean the *graf* or trench of *Garri*, a personal name, which, with slight variations, is still retained in the district and elsewhere, not only as a personal but also as a place-name. In the latter respect, for example, there is an old village called Garrigill, near Alston, in Northumberland, which has similarly an ancient chapel.

The parish of Gargrave, which includes Coniston, Eshton, Bank-Newton, and Flasby-with-Winterburn, contains 11,358 acres, and from an unpublished record of half-a-century back, (1841), we find it apportioned as follows : Meadow and Pasture, 10,427 acres ; Woodland, 483 acres ; Common land, 246 acres, (of which 223 were at Winterburn) ; and Arable land, 201 acres. Of land in furrow there is now, as before

Gargrave Church.

stated, but very little. It is interesting, however, to compare
the present absence of tillage with the state of things say
five centuries ago, when the monks of Sallay held the lands
here. In 1381, according to their *Compotus*, they received
tithes of 41½ quarters of wheat, 62 qrs. of barley, 5½ qrs. and
3 bushels of beans, 208 qrs. of oats, and 40 stones of wool.
Multiplying these quantities by ten, and assuming, says
Dr. Whitaker, that every statute acre yielded three quarters,
we get at an approximate idea of the amount of land in
tillage at that time, which would not be less than 1000 acres.

Of the **Church**, the most interesting feature of the
village, nothing now remains of the previous structure but
the tower, built, according to a date upon an oak board
preserved there, in 1521. With this exception the church
was wholly rebuilt in 1852, and its present spacious interior
is one of the most beautiful and interesting among country
churches in Yorkshire. There is no doubt a chapel existed
here long before the monks of Sallay, its early owners,
founded their abbey in A.D. 1147. A Roger, *clericus de
Gerigraf*, was witness to a charter before the foundation of
that house. In the vicarage garden we have had shown to
us portions of ancient Saxon crosses, the heads of two being
pierced with triangular holes, about two inches at their
broadest diameter, and the shafts are ornamented with Saxon
knotwork and a mutilated *Agnus Dei*. There is also the
base of a Norman pillar ; and another very perfect oblong
stone, about 40 in. in length and 10 in. in thickness, bears
the incision of a floriated cross on the top and a sword on
one side. Another (broken) stone has the representation of
a bow and arrow carved upon it, a memorial stone, doubtless,
of some Saxon or early Norman archer. These were all
recovered at the restoration in 1852, and point to the
existence of a building antecedent to any historic notice we
possess of the church. Of the Manor House here at this
early period we know nothing, excepting that it occupied
a piece of land near the present National School, called yet
Garris Close, a name suggestive of what has been said above,
and where are indications of a deep moat that once
apparently surrounded it. At the end of last century there
was found here a singular relic of brass and steel (engraved in

Whitaker), supposed to be the girdle of a purse of Henry II.'s time. The old Tithe barn which formerly stood near this site was taken down about sixty years ago.

There is a tradition that Gargrave had once *seven* churches and that the ravaging Scots destroyed all save that dedicated to their patron Saint Andrew. This belief has probably reference to several chapels-of-ease and chantries anciently existing in the district, of which few or no traces now remain. No visitor to Gargrave should go away without inspecting the very beautiful interior of the present church. The ornamental glass particularly is of a very high order of merit, there being altogether thirty-one stained windows. Those who have recollections of the great Exhibition of 1851, will doubtless not have forgotten the splendid show of illuminated glass by Hardman, of Birmingham, which extended nearly half-a-mile in length. On that occasion he was awarded the first prize for English stain-glass. The whole of the windows (twelve in number) in the nave of the church are by that firm, and these illustrate in a connected manner the story of the Life of Our Saviour. When the church was re-built in 1852, it was resolved that all memorial windows in the nave should be apportioned in rotation of the subject already fixed upon. This design has been carried out, and beneath each of the windows there is now a neat memorial brass. Several of the windows are by Capronnier of Brussels, that on the east side of the north aisle being the first erected by him (in 1854) in England. There is a handsome reredos in Caen stone, and mural tablets to the Wilson and Coulthurst families. One of these is to the memory of Mathew Wilson, and Frances, his wife, (ob. 1798), sister of the first Lord Clive, whose only surviving daughter Margaret, married (1) the Rev. Henry Richardson-Currer, Rector of Thornton, and (2) Mathew Wilson, Esq., J.P., D.L., her first cousin, a Solicitor in London, and father of the late Sir Mathew Wilson, Bart., M.P., D.L., of Eshton Hall, who was born Aug. 29th, 1802, and died Jan. 18th, 1891. The registers of the parish date from 1557. The only piece of ancient church plate preserved is a silver chalice bearing a Latin inscription (undated), the gift of Henry Coulthurst, Esq., of Bank-Newton, who died in 1656, leaving a son Henry, who died in 1706. The living of the church has been in the gift of the Marsdens, (neè Lister), of Wennington and Giggleswick, since 1673, and since 1852 the Rev. Chas. J. Marsden, M.A., has been incumbent. Mr. Marsden, who is in his 77th year, is, we believe, with the exception of the Rev. J. Mann, the venerable Vicar of Kellington, (aged 86), the oldest beneficed clergyman now living in our Dale. The Marsden family, it may be added, were lords of the manor of Bradford, from 1667 to 1795, when John Marsden, of Hornby Castle, conveyed it to Benjn. Rawson, of Bolton-le-Moors, in whose descendants it is now vested.

Most of the buildings at Gargrave are comparatively modern, and amongst them the Methodist Chapel is a conspicuously neat edifice. There are several inns and old houses, and the Aire bridge here is moreover a structure which carries with it a history probably as far back as the foundation of the church. The oldest dated house is one inscribed 1693, besides which, at the north end of the village, is the Old Hall, a large, roomy dwelling, rough built of water-smoothed limestone and sandstone cobbles, evidently taken from the bed of the Aire. It is now occupied as cottages. A wide carriage entrance (now walled-up) once fronted the road on the south side of the garden. One of the windows bears an old incision, 'Cromwell 1709'—an evident anomaly. Yet the troops of Cromwell are said to have actually occupied the building as a barracks during the siege of Skipton Castle. There is good ground for this assumption for we find ' bold Capt. John Hodgson ' writing in Aug. 1648, that the enemy "marched towards Kendal ; we towards Rippon where Oliver met us with horse and foot. We were then betwixt 8000 and 9000, a fine smart army, and fit for action. We marched up to Skipton * * * *—at which time Captain Currer, a dreaping commander we had in these days, should have delivered up the castle to Langdale, if he had come on, but stout Henry Cromwell commanded the forlorn to Gargrave, but the Langdale's over-run him. The next day we marched to Clithero." From remains that have been found there was no doubt some fatal skirmishing in the vicinity of Gargrave at this time. Several adult skeletons have been unearthed during the process of grave-digging in a piece of ground added to the east side of the church-yard about twenty years since ; and on removing a large ash tree in a field near by, three human skeletons were discovered lying parallel beneath the roots ; victims no doubt of the same great Civil fight. The tree had probably been planted over their bodies *in memoriam.*

There are several fields at Gargrave belonging to the poor of the parish. The charities (dating from 1669) now amount to about £98 yearly, derived chiefly from land and the inn at Hellifield.

There are two or three cotton mills in this neighbourhood, the principal of which is run by Mr. Henry Bracewell. On Jan. 31st, 1874, this mill was burnt down, and damage sustained to the extent of £60,000.

Robert Story, the poet, though a native of Northumberland, was long resident at Gargrave, where he built a row of cottages in South Street, in one of which he first lived (about 1822) when master of the School, then conducted in the old Wesleyan Chapel behind. Afterwards he took a larger and better house in the village, where the school was continued until his removal, through Sir Robert Peel, to London in 1843, where he remained until his death in 1860, aged 65. It was at Gargrave, however, that his best work was written.

Gargrave to Eshton, 1½ m., **Airton,** 5 m. Near the *Swan* Hotel a field path leads over the canal bridge and on to the Eshton road, which passes through richly wooded park-land belonging to Eshton Hall. Here we find but little oak. though the ash and sycamore and common thorn attain a large size. Turn *l.* along the Malham road (forward one goes to Flasby and Rylstone) by **Eshton Hall,** (Sir. W. M. Wilson, Bart., J.P.), the ancient and beautiful seat of the Wilson family, which for many years until his death in Jan., 1891, was occupied by Sir Mathew Wilson, Bart., first elected (1885-6) Member of Parliament for the Skipton Division, and whose statue adorns the principal street in Skipton. The Hall property was bought by an ancestor of the present owner, Mr. Mathew Wilson, a London merchant, in 1642. It is a very ancient manor-house, dating back to Norman times, when the family of De Eston were the mesne lords. The building is of different periods, the latest portion having been added in 1825-6, and it contains amongst its varied collections one of the largest and finest private libraries in England. These include many important historical manuscripts and rare printed works, the collection chiefly of the late accomplished Miss Frances Richardson-Currer. There are also some valuable paintings, including portraits.

&c., by Rubens, Vandyck, Rembrandt, Turner, Sir Peter Lely, &c A portrait here of Charles the First by Vandyck, is, says Montague, "the best I ever saw of this *murdered* monarch." The pleasure grounds comprise about thirty acres, all laid out and planted during the lifetime of the late owner, and with consummate taste and skill. The timber in the park is now well-grown and presents an aspect of great luxuriance. Visitors are frequently admitted, but previous application should be made. About 1½ m. further on our way **Eshton Tarn** is passed in the hollow on *r.*, which from the spongy nature of the ground around it must formerly have been three or four times its present size. It is now less than a mile round. Abounding in excellent fish, it was in ancient Catholic times, an important source of revenue to the lords De Eston, to whom it was granted by Edward I., about A. D. 1280. Crossing shortly the Aire bridge the handsome and imposing mansion of New Field (H. Illingworth, Esq.) is seen upon a verdant elevation to the right, whence the road continues direct to Airton for Malham, &c., (*see* p. 45).

Gargrave to Winterburn, 3½ m., **Airton,** 6 m. This is a delightful walk. By the last route to Eshton Hall, and ½ m. beyond, at Eshton House, (M. A. Wilson, Esq., J.P.), an old flowery lane turns *r.*, and winding, shortly dips into the hollow on *l.*, where is an ancient and copious spring called **St. Helen's Well,** so named from an old endowed chapel-of-ease dedicated to that early Christian saint, and which is mentioned in a commission relating to the manor of Flasby, in 1429. No vestige of the building remains, but the adjoining site is still known as Chapel Field. Probably a cross stood here, and an alms-box to receive the passing charity of those who drank at the well. The water is very pure and cold, and bubbles up with remarkable regularity and force, at the rate of several hundred gallons an hour. At its junction with Eshton Beck, a short distance lower down, the water is said to petrify. The stream side is starred with the beautiful grass of Parnassus, and other marsh-loving plants, not very commonly met with. Crossing here the Nappa Bridge, we are soon in sight of a large and picturesque old mansion called **Friars Head,** which since the death in 1886 of Mr. Dawes, a nephew of the Dean of Hereford, has been occupied by his widow and another family. The house is the property of the Wilsons of Eshton, having been purchased by the late Sir Mathew Wilson's father about 1825, from Mr. Townley Parker of Cuerdon, Lancs. It is a stately looking 16th century building, comprising four front gables of three stories, and there are said to be no fewer than 1470 windows around the house. These had formerly all leaded, diamond panes. The rooms are large and lofty, but the interior fittings are now all altered and modern. One of the upper rooms is stated to be haunted, but by whom or what we have not been able to ascertain. Near the roof is an unlighted apartment called the Dungeon, reported to be the place where the monks consigned their refractory,—possibly the lurking place of the traditional ghost! Originally a grange and hunting-box to Furness Abbey, we find Friars Head valued at the Dissolution at £8 3s. 4d., or about one-sixth of the whole value of the Furness estate in the manor of Winterburn. We are told that after his submission to King Henry VIII. the last Abbot (Pyle) passed a night here on his way to the Consistory at York. Adjoining the house is an orchard which is supposed to have been the monks' burial ground. A few years ago in making a new road to the house a number of

FRIARS HEAD, WINTERBURN.

bones were dug up, which corroborates the belief. Doubtless there would be a private chapel attached. On Scarnber Hill, above the house is the well-preserved outline of an extensive earthwork, probably Danish, forming an elliptic about half-a-mile in circumference. The view from the summit (670 ft.) is very beautiful, comprising Pendle Hill and the ranges westward.

From Friars Head **Winterburn** is reached by a pleasant walk of ½ m. The village lies immured in the lap of gentle hills over-shadowed by such dense foliage as to form in reality a perfect bower, —a retreat fit for the Dryades! It is recorded that upwards of 3000 persons die annually in New York from effects of heat, arising mainly from the city lacking trees; at Winterburn they must surely perish from the opposite cause, for it would be difficult to conceive a place more completely protected from the sun's rays. Amid this bowery landscape the songs of many birds mingle their music with that of the on-flowing crystal, pebbly trout-beck beneath, so deliciously cool and clear that you can hardly resist the temptation to stoop over its murmuring waters and drink! The birds haunting this woody wilderness include, as might be expected, many beautiful and uncommon kinds, such as the jay, kingfisher, wagtails, brown and snowy owls, pied-flycatcher, &c. And in the stillness of a fine

Autumn evening we have stood on the little rustic bridge and watched the shy heron winging its way lazily beside the trout-dappled stream within a few yards of our abiding place. It is a curious instinct with this bird to know, as it evidently does quite well, that fish avoid a shadow, for it seldom if ever preys in sunshine. On the bank near stands a large ash tree divided into two main branches, the base of the trunk up to this division having a cavity so large that a tall person may enter and with the aid of a walking-stick not be able to touch the top of it. The tree maintains an appearance of vigour in spite of this extensive decay. Such canker is very often prevented from spreading at the outset by that useful bird, the strong-billed woodpecker eating out the fungoid particles, when new wood heals up the wound, and the tree is saved from further injury. It is erroneous to suppose, as many do, that the woodpecker 'taps' sound wood to the detriment of the tree. The manor of Winterburn, which included the townships of Hetton, Eshton, Flasby, and Airton, belonged as already stated to the monks of Furness. At the Restoration it was claimed by Thomas Wilkinson, Esq., ancestor of the present owner, T. C. Wilkinson, Esq., J.P., of Newall Hall, Otley. The manor hall is now under a separate tenancy. The old **Independent Chapel** at Winterburn is interesting from its association with the family of Major-General Lambert, one of the most conspicuous characters in the Parliamentary wars. The Lamberts lived at Calton Hall, which will be presently mentioned. The chapel was founded by Lady Lambert, wife of the general's son, probably soon after the repurchase of the family estates. She was an ardent Presbyterian, whilst her husband, John Lambert, who was Sheriff of Yorkshire in 1699, was an equally zealous member of the Church of England, and regularly attended Kirkby-Malham church. It is said that Cromwell, whose signature appears in the Kirkby parish registers in 1655, attended service here, but this is not likely as Cromwell died in 1658, and the chapel would not be founded until some years after that. The first ordained minister, however, was the Rev. John Isott, who was appointed in July, 1678. At that time the sittings consisted of rude benches, whilst the floor was strewn with rushes. It is now neatly pewed, with accommodation for about 150 worshippers. Since 1882 the little building has been rented by the Vicar of Gargrave, who holds a service here every Sunday afternoon. There is no burial ground attached, the nearest being at Rylstone and Gargrave, about three miles off.

From the stone bridge, Winterburn, a country lane winds at easy gradients 1¾ m. to Calton Hall. About midway the farmhouse of Cowper Cote, where the Craven Harriers sometimes meet, is passed on *r.* Cowper Cote, as part of the possessions of Furness Abbey, was valued in the 'First Fruits' at the Dissolution at £8 10s., about £80 of present money. From the summit of the road (Abbey Hill) near here an excellent retrospective view is obtained of Flasby, Rylstone and Cracoe Fells, with the encampment prominent on Scarnber Hill above Friars' Head. The original **Calton Hall**, occupied by the celebrated General Lambert, was burnt down during

D

the lifetime of his son, who erected a plain stone mansion on its site.
The building having fallen into decay was replaced in the early part
of this century by the present white house.   It occupies an elevated,
yet retired position, such an one as a military commander, might
choose with obvious advantage. From the lawn is derived an expansive
and very beautiful view extending from Flasby Fell westwards to
Pendle Hill. Here is preserved an ancient Sun-dial, inscribed IL.
(John Lambert) WF. (Wm. Fairfax) 1688 ; the only relic of the old
family now remaining here.   The great Parliamentary commander,
John Lambert, sixth heir-descendant of John Lambert, of Preston,
Vice-Chancellor of the Duchy of Lancaster, was born here Sept. 7th,
1619.   At the age of twenty he married a daughter of Sir William
Lister, Kt., of Thornton, another chief militant of the great Civil
strife. In the twenty years of his life that followed the event of his
marriage, Lambert stands out in bold relief in history as one of the
wisest of leaders, yet upholding staunchly the rigorous discipline of
that stormy period.   A man of iron resolve, of firm and independent
character, (after Cromwell's own heart), cool, calculating, and
discerning, these lines of Smollett may not inaptly be applied to
him,

> " Thy spirit, Independence, let me share,
>   Lord of the lion-heart and eagle eye,
>   Thy steps I follow with my bosom bare,
>   Nor heed the storm that howls along the sky."

The successes of Cromwell in the open field are in large measure due
to the skill and determination displayed on all occasions by this
brave young chief.   In his thirtieth year he was advanced to the
Commissary-Generalship of the northern army, and in 1655 appointed
one of the twelve Major-Generals installed by the Protector for the
military government of England, an office which all authorities allow
he deservedly held, and it is certain he acted with great circumspection,
wisdom, moderation and justice.   At this time Cromwell appears to
have visited him, for, as mentioned above, the Lord Protector's
autograph as witness to a notable local wedding is found in the Kirkby
church registers for that year. Lambert sat in Parliament during the
Protectorate, and on the death of Cromwell in 1658, and subsequent
retirement of his son Richard, he parried, we might say, single stick
with Hazelrig for chief dictatorship. His fortunes, however, were soon
reversed, for in 1660, at the Restoration, he was apprehended on a
charge of high treason, imprisoned, and ultimately condemned to
perpetual banishment in the island of Guernsey, where he died some
thirty years after, at the age of 75.   His forfeited estates in Craven
were afterwards re-purchased by his son, John Lambert,* father of

---

* The famous General's son does not appear to have been exempt from the
roisterous bacchanals of the time, to judge from the following lively bit of gossip
extracted from the Diary of the Rev. Oliver Heywood, A.D. 1681 :
  "1681.—Mr. Lambert, of Caulton, Mr. Heber, Col. Carre, Sr Walter Hawks-
worth, &c., drunk at Skipton, 10sh. a-piece in wine, were laid aside to sleep,
amongst whom was Mr. Sutton, preacher at Skipton and Carleton, he grew very
abusive, he played upon Col. Carre, who left them, then upon Mr. Heber, told him
his father had been a traytour, but his own father (Mr. Sutton, formerly minister

the last heir male, who died young, March 9th, 1675-6. Frances Lambert, sole heiress, married in 1699, Sir John Middleton, of Belsay Castle, Northumberland.

But, as it was with Lambert, so it is with most people,

> " Life is a journey,—on we go
> Through many a scene of joy and woe,"

so leaving Calton Hall on *l*. we emerge on the road (9 m. to Grassington) and wind down a picturesque thoroughfare to the substantial Aire bridge at Airton Mills. A path hence by the river leads by Hanlith Mill to Malham (3 m.). It should also be stated that from Winterburn Malham may be reached (6 m.) by the route described on p. 27.

Gargrave to Bell Busk by the Pack-horse road, 2¼ m. A pleasant deviation from the ordinary highway through Coniston may be made by leaving Gargrave station and crossing the Aire bridge, and up West Street over Ireland (canal) bridge, whence the road runs through the magnificently wooded park (about 800 acres) of Gargrave House, (J. Coulthurst, Esq., J.P., D.L.), where the stately beeches and sycamores are seen rising from thirty to forty feet in height before a branch is given off from their straight boles. Ascending the lofty avenue the road passes a barn and shortly developes into a grass-covered way between walls, with nice open view north of Malham Cove, Kirkby Fell, Ryeloaf, and part of Fountains Fell. This road was anciently the old pack-horse road from Skipton to Settle, and continued to be the regular highway until the new road was cut through Coniston about 1820. An old dwelling called Granny House is passed on *r*., which up to that time was a 'public,' and a familiar rendezvous of the packmen in ancient days. It is a stout old edifice which has braved the winters of, we should say, a round three centuries. In a quarter-of-a-mile the Aire bridge, and shortly the Red bridge (so called from the colour of the stone) are crossed, whence *l*. to Bell Busk station, or *r*. to Malham, 5 m. About fifty-five years ago the Aire bridge was almost too narrow for a single cart to pass ; it was then widened by the County authorities, but is still narrow. It is one of our oldest pack-horse bridges, and has existed now a good many centuries.

at Skipton) was a loyal person, a good man, gone to heaven, and there prayed for him every day, saying God will hear his prayers, &c. He again abused Mr. Heber, who gave him a blow on the head, they squabbled, they turned Sutton out of door as not fit for their company. He is a strange man—he will drink till 3 or 4 o'clock on Sabboth-day morning, yet preach and rant it agt drunkennes notably in the pulpit, he sth himself that he hath the knack of preaching ; oh, dreadfull, other sad storys I hear of a debauched clergy, yet hector it strangely agt Presbiterians."

GARGRAVE TO BELL BUSK.

Through an umbrageous country from the bridge opposite the *Grouse* and *Swan* Inns the road descends under the railway and crosses the Aire to Coniston Cold, 2 m. Just above the bridge the river makes a curious natural bend locally known as the Coniston S, which is also seen from the railway. A few years ago the proprietor of the Haw Crag quarries, who held the land in which this remarkable curvature is situate, in order to prevent or mitigate flooding, caused a straight channel to be cut through one portion of it and a retaining-wall built, so that this end now makes an island, which would have been washed away but for the stone banking. Below the bridge there is another bend where the river passes over damstones constructed for a water-hold used for driving the wheel at the old corn-mill lower down. The mill, which has not been run these sixty years, is now a ruin, but the old mill-goit is still intact.

Coniston in our earliest charters is spelled *Conigston* and *Conyngeston Cald*, (Saxon, *conyng*, a King), from having been royal land in Saxon times. The meaning of the distinctive appellation *Cold* is obvious; a name, however, that is hardly deserved at the present day, for the village lies snugly amid well-wooded and picturesque surroundings. These plantings were effected about a century ago when the Garforths came into possession of the manor, whose descendants, now represented by A. A. Tottie, Esq., of Coniston Hall, still hold the same. Its previous history is traced by Whitaker. In the Subsidy Roll of 2 Richard II., Coniston we find paid a poll-tax of 9s. 4d., or about the same as Linton and Addingham, and a third less than its namesake in Kettlewell-dale.

From Coniston to Bell Busk (1 m.) we go along a leafy road by the Hospice Howe Plantation and the handsome modern church, founded by the late J. B. Garforth, Esq., in 1846, and following the course of the river reach Bell Busk station by the large silk mills of Mr. C. A. Rickards.

BELL BUSK.

BELL Busk is not one of those places enshrined in
the pages of *Domesday*, nor even in documents
of a much later period. It does not appear
on Speed's Yorkshire map of 1627, although
Otterburn, the next hamlet does. The fact is Bell Busk
consisted anciently of a single house situate on the east
bank of the Aire near its confluence with the Otterburn
and between the ancient bridge and still older ford. The
present village is of comparatively new growth, having
sprung into existence with the mills erected towards the end
of last century. The old house mentioned lay near a track
used from the earliest times, in passing between Skipton and
Settle and the north, and in pack-horse days we are led to
understand a *bell* used to be suspended in a conspicuous
bush, and rung as an indication of the route to be taken, or
as a warning after dark that the waters were out. Then as
now this was the central and most thinly populated part of the
whole Deanery of Craven, and in such a lonely spot a 'guide'
of this kind would be very acceptable. Hence this is how
the place is believed to have got its name, and the Good
Templars of the village have in consequence called their
association the "Bell in the Bush Lodge." Such another
'out-of-the-way' village called Bell-on-the-Hill lies about
midway between Whitchurch and Malpas, in Cheshire,—
Malpas by the way signifying *Malsus Passus*, or 'bad
passage or road.' The custom of bell-ringing, like horn-
blowing, as a guide to benighted travellers is very ancient,
and was one of the usages prescribed and long practised by
the Knights Hospitallers of St. John of Jerusalem, and has
doubtless in various combinations given name to both places
and persons. But as doubt has often been expressed as to
this having been the true origin of the name Bell Busk, we
have in vain sought for a possible explanation of it in the
sign of an inn. Such signs have frequently originated

place-names, and at Oswaldtwistle, near Accrington, is an inn called the ' Bell in the Thorn,' but this it should be stated was named after the man who originally kept it, *Bellthorn*. But there has been no such inn that we can ascertain at Bell Busk.

A more likely theory is that of the Celtic *bal* or *bel*, a dwelling, or place of sacrifice, near a *bush*. We have seen that all along the valley of the Aire (as at Baildon) such places with the root-word *Bel*, lying adjacent to remains of remote antiquity, lend much countenance to this belief. Here about Bell Busk we have traces of pre-historic barrows, cairns, and earthworks ; relics undoubtedly in some instances of an age when Baal worship prevailed in this country. Ten years ago two broken urns were unearthed on an eminence called Lingber, about a mile south of Otterburn, and which contained cremated ashes, along with a copper dagger or knife, the whole being overlaid by a slab of gritstone. In the pit close by a farmer had previously picked up a thin silver coin, and a beautiful gem of amethystine quartz, incised with a figure, the latter being of good Roman workmanship. In an elevated pasture, about a mile north of Bell Busk, on the way to Airton, another barrow was opened in 1887, and found to contain a rude urn enclosing calcined bones of a human subject, with fragments of charcoal. Again, upon an eminence a mile north of Otterburn, is a large earthwork that probably occupies the site of a temple when the ingle fire burned in commemoration of the Druidical god Baal. The stream that descends to the Pot Ho. at the foot of the hill is still called Ingle beck. But whether these early evidences of Celtic occupation gave rise to an older derivation than that of the ' Bell in the Bush ' cannot, we think, with any certainty be ascertained. A perfectly tenable origin may still further be advanced by the fact that the word *bel* is often found in conjunction with other words to signify *a ford*, such as Belfast, (anc-*Bel-feirsde*), meaning the *ford* of the *farset* or sandbank ; Belclair, the *ford* or entrance to the plain ; Lisbellaw, the fort at the *ford* mouth ; &c. We have already referred to the ancient ford here. Bell Busk may, therefore, mean simply the *ford* by the *bush*.

The little rustic village possesses nothing specially noteworthy. The silk-spinning mills belonging to Mr. Rickards
are the principal source of employment to the non-farming
class, and there is also some quarrying at Hawcrag Rock.
In Jan., 1877, an enormous blast was discharged at this
quarry, when upwards of 30,000 tons of stone were removed.
Bell Busk was an early seat of Yorkshire Quakerism, and
under the Toleration Act licence was obtained in 1689 to
hold meetings here and at other villages in Craven.

Bell Busk to Otterburn, 1½ m., **Settle**, 7½ m. This is by the
old pack-horse route described on p. 39. From Bell Busk the road *l.*
crosses Otterburn beck direct to **Otterburn**. This we may remind
the reader is not the Otterburn of the well-known ballad of *Chevy
Chase*, which is in Northumberland. The name is obviously derived
from that amphibious creature the otter, which, whatever may have
been the warrant in early times (and *Otreburne* is included in
Domesday in the parish of Kirkby-Malham), is now seldom if ever
seen here. The district is richly wooded, but a century ago there
was hardly a tree to be seen. Now the pleasant trout-beck courses
through the village in summer-luxuriant shade, where revels the gaudy
dragon-fly, and where the quick-eyed kingfisher darts with painted
wing beneath the old stone bridge spanning the stream. The present
bridge was built to replace an older one about 1813, when the
common land was enclosed. Anciently the greater part of Otterburn
belonged to the monks of Fountains, who had probably a small
chapel or cell here. In A.D. 1257 we find the following local
confirmation of a grant of land to that monastery. "Ric. de
Otterburn, Clerk, son of Hugh de Otterburn, confirmed all that
Thomas, son of Willm. de Malghum had given, and also gave lieve
to enlarge and repair the conduit at Malghum [Malham]." The old
Hall here was rebuilt early this century by Robert Nightingale,
father of the late Judge Nightingale, the well-known coursing judge.
It is now attached to an extensive farm. Many of the better-class
old houses in Craven were built in ' stirring times' of inordinate
strength, no doubt for defence. Such an one is that occupied by Mr.
Wm. Gomersall, at Otterburn. The parlour has cupboard recesses
5 ft. deep, behind which are 3 ft. thick walls. Formerly the house
had large open fire-places fit up with mediæval "bee-hive" ovens
similar to those found in our old abbeys. Mr. Gomersall, whose fame
as a scientific writer and local investigator has been long established,
possesses a unique collection of Craven fossils, amongst which we are
pleased to note the uncommonly rare *Pleurorhythicus minax*, from
the neighbouring Yoredales.

The tourist leaves Otterburn by a rustic shaded lane, (the old
pack-horse route to Settle), emerging in a good ½ m. from between a
plantation on an open field, which he must cross up to the gate, and
ascend field again to the two gates at the top. Entering *l.* descend the

moor to a gate which opens on to a lane—a broad grassy lane, which
in ½ m. passes Bookilber Farm and the extensive rabbit-warren
belonging to Mr. Harrison. From the farm (which commands an
extended view over Airedale to Pendle, no house is now passed for
over three miles,—the road continuing between low hills where the
botanist may find diversion among the various kinds of plants.
These include the interesting little butterwort, St. John's wort, grass of
Parnassus, mt.-willow-herb, scabious (*S. succisa*,) &c.,—all beside
the stream bordering the way. After crossing the small beck dividing
the parishes of Settle and Long Preston, the terraced heights of
Langcliffe Scars come finely into view, when a descent is made upon
Scaleber Bridge (1010 ft.) at the Waterfall. A path from the stile
on *l.* makes a somewhat precipitous descent into the finely-wooded
ravine. The scene is extremely grand. The Scaleber beck (which
enters the Ribble below Long Preston) here comes over lofty cliffs in
two broad cascades of about 20 ft. and 30 ft. respectively, whose wild
environment luxuriates in various spray-spangled greenery. A large
mossy and many-hued rock in the bottom must be a perfect feast to
the eye of the artist. During a hard winter, like the last (1894-5),
when King Frost mantles tree and stone with the most exquisite and
delicate tracery, and about the half-frozen waterfall huge pendant
icicles gleam like silver in the mellow sunlight, a fairy-like scene of
wondrous beauty is revealed, worth coming a long way to see.

Proceeding, the junction of the road to Malham is soon reached
(*see* p. 69), where is a defaced ancient encampment, which once
contained a large water-cistern, doubtless used by the Roman soldiery
stationed here. Their road went (as now) by Scaleber and Ebor Gate
on High Side, connecting the Roman roads of Settle with upper
Airedale. Fragments of deer bones have also been dug up at this
camp. The tourist now descends to Settle, 1 m.

BELL BUSK TO MALHAM.

AIRTON, 2 m.   KIRKBY MALHAM 3½ m.   MALHAM 5 m.

J UST above the peculiar Coniston S, previously described, the river takes an abrupt turn from the east, and for the remainder of its six miles' course runs due north.   It traverses a landscape half-wild, half-beautiful, consummating in lofty scars and mountain scenery of unrivalled grandeur and scientific interest.   Were this valley filled with a large lake, (such as doubtless to some extent once existed), following the sinuosities of the hills, the view revealed would not be inferior to any of the grand lake scenes of similar extent in Cumberland.

If no conveyance has been ordered, the tourist may shorten the road to Airton a little by taking through the gateway at the bottom of the station road, and following the field path into a rustic lane which emerges on the Settle and Hellifield road at Airton.   This is a pleasant walk if fine. About midway the stream at Kirk Sike is crossed ;   Kirk Sike being the traditional site of a Christian place of worship before the building of Kirkby Church, and the adjoining pastures are curiously enough still known as Great and Little Church Door and the Parson's Crook (or Crozier).

AIRTON AND SCOSTHROP.

From the time of *Domesday* these have been separate townships, though only the road (or sike) divides them. Whilst the Wesleyan Chapel and the Post Office are in Scosthrop the houses opposite are in Airton.   After the Conquest the manor of Airton was held by Robert de Bulmer, and that of Scosthrop conjointly by the Abbot of Dereham and Thomas de Scostrop.   There are several old dated houses in the locality.   Garris House on the Hellifield road, is

probably like that of the same name at Gargrave, a survival
of the residence of the ancient lords of the manor. The
present edifice is said to have been built in 1602 by John
Topham, founder of the Free Grammar School in 1606.
Another old house is inscribed EWA 1696. From the time
of Henry VIII. (*ca.* 1540) until its confiscation after the
Civil Wars, the manor of Airton, with half that of Scosthrop,
was held by the Lamberts, of Calton Hall, whose history we
have already traced on pp. 37-39. According to a deed of gift
to Fountains Abbey, confirmed 10th Richard I., or A.D. 1198,
there was a corn-mill at Airton thus early. The mill most
probably stood on the site of the old portion of Messrs.
Dewhurst's cotton mill down by the river side. This is known
to have been a water corn-mill in former times. Calton it may
be remarked, was originally wholly abbey land, belonging to
Fountains, Dereham (in Norfolk) and Bolton, and the monks
would have part of their corn ground here, as there was at
least one Cell in the neighbourhood. At present there is no
inn here, but post-horses and conveyances may be obtained at
Berry's in Scosthrop. The minimum charge for horse hire
from Bell Busk to Malham is 2s. 6d.

The pedestrian may take the river-side route from
Airton Mill, crossing the plank-bridge on to Hanlith Mill.
Hanlith Hall, picturesquely situated on the hill side
above, is the ancient seat of the Serjeantson family, who
have been local property owners for fully three centuries.
The manor in the 16th century was held by the Metcalfes, of
the historic family of Nappa, in Wensleydale, by whom it
was sold to the Listers, of Midhope, and acquired, about
1615, by Josiah Lambert, of Calton Hall, father, by his
third wife, of the celebrated Parliamentary General (*see* p.
38). A stone on a lathe (near where an old tithe-barn
stood) bears the date 1694. Seven horse shoes have long
been suspended before the hall door, an interesting relic of
Craven folk-belief in their efficacy as a charm against ill-luck.
Such signs are still not uncommon in Craven. The tourist now
crosses the stone bridge between the hall and the mill and
wends his way onward about a mile through flowery meads
to Malham, passing about midway the two springs of Airehead near two conspicuous ash trees (*see* p. 57.

From Airton by the road to

KIRKBY MALHAM

we pass an old house, with a sun-dial on its west gable, called Skellands, built by the family of King, now about two centuries ago. Thomas King, of Skellands, gent., married a daughter of Wm. Serjeantson, Esq., of Hanlith, in 1714, whose five grandsons were, with one exception, all eminent church dignitaries. This exception was the celebrated James

KIRKBY MALHAM.

King, LL.D., F.R.S., a captain in the Royal Navy, who accompanied Captain Cooke on his last great voyage of discovery round the world, of which he wrote an able and graphic account. Dr. King died in 1784, at the early age of 31. A long epitaph on the family may be seen in Kirkby church.

The parish of Kirkby-Malham comprises the whole valley from Otterburn on the south to Malham Moor on the north, and has an area of 23,727 acres. The population in 1881 was 821, or an average of nearly 29 acres to every soul.* The Domesday name *Chirchebi* premises the existence of a church here in Saxon times, but it was probably ravaged by the Danes, and at the time of the Conqueror's survey practically non-existent. The first legal mention of it occurs in a charter of confirmation by King John, in 1199, to the Abbot and Canons of West Dereham, in Norfolk. In possession of this monastery the rectory and advowson remained until the Dissolution, when it was granted to George, Earl of Shrewsbury. In 1621 we find Sir Thos. Wentworth, afterwards the great Earl of Strafford (who died upon the block), patron of the living, and who about the above date had married a daughter of Francis, 4th Earl of Cumberland, of Skipton Castle ; whose niece, Elizabeth Clifford, married in 1634, Richd. Boyle, Earl of Burlington, from whom is descended the present noble family of Cavendish. To this house the patronage was subsequently transmitted, and is now held by W. Morrison, Esq., M.P., of Tarn House, Malham. The church underwent a thorough restoration some few years ago. It is in the Perpendicular style of the time of Henry VII. The roof is only partially battlemented, and on the tower are some shields and the initials G.N.R., probably those of Geo. Norwych, the vicar in 1485. The interior pillars have on their western faces canopied niches, which in the old Catholic days no doubt held statues of saints. This is a peculiarity found only in the churches of which the Tempests were principal benefactors, namely at Broughton and Bracewell, in Craven. About fifty years ago several interesting old frescoes were partially restored from beneath coats of whitewash which had concealed them. The ancient font here exhibits an admirable example of the dog-tooth ornament, and is probably of Saxon age. The registers, dating from 1597, possess an uncommon interest in that they contain the autograph of England's

* Compare this population and area with the manufacturing districts of mid Airedale (*see* p. 121 of *Airedale, Goole to Malham*).

Lord Protector, **Oliver Cromwell.** He has written his name as witness to a 'capitulation' of a very interesting kind, - to wit, the marriage between 'Martine Knowles, of Middle House in this parish and Dorothy Hartley, of West Marton,' on 17th Jan., 1655. At this time Cromwell was on a visit to General Lambert, at Calton Hall (*see* p. 37), and may we not imagine the great " uncrowned king " forgetting for an hour the turmoils of state and enjoying the pleasing ceremony,—nay, perhaps, amid flowing bumpers proposing the health and happiness of the newly-married pair ! An old house at Kirkby goes by the name of Cromwell House, doubtless so called in honour of his visit. The church, containing memorials of General Lambert's family, was doubtless garrisoned in his service during the Civil Wars.

In the picturesque Kirk Gill, about ten minutes' walk from the village, is a Spa Well, situate at the foot of a small Yoredale-limestone cliff, and which is said to possess virtues similar to the waters at Harrogate. In these woods the botanist will discover many rare species. Here also may be found in Spring, the pink and white varieties of the common blue-bell, besides other attractive kinds of wild flowers.

Ryeloaf (1790 ft.) may be most conveniently ascended from Kirkby, and a descent made to Malham. Time required, 2½-3 hours. Ascend the Settle road about 1 m. to the 'red gate' at the guide-post (4½ m. to Settle), whence alongside the plantation of Acraplats, as described on p. 66. The summit is plainly seen, and from it is obtained, perhaps, the finest view in upper Airedale.

From the Hotel *(Victoria)* at Kirkby a pleasant run of 1½ m. brings us to Malham, the *Ultima Thule* of our journey up Airedale.

MALHAM.

"A realm of mountain, forest haunt, and fell,
　　And fertile valleys beautifully lone,
　Where fresh and far romantic waters roam,
　　Singing a song of peace by many a cottage home."
　　　　　　　　　　　　　　　　　J. C. PRINCE.

NOT the least charm about Malham is its complete retirement from the distracting influences of town life. Its soothing, wholesome environment seems to breathe of perpetual quietude, especially felt in the long, hot days of summer, when the unobstructed sun-rays flush the white scars with radiant light, the cloud shadows lie motionless, and a drowsy stillness fills the warm air,—a stillness broken only, perhaps, by the bleating of mountain sheep, the lone cry of the curlew, or perchance the familiar voice of some lingering cuckoo heard afar off among the treeless fells !　The place, however, is not always in this happy and tranquil atmospheric mood ; sometimes the storm-clouds lower and vaporous rains and wind rush along the wild hills grandly, but in a manner which most people, we opine, would much rather simply witness than bodily experience.

The straggling little village, through which the first waters of the Aire pour, stands (640 ft. above the sea) at the foot of its guardian hill, Cowden (1000 ft.) (locally *Cawden*), whilst on either side tower the familiar cairns on Gordale Crag and Piked Haw, from all of which there are capital prospects.　Perhaps the best convenient view of the place is to be obtained from the Tranlands road behind the Wesleyan Chapel.　The village wears a weathered, mountain look, in keeping with its situation and surroundings, and the houses are for the most part substantially built of native grit and limestone.　There are two comfortable hostelries, the *Buck* and *Lister's Arms*, besides several very good temperance hotels and private lodging-houses. The terms vary from about 30s. to 50s. per week inclusive.

The chief attractions of the place are, of course, the majestic amphitheatre of the Cove, and Gordale Scar, but there are other scenes and walks, to be hereafter enumerated, in the neighbourhood which well merit the visitor's attention. With respect to the origin and history of Malham, the opinion expressed by Dr. Whitaker that it received its name from *Malgh* its supposed Saxon owner, has been generally quoted and accepted. But in a place so removed, and so predominant

MALHAM.

by its physical aspects, we are disposed to look for an appropriate descriptive nomenclature, as is the case with all the other townships in this extensive parish. The earliest spelling of the name we find occurs variously as Malgham, Malgum, (in *Domesday*) Mawlam, Mawm. The latter carries with it a pronunciation which the place has always borne. Consequently if we allow for the misapplication of sound in the Saxon *sub.* Norman spelling of the word (a circumstance of common occurrence in early charters) we arrive at a very different meaning to that usually accepted, for places compounded of

Maum, Moym, and *Mam* are from the Celtic-Irish *madhm, a mountain pass or chasm;* thus Maum-Turk, *the boar's pass,* Maumakeogh, *the pass of the mist,* Mam Tor, the hill pass, (above the Windyats, Derbyshire) and Malham, locally Mawm (*the way* to or at) *the pass,* now *the village or hamlet of the pass or gorge,* in allusion either to Gordale or the narrow approaches to the village. The crooked ascent from Malham on to the Gordale road bears the name of Finkle Street, evidently from the Danish *vinckl* (Belgic *winckel*), an angle or corner, a very meet term for this part of the road. Other similar thoroughfares in and about Airedale (as at Selby and Armley) are also known by this singular name, and in Cheshire is a romantically situated little village called Wincle, and below Wincle Grange is the old Dane's Bridge.

Of the Celtic occupation of Malham there is undoubted evidence in local cave deposits of animal remains belonging to a primitive people, and in stone circles and cairns which, however, have never been sufficiently investigated. About forty-five years ago a large barrow containing human bones was opened on the upper east side of the Cove. It had never hitherto been disturbed and was locally known as the Friar's Heap or Monk's Grave, but it is much more likely to have been a British or Danish burial mound.

In Saxon times the great Earl Edwin belonged lands in Malham, and at the Conquest the manor of East Malham was bestowed upon the Norman William de Percy, and soon after the place gave name to its mesne lords the notable family of Mawm or Malham, who died out in Craven at the close of the seventeenth century. The Mauleverers were also lords of thirteen carucates (probably not less than 5000 acres here) in East Malham, of which twelve oxgangs (eight oxgangs constituting a carucate) were early given by them to the Priory of Embsay, afterwards Bolton. Prior Hall, the oldest building now standing in Malham, doubtless retains the original site of the edifice first occupied by the monks of Bolton, where they remained till the Dissolution, and where their courts were held. But the Courts Baron, tradition avers, were held within the sheltering corridors of Gordale, a spot (if this were so) that may readily be imagined would contribute not a little to the impressiveness of the ceremonial.

East Malham, together with a moiety of the manor of West Malham, was after the fall of the monasteries acquired by the Lamberts, and afterwards, about the middle of the 17th century, alienated to the Listers, Lords Ribblesdale. West Malham, originally also held by William de Percy, founder of Sallay Abbey, included the Tarn, and was in possession of the monks of Fountains, whose vast estates, extending from Ripon on the east to Fountains Fell westward, comprised in Craven an area of not less than 60,000 acres. Their lands in this district were appropriated mostly to the grazing of sheep, and on Fountains Fell they had a spacious bercary or lodge, at one time occupied by five shepherds, and in East Malham the monks of Bolton had a similar establishment, to which were attached pens, folds, and wash-pits, besides every other requisite of a great sheep-farm. Frequent reference is made to the repair, &c., of this bercary by the Bolton monks in their Compotus from A.D. 1290 to 1325. Yearly the herdsmen of Fountains drove their flocks over the high moor down to Kilnsey, in Wharfedale, where the animals were clipped, and whence the wool was afterwards conveyed in wains drawn by oxen with a pole, as was the custom then, all the way to Fountains Abbey. Stone crosses, the sockets of which may still be found, served to guide them, or any passing pilgrim, over these wild moors. At the Dissolution West Malham was granted by the King to Sir Richd. Gresham, Kt., and his heirs for ever, who however disposed of it ; and in 1560 it came into the hands of the Assheton family, by whom it was devised to the noble house of Ribblesdale as stated above.

The former possessions of the old monks of Fountains and Malham, are preserved now only in such names as Prior Rakes, (the extensive pasture between the Tarn and Cove), Abbot Hills, Friars' Garth, Cross Field, &c. In the time of the Asshetons there was a deer park, still known as such, adjoining the west side of Prior Hall, where some sixty head of deer were kept, and whence an animal was occasionally liberated for a stalking-hunt over the hillocky scar-rent mountains as far north as Langstrothdale Chace.

Touching the subject of wild animals, besides the fox. rabbit, stoat, and weasel, little is seen here now. But seven

E

years ago a badger was observed above Malham, and hunted down to Hanlith, where it was captured, and it is now in the possession of Mr. Rickards, of Bell Busk. Also another of these rare animals was in February, 1891, taken on the high ground at Stockdale, between Malham and Settle. But the district is more especially noted for its rare birds, plants, mosses, lichens, &c., and in this respect is one of the finest hunting-grounds of the naturalist in Britain. We shall make further mention of this subject later.

Malham has a very old and great reputation for its sheep-fairs, as many as 80,000 head having been exhibited on a single fair-day. There are three fairs annually ; the first for lambs on June 30th, the second for lambs on the second Thursday in Aug., and the third for sheep on Oct. 15th. But besides sheep and cattle rearing there is another local industry of some consequence, viz. : lead mining. The veins are worked under Piked Haw, and are upon the whole highly metalliferous ; the "Rich Groove" mine here having, we may add, yielded an abundance of very good metal. In April, 1887. a block or "knocking" of lead was brought to the surface weighing upwards of a ton, and containing 85 per cent, of lead, 4 oz. of silver to the ton, with a surface of carbonate of copper. This fine block was afterwards sent to the Newcastle Exhibition. At the beginning of the century occupation was found for a portion of the inhabitants at a small cotton-mill, situated on the stream near the Pan Holes waterfall, a little north of the village, but the mill having been given up some years ago, it fell into ruin and has since altogether disappeared. The old free school at Malham is now also a thing of the past, yet the building still stands beside the road near Prior Hall. It was founded by Rowland Brayshay in 1717, and endowed by him with land valued now at about £110 a year. This endowment, with others, is now applied under the late Act to the maintenance of the Kirkby-Malhamdale United School, conducted since 1877 in a good building situate midway between Kirkby and Malham. For many years during the last and present centuries, Thomas Hurtley, author of a quaint and entertaining volume entitled, "A Concise Account of some Natural Curiosities in the Environs of Malham in Craven," was master of the village school. His book, which is now scarce, was published by the help and patronage of the first Lord Ribblesdale in 1786. It contains some curious and, of course, long exploded notions, not the least remarkable of which are the altitudes quoted of British hills, proving "unquestionably" that the 'mountains of Craven' top the rest of the United Kingdom. This is a statement for which at that era the author himself was not wholly responsible, yet the comparisons at this day possess a peculiar interest, and some may be mentioned; thus Whernside (2414 ft.) is stated to be 5340 ft.; Ingleborough (2373 ft.) as 5280 ft.; Penyghent (2273 ft.) as 5220 ft.; Snowdon (3571 ft.) as 3568 ft.; Skiddaw (3058 ft.) as 3270 ft.; and Benewewish (Ben Nevis, 4406 ft.) as 4350 ft. It is noteworthy that while the Yorkshire hills have their true altitudes more than doubled, the other British 'monarchs' are if anything underrated. But the Yorkshireman is proverbially proud of his county, and if his hills are not 'in the run' among British mountains, they at all events cover plenty of ground, so he may still boast that what they lack in height they make up for in breadth! Hurtley died about 1835 and was buried in Kirkby churchyard. His granddaughther, Miss Hurtley, lives at Malham now. She is an active, chatty old dame, (in her 80th year) and keeps a small lodging and refreshment house on the Gordale road.

Malham Cove, which we must now describe, is about 15 minutes walk from the village. It is one of the grandest inland cliffs in Britain, and has certainly no parallel in Yorkshire, having been likened to the great cliff which rises above the fountain of Castalia at Delphi, in Greece. It is caused, we may remark, by the great Craven Fault which has thrown down the limestone southwards from about 1200 ft. at Malham to at least 3000 ft. at Ingleton. Here the white rock * is exposed for nearly a quarter of a mile in a crescent-shaped battery rising perpendicularly to a height of 286 ft., and the limestone descends still another 200 ft. below the base of the cliff. It is formed of three

---

* This singular *whiteness* is caused by the perpetual action of the water dissolving the carbonate of lime which so thoroughly "white-washes" the surface as to render it very clean and often distinctly visible at very long distances.

successive narrow ledges, along which small animals have strayed, and helplessly perished in the attempt to return. Such an incident occurred many years ago when a fox and dog in full chase got on to the narrowest point of the middle ledge, and being unable to proceed further or turn round, both were precipitated into the bottom and killed. The cliff is the habitat of innumerable jackdaws, and is also one of the few natural breeding places of the house-martin. The vicinity of the Cove also abounds in many botanical rarities,

MALHAM COVE.

—too rare indeed to be specially localized as some are now unfortunately nearly extinct. In inaccessible crannies of the limestone pavement above, grow the maiden-hair spleenwort, green spleenwort, harts-tongue and other beautiful ferns, which at one time were very abundant on the surrounding moors. But large quantities have been carried off, only to perish beneath the smoky canopies of large towns. This is a great pity, as fern and flower in profusion in their natural haunts give unspeakable charm and interest to a place, of untold value to

the beholder in many a dull after-day. Ruskin once visited
Malham, and this is what he wrote of the Cove in the
Parable of Jotham (Prosperina). " In Malham Cove the
stones of the brook were softer with moss than any silken
pillow ; the crowded oxalis leaves yielded to the pressure of
the hand, and were not felt ; the cloven leaves of the
herb-robert and robed clusters of its companion overflowed
every rent in the rude crags with living balm ; there was
scarcely a place left by the tenderness of the happy things
where one might not lay down one's forehead on their warm
softness and sleep."

The **Source of the Aire** is popularly accepted to be
Malham Cove, but frequent experiments have been made
with the result that the bulk of the waters issuing from the
base of the Cove are found to be derived from the stream
flowing from the Tarn and disappearing at two ' swallow
holes ' a short distance below. The Tarn again is fed by
other streams descending from the neighbourhood of Capon
Hall, Fountains Fell and Hard Flask. There are also two
springs known as 'Airehead,' about a half-mile below Malham
village, and strange to relate, when the waters of the tarn
have been held back and suddenly liberated these springs are
found to be ' flooded ' fully half-an-hour before the Cove
water, although the latter is a mile nearer the ' sinks ' below
the tarn. This can only be explained on the supposition
that the passage to Airehead is comparatively straight and
rapid, whilst that to the Cove is over a series of lofty
waterfalls (the drop from the tarn to the base of the Cove
being about 600 feet) into deep or expansive pools or
reservoirs, and along a channel, broad, shallow and cavernous ;
and from the ordinarily sluggish and tardy exit of the waters
at the Cove, it would appear to indicate the presence of some
such stupendous wide-spreading cavern behind the face of
this cliff in which is one or more lofty cascades. During the
great floods of 1775 and 1824 when the tarn overflowed and
choked the " sinks," the water poured down the open gorge
and over the depression in the middle of the Cove in a broad
magnificent cataract, "superior," says White in his *West
Riding of Yorkshire*, "in depth and little inferior in grandeur
to the falls of Niagara." Such indeed was the volume of water

(stated by an eye-witness to have been nine yards in width)  and expanse of spray that spectators were unable to approach within a hundred yards of the fall without being drenched through. But to return ; we may observe that the underground limestone appears to be so fissured and bisected with hidden unknown streams, that to determine accurately the sources and directions of the many springs that go to feed the Aire seems practically impossible. Still many useful experiments may be tried. The stream, it is worth noting, descending near the old Smelt Mills on Malham Moor was long considered to be identical with that appearing at the Cove, but on analysis the upper current was found to be from two to three degrees harder than at its issue, notwithstanding its subterranean passage over a limestone bed of at least $1\frac{1}{2}$ miles ; a degree of hardness we may add approximating nearly to that of an old well situated in front of Prior Hall. This well is 42 ft. deep, and maintains a degree of extreme coldness even in the hottest weather, and is regularly resorted to at such seasons by local farmers for use in butter-making. It is supposed to flow from a spring rising in Cowden Hill, but singularly another well in the same direction close by is often found to be dry when the other has preserved its never-failing supply. A very remarkable phenomenon is also attached to this hill. About every five years we are told a body of water rushes out of the foot of Cowden and down Finkle Street to the *Lister's Arms* Inn, with such violence as to tear away the macadam of the road in parts down to the rock. This torrential discharge continues for seven or eight hours, after which the scene resumes its wonted stillness and the grass reclothes its denuded slopes. The Sabbatic river of Syria, which in the time of Josephus flowed every Sabbath day, but now flows every third day, is an analogous phenomenon. In the Autumn of 1890 there was a slight eruption, but it is now about ten years since any serious damage was done by this singular freak of Nature.

Malham Tarn may next claim our attention. It

is situated on Malham Moor at an altitude of 1250 feet ; the beautiful Tarn House (W. Morrison, Esq., M.P., J.P.) above its northern shore, clothed with luxuriant wood, having an elevation above mean sea-level of 1314 feet. It was built and occupied as a summer residence by the first Lord Ribblesdale. The lake (the largest natural expanse in Yorkshire) covers about 150 acres, and occupies a shallow basin of impervious Silurian slate, overlaid by a loose conglomerate, which thus holds the water—nowhere more than 14 feet deep. It abounds in fine trout and perch, "the best fishing," declared Charles Kingsley, "in the whole earth." Trout of 11 lb. and perch of 5 lb., observes our old friend Hurtley, have been taken from its waters, but unless the author's native pride, already alluded to, which doubled the heights of the Craven mountains likewise doubled the weight of the fish, they must have very much deteriorated, for ordinarily the trout (of two kinds) run from 1 lb. to 3 lb., sometimes a little over. The fish were probably introduced by the monks of Fountains, to whom the tarn was a valuable means of income. The shingly margin of the lake is fringed with the creamy flowers of Parnassus, and other rare and damp-loving plants. Over the waters skim or dive numbers of coots, moorhens, teal, and occasionally a few mallard. The wood wren, little grebe, and (on one occasion) the tufted duck, nest in the vicinity of the tarn. In winter-time many rare migratory birds also visit this interesting neighbourhood. Just above the north shore are a couple of small but beautifully-incrusted caverns.

Gordale Scar, about a mile east of Malham, though formed by the same natural convulsion which produced Malham Cove, is as a scene much more impressive than it, inasmuch as it creates a feeling of wonderment almost akin to horror on first beholding "its ponderous and marble jaws." The visitor unaware of the approach to this sublime scene is taken by surprise, for suddenly, as by the power of some giant necromancer, the angle which bounds the desolate valley is turned, and the spectacle of astonishing grandeur stands revealed. As a rock scene it has few if any peers in these islands, and no less an authority than the great traveller Bishop Pocock, declares that during the whole of his wanderings in Syria and the East, he never met with anything

so sublimely impressive.　The overhanging cliffs on the left
tower to a height of 300 feet, in gloomy weather touched by

GORDALE SCAR.

floating clouds, whilst the opposing massive stone walls of
scarcely inferior altitude likewise project, thus forming as it

were, a great roofless cavern. Hundreds of sable-plumed jackdaws make the gloomy place their home, whilst from the yew-clad, dizzy, topmost heights, a quick-sighted kestrel may now and then be seen darting down upon its unsuspecting prey. The centre of the ravine is piled up with boulders and loose fragments of stone, the accumulated debris of countless centuries, denuded from the encompassing strata. Coming from the moors above a body of water rolls down about a third of the height in a series of foaming cascades, which in times of flood present an unusually wild scene, blowing their "hoarse trumpets from the steep" with deafening noise. And particularly so after the autumn rains, when the volume and sound of the water, combined with its gloomy environment, renders the scene inexpressibly grand, and far exceeding in impressiveness the famous cataract of Lodore, in Cumberland. Ordinarily it is quite practicable to ascend the chasm and reach the moors above by crossing the stream and climbing the rocks by footholds on the left side of the waterfall. This is frequently done by ladies at the risk, perhaps, of a little wetting by the ascending spray. The present course of the stream was occasioned, about the year 1730, by a terrific thunder storm bursting the rocky barrier through which the current is now diverted. Formerly it descended the centre of the pass above, as is evident from the coating of tufa or thick limy deposit covering the large rock in the middle of the old channel observed on the way up. The water is of a decided buff colour, caused by its holding in solution the lime dissolved and re-deposited on its passage downward ; these incrustations in the bed of the stream giving it a very clayey appearance. The action is what is erroneously called 'petrifying ;' objects immersed in the water becoming in time incrusted (not permeated) or fossilized with the carbonate of lime. The whole of the cliffs forming this stupendous chasm consist of carboniferous limestone, excepting a bed of older Silurian grit exposed at the foot of the gorge. The original dislocation must, one would think, have involved a dynamic power sufficient to shake the whole earth. That it is due in the first instance to a 'fault' or throw in the strata, and subsequently to the slow operations of Nature, is perfectly evident. Several minor 'faults'

are observable in and around the chasm ; one such appears
at the top of the first fall where the rock is divided by a gap
a few inches wide ; the throw being slight, and is well seen
higher up,—not the result of water separation, but an obvious
dislocation caused at the great upheaval. The worn and
cavernous character of the base suggests the battery of
sea waves at some time.   That both sea and ice have
filled this valley (as they have covered the rest of Yorkshire)
is of course admissible, but the period of such attrition is too
remote to have left sufficiently identifiable traces of their
intrusion at this spot. The stones of the dry bed are sharp
and angular and not water-worn, and every appearance of
ice-scratchings must long since have weathered off.   The
appearance of the gorge must in fact be attributed to the
combined chemical and mechanical agency of the atmosphere ;
to frost and rain, and the erosive power of water, which are
grinding it back, so that in ages yet far remote the chasm
will become a huge winding defile in the mountains.   There
is no doubt, however, that it was originally a great cavern,
the roof having fallen in when worn down to a mere shell.
It was then much higher than at present. The laureate
Wordsworth wrote a sonnet on the place, and the poet Gray
(whose description of it appears in almost every account of
Gordale) said that it made an impression upon him that
would " last with life."

As already stated the district is singularly rich in plant-
life, and the following list of specialities will be useful to the
botanist.   It will be noted that among the species named
several Arctic and maritime types occur.

Flowering Plants.—*Thalictrum montanum, Armeria maritima,
Actæa spicata, Cochlearia alpina, Draba muralis, D. incana,
Thlaspi occitanum, Viola lutea, Alsine verna, Hypericum
montanum, Geranium sanguineum, G. sylvaticum, Hippocrepis
comosa, Rosa tomentosa, R. pimpinellifolia, Poterium sanguisorba,
Alchemilla montana, Potentilla alpestris, Rubus saxatilis,
Geum intermedium, Pyrus rupicola, Ribes petræum, Saxifraga
hypnoides, Sedum villosum, S. telephium, Galium boreale, G. sylves-
tre, Scabiosa columbaria, Carduus heterophyllus, C. nutans, Taraxa-
cum erythrospermum, T. palustre, Antennaria dioica, Hieracium
Gibsoni, Vaccinium oxycoccos, Polemonium cœruleum, Pinguicula
vulgaris, Calamintha acinos, Myosotis sylvatica* (a mountain
form), *Primula farinosa, Salix phylicifolia, Taxus baccata,*

Potamogeton densus, P. lucens, P. perfoliatus, Orchis incarnata, Gymnadenia albida, Serratula tinctoria, Convallaria majalis.

Mosses.—*Sphagnum deflexum, Gymnostomum curvirostrum, G. tortile, Dicranum calcareum, Seligeria pusilla, Trichostomum tophaceum, T. mutabile, T. crispulum* and *v. elatum, Barbula recurvifolia, B. intermedia, Zygodon viridissimus, Z. Nowellii, Ulota Bruchii, Orthotrichum Lyellii, Splachnum sphæricum, S. ampullaceum, Funaria calcarea, Philonotis calcarea, Breutelia arcuata, Zieria julacea, Bryum roseum, Cinclidium stygium* (at the north-west of the Tarn, one of its three English stations), *Mnium cuspidatum, M. affine, M. serratum, M. subglobosum, Fissidens crassipes, Cinclidotus fontinaloides, Fontinalis gracilis, Antitrichia curtipendula, Anomodon viticulosus, Pseudoleskea catenulata, Cylindrothecium concinnum, Orthothecium rufescens, Brachythecium rivulare, Eurhynchium pumilum, Rhynchostegium murale, Hypnum rugosum, H. virescens, H. giganteum, H. stramineum,* and *H. scorpioides.*

Lichens.—*Leptogium lacerum, Ramalina calicaris, R. fastigiata, Peltigera polydactyla, Parmelia perlata, P. olivacea, Squamaria crassa, S. gelida, S. saxicola, Placodium murorum, Physcia tenella, Solorina saccata, S. limbata, Ramalina farinacea, Evernia prunastri, Lecanora rupestris, L. calcarea, Lecidea cupularis, L. concentrica, L. exanthematica, L. cœruleo-nigricans, Endocarpon miniatum* and *v. complicatum, E. fluviatilis, E. rufescens,* and *Graphis scripta.*

The walks and drives from Malham are many and varied. For the day visitor the following are recommended.

Malham to the Tarn and Water-Sinks and back by the Cove; or by Janet's Cave to Gordale, climbing the Scar (*as described on p.* 61) **and across the Moor to the Tarn, and back by the Cove.** Time required in either case about three hours. To the Tarn ascend the Cove road about 1¼ m. to the gate at the road top, which enter and proceed to the end of the pasture, whence the path diverges *r.* to the Lower Tarn Ho., and the water side is reached in view of the Tarn Ho. on its north slope. After viewing the **Tarn** follow the stream at its outlet about ¼ m. down to the **Water-Sinks,** (1250 ft.), where the water may be seen in two places, divided by the wall, disappearing amongst limestone pebbles at the foot of a low hill. The water is clear and drinkable. Hence the wall may be followed straight down 1¼ m. to the Cove, following the old channel of the stream that once ran over its summit, but the limestone is now so much 'denuded' and abounding in 'sinks,' that the chances of a repetition of such a scene as we have mentioned, as witnessed twice within the last century, are becoming day by day more remote. This gorge is very rough and in parts precipitous. The better way from the Aire-Sinks is to round the hill (where the upper water drops) by a distinct track, and follow the wall side east about 100 yds. to the stile. Here a well-defined path continues beneath the

scars about ¾ m. until a field is reached on the east side of the **Cove**
top, which is descended to a gate that opens on to the summit
pavement (1000 ft.) The view hence over Lancashire as far as Pendle
Hill (whence the Cove is visible) and the long range of the Pennines, is
very fine. The sharp top of Flasby Fell to S.E., and the peculiar
glacial knolls about Gargrave stand out very conspicuously. Crossing
or skirting the outer edge of the deeply-fissured pavement, the wall
may be followed a short distance and the grassy slopes descended (try
the echo !) on the west side to the foot of the Cove. The Cove,
Tarn, &c., are described on the preceding pages.

**Malham through Little Gordale to Janet's Cave and
back,** 2½ m.   About a ¼ m. above the last houses on the Gordale
road a step-stile on *r.* (op. a row of thorns) leads down fields towards
a barn, near which a foot-bridge crosses the Gordale beck, with the
fine woods of Hanlith Gill in front. By keeping this side of the
stream, a walk of little more than ½ m. conducts through the wooded
ravine of Little Gordale to **Janet's Cave**, a charming sylvan retreat,
of which, in the words of Milton, we may justly exclaim,

> "In shadier bower
> More sacred and sequestered, though but feigned,
> Pan or Sylvanus never slept, nor Nymph
> Nor Faunus haunted."

A small cascade set within a living framework of moss and foliage,—
in Autumn the scarlet berries of the rowan or witch-tree contrasting
beautifully with the white foam, renders the scene exceedingly
attractive. And what more fit abiding place than this for Queen
Janet and her airy little people, whose humble dwelling, guarded by
the oft-swollen stream, we see in the rock above ! Imagination alone
is left to picture the lone witching hour when the moon-silvered
waterfall pours forth its music to the dance of the fairies ! Emerging
from this cool and shady recess the visitor descends a field path to a
small gate, whence the return to Malham may be made *l.* by the highroad ; or *r.* to Gordale Scar.

Malham to Tranlands Gill and back by Kirkby, 3½ m.
Round by the Wesleyan Chapel and up an old lane *r.* and then *l.*,
proceeding through the gate-way at the top to Tranlands House, with
its witch-scaring horse-shoe conspicuous on the door. Many other
houses around Malham may be found with one or more such horse-
shoes nailed to their doors, in accordance with a belief, still more or
less prevalent in Craven, in their power to act as a charm against the
evil doings of witches and wise men ; and associated likewise from an
unknown era in the minds of most people at the present day as omens
of good luck.   Lord Nelson, we are told, had a horse-shoe nailed to
the mast of the *Victory*—for luck !   But, alas ! it ill-requited him on
the day of Trafalgar. From the house the Gill can be descended,
and the stream followed to its head, about half-a-mile. The water
flows beneath crumbling Yoredale shales, by a larch plantation, and
the grassy way is strewn with wild geraniums, stitchwort, milkwort,
and other floral treasures, and in the Spring-time primroses, violets,
and flowering thorns display their odorous bloom. A rough track

hence leads up to Acraplats House and on to the Settle road, whence a descent is made to Kirkby (1 m.) and back by the main road.

Ascent of the Weets (1380 ft.) **by Hanlith Gill and back.** Time 3-4 hours. The rugged woods of Hanlith Gill constitute an attractive walk in themselves. Proceed by the route described to Janet's Cave as far as the foot-bridge near the conspicuous barn. The watercourses forming the acclivitous Gill give it some likeness to a large W, the left lateral branch shaping the ravine of Little Gordale, already mentioned, whilst the tripartite eastern branches, rising before the spectator, form the Gill proper. The woods are very luxuriant, and reveal many pretty glimpses of dell scenery. In Autumn they teem with hazel nuts, blackberries, and groups of scarlet-fruited ash, which, amid the various tinted foliage, conspire to make up a delightful picture. To the top of the Weets from the foot-bridge we must keep on the left side of the middle gill, ascending the open grassy slope with this gill on our *r.*, and so round the top of it, and through the pasture that lies just below the moorland ridge which forms the summit of the Weets. A few dark weathered gritstones mark the top. The view is very fine, especially southwards over the fells and villages of the Lancashire border country. In this direction we see Pendle, Boulsworth, and various points of the south-western Penines, with the moors about Hebden Bridge, Haworth, and Keighley. Westward, Ryeloaf, Kirkby Fell, and the cairn on Pike Daw are conspicuous, whilst that on Gordale Crag stands a little north of our view-point. Eastwards, the eye takes in a wide range of country bounded by Gt. Whernside and the Wharfedale hills, with the white-quarried summit of Boss Moor intervening. To the south-east the sharp cones of Flasby Fell appear, and the fertile district of middle Craven. The tourist may descend by the way he came, or pursue a track northward about ½ m. on to the Gordale road 1½ m. from Malham.

Ascent of Ryeloaf (1790 ft.) **and Kirkby Fell** (1790 ft.)

and back by Kirkby. Time about 4 hours. This is a capital half-day's outing, the views, especially from Ryeloaf, being unsurpassed in interest and extent by anything in Craven. Opposite Armstrong's Temperance Hotel a stile is entered leading up to a lane, which cross and ascend the lane, forward through fields by a path and stiles all the way until the stone barn in the hollow is reached, with the cairn on Pike Haw up on *r.* Cross the Sell Gill burn (a tributary of the Aire) here, and continue straight up the fields by a path skirting the wall-side, with a small plantation a short distance on *l.* By this route no more complete or characteristic view of Malham Cove can possibly be had ; its entire circumference being exposed almost from base to summit. The whole of the rock on the north side. it will be observed, is composed of the scar limestone, which is cut off by the 'fault' that brings up the grits southwards to the line of scars. When opposite the plantation an early outcrop of the sandstone grit may be seen in the stream by the wall side. Follow the path up to the broken gritstone summit, which the path skirts on *l.*, and make straight for the wall and on to the heather, whence the cairn on **Kirkby Fell** is reached in five minutes. The view is very fine but scarcely equal to that from **Ryeloaf**, which is soon reached by crossing the depression opposite (to the west). Here our stand-point (1790 ft.) is central. and in every direction unobstructed. Northwards the whole of Hard Flask is spread out, looking in any weather magnificently wild. From Kirkby Fell the Tarn House and all the watery expanse before it can be seen, but from here no house or sign of visible life appears to break the impressive solitude of the vast plain. Far away it stretches until the scars of Littondale separate it from the huge bulk of Great Whernside, seen towering to the north-east, and divided by the depression in upper Wharfedale from the conspicuous eminence of Buckden Pike. Eastward the Great Wham caps the summit of Grassington Moor, and S.E. we are able to descry the craggy top of Simon's Seat, with the intervening range of Cracoe and Rylstone Fells as far south as Embsay Crag. South again we have Pendle and the Lancashire moors, whilst the volcanic-like cones of Flasby Fell look extremely picturesque. with the broad vale of Airedale narrowing down to Bingley, and backed by the heights of Baildon and Idle Hill. To the north and west the view is wild and grand, including four principal Craven mountains, viz. : Whernside (2414 ft.). Ingleborough (2373 ft.), Penyghent (2273 ft.), and Fountains Fell (2170 ft.), with a vast tract of upper Ribblesdale reaching almost to the confines of the Lake District. Lunesdale, and when sufficiently clear, the sea off Morecambe are also discernible. After enjoying this extensive and magnificent prospect, a descent may be made towards a plantation S.E., and the wall-side followed down by a streamlet to a gate, whence a good grassy road goes alongside the plantation (Acraplats) and through a number of gateways (*please shut the gates*) until the Settle road is reached at the guide post. A descent of 1 m. will bring the visitor to Kirkby, and thence straight to Malham.

Ascent of Fountains Fell (2170 ft.) The southern slopes of this Fell form the northernmost gathering ground of the waters of the Aire, and the tourist, so inclined, may amuse himself by tracing their several courses with a view to elucidating the long-vexed problem of the source of the Aire. A fine whole day should be selected for this trip, and suitable provision taken, as the only 'restaurants' likely to prove serviceable in this sparsely inhabited region are the open-air ones provided by Nature among the clear springs of the mountain sides. The distance from Malham to the top of the Fell may be reckoned at 6 m., covering a rise of about 1500 ft., chiefly at the beginning and end of the walk. Take the

Cove road and leave the Tarn on *r.* to Capon Hall (farms). Between the Lower Train Ho. and the Higher Train Ho. passed on the way is a run of level ground (about a mile) called the Streets, where in old times horses used to be trained for racing, &c. It is the longest piece of open level ground to be found in this wide, rugged district. A century or more ago, when Boss Moor Fair was one of the great farming events of the year in Craven, whole armies, literally, of Scotch drovers came this way with their herds of black cattle, ponies and sheep. They traversed these wilds from the Highlands every Autumn for the big fair held on the lofty summit of the moor (1080 ft.), some two miles north of Hetton, and many strange tales are related of the cute things said and done at these famous annual gatherings, and of deeds perpetrated too, we opine, not always of the most peaceable character. Indeed, more than one human skeleton has been found with bones rotting beneath some cavernous rock on these wild moors, which ominous discoveries would appear to point to one aspect at least of these lawless times. It is now nearly a century since an old public house called the *Waste* Inn, which stood at the top of the lane near the Druids' Circle at Bordley (*see* next route) was taken down, as was another, appropriately named *Lone Head* Inn, a little to the south, also frequented by the drovers in the old days.

About half-a-mile past Capon Hall a long wall runs due north to the south summit of Fountains Fell, which may be followed and along the top as far as the Tarn. On the north-western declivity is a 'swallow-hole' in the limestone called Jingling Hole, into which a stream from the gritstone fell above is lost, to appear again at Neals Ing, about a mile lower down. Stones thrown into the chasm produce a sound like breaking china, hence the name of it. Just above the Hole is a pretty large cave. The bulk of the mountain is built up of main limestone, with a cap of millstone grit, and intervening is a thick bed (580 ft.) of Yoredale shales, &c. The view is similar to that which we have described as obtainable from Ryeloaf, excepting that the contiguity of Penyghent shews the precipitous mass of that mountain to greater advantage, and also the wild extent of country northward over Langstrothdale to the summit ridge of Wensleydale, with the lofty heights of Crag Moss, Gt. Whernside, and Upper Nidderdale, is seen better than from the more southern hill named. From Jingling Hole a descent may be made by Thornah Gill to Rough Close and Westside Ho. by a track on to the Capon Hall road for Malham. The east side of Fountains Fell is steep, and consequently the ascent from Higher Train Ho. over Knowe Fell is not recommended.

Malham to Grassington by Skirethorns, 8 m. By the Gordale road direct to Lee Gate House (2½ m.). The road is hilly, the highest part between Malham (640 ft.) and Gordale bridge is 827 ft. Janet's Cave (1 m.) may be visited on the way, and also Gordale Scar by leaving the road at the farmhouse. From Lee Gate (1200 ft.) the rambler may shorten the distance a little to Skirethorns (3½ m.) by crossing to Bordley (1 m.) and thence by Height Farm ; but if he prefer to follow the straighter path he must continue to

ascend a short distance past Lee Gate Ho. on *r*. to the guide-post
(8 m. to Settle ; 3¼ m. to Kilnsey). A wild prospect is obtained of
the limestone fells in front, with Hawkswick Clowder (1350 ft.) and
the Parson's Pulpit (1760 ft.) conspicuous ; and hereabouts the lover
of wild flowers will be delighted with a great profusion of the pretty
yellow mountain pansy. Turn *r*. along the lane which terminates in
an open pasture opposite a plantation, with Kilnsey moor on *l*. To
Kilnsey the *l*. wall should be followed ; whilst our route is by the
long wall on *r*., obtaining a good view southwards of the pointed
summit of Flasby Fell and the bossy end of Rylstone Fell. Near
the second gate-way (through which we have to pass) is the remains
of an ancient (supposed) Druids' temple, consisting of a mound 3 ft.
high and about 150 ft. in circumference, where was formerly a
complete stone circle with a large flat stone at one end called the
Druids' Altar. The circle appears to have been destroyed in
building the adjoining wall, and all that is to be seen now are three
upright stones raised above the earthwork. We now enter a long
lane and in about ½ m. observe on *r*. a three-arched cave situate in a
low limestone cliff above the lonely **Height Farm** (1200 ft.). The
occupant of this farm was tempted out of a natural curiosity to open
this cavern in the Spring of last year (1890). On digging some ten
yards into it numerous remains of foxes and deer, and skulls, bones
and teeth of various extinct animals and birds, were found embedded
in the stiff clay which blocked the passage into the cavern.* They
are at present in possession of the farmer. There seems little doubt
but what at some distant period the cave has been inhabited, for in
the immediate vicinity an iron spear-head and fragments of rude
earthen vessels have also been turned up, relics, evidently, of the
aboriginal tribes who once roamed over these wild hills. The cave
faces the west, and growing upon the scars about it are various kinds
of ferns, as the wall-rue, polypody, and black-stalked spleenwort. In
a neighbouring pasture, called Long Close, is another (doubtless
ossiferous) cavern, but not yet opened. We now descend upon the
picturesque and pleasantly-situated little hamlet of **Skirethorns**,
with its magnificent plane-tree, covering probably a circumference of
shade from 200 ft. to 250 ft. In the Bell Bank wood opposite, near
another large and conspicuous plane-tree, there was found in October,
1880, the skeleton of an adult male person. It was stripped of every
article of clothing, and there was absolutely nothing left by which
the body might be identified. No one from this neighbourhood had
been missing within living memory, and how long the body had lain
there it is impossible to tell. It was ultimately buried in Linton
churchyard. From Skirethorns the Kettlewell road is reached,
whence *r*. to the Primitive Methodist Chapel, and sharp *l*. over the
substantial five-arch Wharfe bridge up to Grassington.

　　　Malham to Settle, 6 m. By the main road *via* Kirkby it is
7 m., but to those who are not afraid of a little rough walking the
bridle route will be preferred. Ascending the Cove (or Capon Hall)

---

* The discovery was announced by the author in the *Naturalist* for July, 1890.

road about ¾ m. a sharp turn *l.* is made towards a gate in the corner, and the next gate above it (250 yds.), at foot of which is a line of stones, is the point at which to leave the road.   It is directly opposite the face of Malham Cove, and a good view of it and of Airedale southwards to Cross Hills is obtained from here.   Open the gate and follow the wall side up ¾ m. to the gate at the top before you, whence a broad grassy track continues under **Kirkby Fell** (1790 ft.), over the middle and most elevated part of the way between Malham and Settle.   From the highest point (1550 ft.) the path goes down beside limestone crags with the cairn on **Ryeloaf** (1790 ft.) conspicuous up on *l.*   The ascent of this notable mountain (*see* p. 65) can very readily be made from here by dipping into the gully and then following the ridge up to its summit, which is visible most of the way.   Continuing beneath the ferny scars we soon arrive opposite the large **Stockdale Farm**, a dwelling whose lonely and romantic situation (1250 ft.) reminds us not a little of Wordsworth's description of the abode of the ' Solitary ' in the poem of the *Excursion*,

" Behold !
Beneath our feet, a little lowly vale,
A lowly vale, and yet uplifted high
Among the mountains ;   even as if the spot
Had been, from eldest time, by wish of theirs
So placed,—to be shut out from all the world !—
A quiet treeless nook, with (two) green fields,
And one bare dwelling ; one abode, no more ! "

When the snows of winter fall heavily on this high land, the solitary mansion is sometimes inaccessible for weeks together. According to an incised stone (S F 1688) the house has been built some two centuries, but it has at various times since been added to and improved.   The farm comprises some 5000 acres, and extends two miles up and two miles down the valley.   Interesting it is to note at this elevation that of bush fruit (especially the rasp and gooseberry) excellent average crops are produced, whilst the soil too seems well adapted for the growth of rhubarb.   Apples on the other hand appear unsuited to this situation and may be regarded as a failure.   Now resuming our descent, we obtain an imposing view of the magnificent Langcliffe Scars, rising terrace above terrace, and culminating in huge round white bosses like the domes of some mighty citadel.   The valley hereabouts bears evidence of excavations by ice, for in the large heaps of mixed gravel we have plain record of that far-back frigid epoch when enormous glaciers ploughed their way down these rugged heights.   Coming to the junction of the roads, (*l.* to Kirkby by Scaleber Waterfall, ½ m., *see* p. 44)   a descent of 1 m. is made past the Roman Catholic Church into Settle.

Many enjoyable walks and drives may be combined with the preceding, or with other routes and places already described, making a stay at Malham of almost any length of time a delightful experience.

F

MALHAM TO HELLIFIELD.

AIRTON, 2½ m.   OTTERBURN, 4 m.   HELLIFIELD, 6 m.

CONCLUDING our survey of the head waters of the Aire we next turn our steps in the direction of the romantic Ribble.   A return from Malham to Hellifield (6 m.) may be made through Airton and Otterburn, this being a very pleasant walk or drive. Approaching Otterburn, a round green hill—the highest of the many green hills in this part of Craven—will be noticed rising northwards above the Ingle Beck that flows down from Ryeloaf.   This is Howber (750 ft.) commanding a remarkably wide and picturesque view, about which the poet of Otterburn, the Rev. W. J. Gomersall, thus tunefully sings :

> Pendle, Sharp Haw, Kirkby Fell,
>   Weald of Craven stretched between,
> Holts that guard each hamlet dell,
>   Brooks that glimpse across each scene,
> Slopes that into woodland swell,
>   Knolls that garb their crests in green.

No better prospecting site than this could have been chosen in those disturbed warlike times when the marauding Danes penetrating our remotest valleys, drove all before them and became for a time usurpers of the land.   Here on Howber they appear to have established themselves, and the earthen vallum of their primitive stronghold is still in parts perfect. The camp is somewhat elliptical in shape, and measures about 200 feet in diameter.   The thrown-up rampart slopes on the west from 10 to 15 feet, and has probably been protected on this side by a stout palisade of piked staves, while the east and parts of the north and south, conforming with the natural ground-level, have been enclosed with a thick quickset hedge like that now remaining.   A little below, in the field called Firbank, are traces of ancient ring-dwellings. One of these early foundations is still almost perfect, the diameter comprised within the circular bank, formed to withstand the thrust of poles for the tent, is 12 feet, and on the south-west, or sunny side, is the door-way three feet wide. The ancient Britons would bask for hours in the sun, and it was a common practice for the aged and the weary to recruit their energies by exposing themselves naked to its recuperative rays. Some have supposed these earthen circles to be relics of the native nomadic tribes who occupied a place only as long as there was pasturage for their herds. Up to 1813 these lands, now green and cultivated, were wild moor, and the adjacent village of Kirkby was, as its name implies, in pre-Norman days a possession of the Danes.

We now stand for a moment on the bridge at the little "city" of Otterburn, (*see* p. 43) and turning northwards look up at the grand dome of "St. Paul's," with which majestic pile the rounded summit of Ryeloaf may not be inaptly compared. The original name of this eminence is Inglehow, which suggests like Ingleborough an ancient look-out post or beacon-hill.

This reposeful hamlet-nook is situated almost in the very centre of the Deanery of Craven. How happy is the bard of Otterburn's description of it :

> Straight I tell thy place of hiding,
> Heart of Craven !
> With thy seven rustic hearths,
> With thy seven apple garths,—
> Triple byways thither turn,
> Link themselves across the burn ;
> Ivied bridge their trysting place,
> Where the lindens interlace ;
> Where the sombre, sable yew
> Veils the passer's nearer view,
> There I tell thee, there thou hidest,
> Heart of Craven !

But Otterburn in early ages was a more populous and important place than it has been for many generations past. Five centuries ago, instead of the "seven rustic hearths" now existing, there were fourteen families resident here, the chief of which, according to the Poll Tax of A.D. 1379, was the blacksmith's, who was assessed at 6d., while every other householder in the township paid 4d. This bygone "smithy" betokened some amount of traffic on the old road through Otterburn, which connected Hellifield and the west country with upper Airedale and Wharfedale.

In this neighbourhood are several barrows or prehistoric
burial-mounds, remains of earthen enclosures, shallow pits
and ring-dwellings,* which prove the early importance of

OTTERBURN.

the site. The most interesting of the barrows may be seen
on the way from Otterburn to Hellifield (2 m.). It is
mentioned in Pennant's *Tour from Downing to Alston Moor*,

* Described in the author's *Craven and North-West Yorkshire
Highlands*, pages 308—311.

in 1801. It is an isolated grassy mound close to the left of the road a short mile from Otterburn. Recently about half its diameter has been removed for the sake of the excellent bed of sand it contains. This is unfortunate as it was one of the most shapely barrows in Craven, forming a perfect circle nearly 100 feet in circumference. It was opened by Mr. Tiddeman of H.M. Geological Survey, and Mr. Gomersall of Otterburn, in 1885, when two large earthenware urns were found in it buried from one to two feet below the surface. One of these contained a very good copper knife or dagger of lanceolate-leaf shape, and pierced with a single rivet-hole, and there was also a sharp-pointed bone, like a packing-needle, 3 inches long, with a hole at the thick end, as well as a small copper-fastening, the use of which cannot be exactly defined. The presence of the copper dagger reminds us of the frequent practice of the ancient Britons of burying the favourite weapon of the deceased along with his ashes, just as the Choctaws used to do within present recollection. The poor fellows thought that such weapons would be needed in the great Hereafter, so impressed were they with the state of existence in this world! The other urn contained a piece of thin metal binding similar to that mentioned. Each urn was covered with a stone slab, and in the earth beneath fragments of several rudely-ornamented potsherds were discovered along with another very perfect vessel of bowl-shape, impressed with diagonal lines, and the base of a similar vessel, upside down, covering burnt human bones. In all four urns were found. A few months previous to these discoveries Mr. Hargreaves of Wenningber, the adjoining farm, found loose in the gravel a very beautiful incised gem of amethystine quartz, depicting a figure holding in one hand a long wand or stick, with a ball at each end, and some shorter and thicker object in the other. It is pronounced to be of good Roman workmanship. Near it was likewise found a silver penny of the reign of Henry III., coined at Dublin. The latter had no doubt been dropped by some 13th century visitor.

HELLIFIELD.

" Change is the very spice of life, which gives
It all its flavour."—*Byron*.

ELLIFIELD has become a busy railway junction
since the opening of the line into south Lancashire.
It is now one of the stopping-places of express
trains for Carlisle and the north, but the rather
elevated and windy position of the station on the edge of
Hellifield Moor is not calculated to " jubilate " the traveller
on a raw night.   There is however, ample waiting-room
accommodation, a book stall, and a refreshment room.

Hellifield, says Dr. Whitaker, is the *field* of *Helgh*, its
Saxon owner, but we are inclined to think, from the Domesday
name, " Helgeflet," that in the terminal *flet*, there is a
suggestion of the Teut. *fleot*, a flush of water or arm of the
sea on which vessels may float, as in Fleetwood.   And as we
stand at Hellifield station and view the flat, low-lying marshy
lands on the south, there appear good grounds for assuming
such a derivation.   An examination of the gravel, sand, and
stones composing the valley bottom in the direction of
Preston in Lancashire, lends great probability to the belief
that this was once an elbow or arm of the sea.   Moreover,
some thirty years ago a perfect vertebræ of a whale was taken
out of the river gravel in the valley about a mile to the west
of Hellifield.   This discovery was made while some draining
was going on in Wigglesworth Ings, and as there appears to
have been a group of bones found together, it really seems
as if the huge animal had been washed up by sea-tides when
the Ings was an estuary.   The spot is in the Ribble basin,
and is now over 20 miles from the Ribble estuary.

A tourist passing this way and hearing of the remarkable
discovery of this whale, the truth of which he seemed to
doubt, sarcastically remarked, " I suppose you will find sharks
in this neighbourhood also ?"   " Oh, yes," replied the man
interrogated, " there's lots."   " Goodness, gracious—living ?"

" Yes," he added,—" the lodging-house keepers !" But this was a really hard and undeserved retort ; the Craven inns and lodging-houses, as we have already pointed out, being everywhere known for their fair and reasonable treatment.

The importance of Hellifield as a railway-junction has led to a good deal of building of late years, and the place wears now quite a modern aspect. Various private houses provide teas and refreshments, and there is also a good temperance hotel with ample night accommodation, in addition to the *Black Horse*, a well-known coaching inn, recently rebuilt, on the old Leeds and Kendal turnpike. When the Act of Parliament was obtained in 1752 for "repairing, amending, and widening" the road from Keighley to Kendal, a contract was made with John Birtwhistle and Thomas Lee for the road making from two roads on the west of Gallaber Slosh to the top of Coniston Moor, at 10s. 6d. per rood. They were also to make an arched conduit over the said Slosh, the breadth of the road, and an arched bridge over Hellifield Beck. On leaving the old toll-bar house the road went to the right to a little beyond the Pan Beck farm, and thence over Goose Mere Height by a thorn hedge through Swinden and Nappa. This is now open field and the old road is grassed over and hardly distinguishable.

Hellifield Peel, the seat of Frank J. Bright, Esq., a nephew of the late eminent politician, Mr. John Bright, occupies a verdant and level mead, about half-a-mile to the south of the village. Erected 5½ centuries ago it is probably, with the single exception of Bolton Hall, the oldest entire mansion now remaining in Craven. Lawrence Hamerton, of Hamerton, obtained in the year 1440-1 royal licence to fortify and embattle his manor of Hellifield, and for many generations the old fortification was their property, being doubtless intended, from its great strength and comparatively small size, for service only as an occasional retreat in disturbed times. The owners lived in great splendour at the neighbouring Wigglesworth Hall.

The manor of Hellifield was originally held by its mesne lords, the De Knolls, of the Knights of St. John of Jerusalem, but about the end of the reign of Edward III., a matrimonial alliance having been formed between the heiress of Elias de Knolle and Adam, son of John de Hamerton, the manors of Knolsmere, Wigglesworth, and Hellifield Peel, descended to this family. Lawrence Hamerton, above mentioned, is buried in the south choir of Long Preston Church. He married a daughter of Sir John Tempest, of Bracewell, Kt., by whom he left a son, Sir Richard Hamerton, who died in 1480. At this time the family estates were of great extent and value and at the death of Sir Richard, his son Sir Stephen Hamerton, became heir to a vast property. He married a Plumpton, and left a son, John Hamerton, who by an Inq. taken April 14th, 1516, was found to have been seized in demesne as of fee, of the manors of Hamerton, Knolsmere, Wigglesworth, Hellifield, and Langfield, and a third part of Rishworth, &c., besides lands in Slaidburn, Newton, Settle, Feizor, Calton, and Coniston-Cold. He was father of the celebrated but unfortunate Sir Stephen Hamerton, Kt., who attainted with many others of high treason, through allying himself with the Pilgrimage of Grace, was "drawn, hanged and quartered" at Tyburn, and the whole of his estates were in consequence forfeited to the Crown, 28th Henry VIII. (A.D. 1537). Subsequently however, the manor of Hellifield passed by fine levied A.D. 1561, to John Hamerton, Esq., son of Richard, younger brother of Sir Stephen, by which it returned once more to the Hamerton family, and to whom it still belongs. The late Mr. Philip Gilbert Hamerton, the celebrated painter and art critic, was we may add, a member of this old family.

The ancient Peel is enclosed with a deep and broad moat. The building is of three storeys with embattled parapets and walls of great thickness. Having undergone restoration and improvement, though still retaining its ancient features, it has now more the appearance of a handsome country seat, than of an old war-proof fortress. Pleasant gardens and luxuriant foliage brighten the surroundings, and there are all the usual out-buildings, &c., that belong to a large modern residence. On one of these—the gardener's house—is a curious well-cut stone, bearing part of a Latin inscription, and on another stone is carved D. I. A., 1694 ; both stones having it is said come from an old house at Swinden, pulled down a few years ago. Another stone with a defaced inscription was brought from Sallay Abbey, and is built into the servants' hall, or new end of the house.

Hellifield to Gargrave by Swinden, 7 m. Follow the Gisburn road ½-mile to Pan Beck farm. On the right just below the Pan Beck barn and close under the plantation, stood the ancient Hellifield corn-mill, long ago destroyed. The Canons of Bolton Priory had the mill at one time, with the tithe of corn, &c. Turn here to the left over Goose Mere Height to the rustic hamlet of **Swinden,** nestling among trees, hardly accessible now by a proper road, though once on a busy coaching route, as already explained. Removed now from the busy highways of the world it seems almost the prototype of Goldsmith's *Deserted Village.* The ancient manor-house here has been rebuilt, and was formerly an inn,—

> Where village statesmen talked with looks profound,
> And news much older than their ale went round.

Near by is an old cottage (now a stable) with some illegible initials and date 1686 over the door. Another old house stood on the hill side above the Hall near some plum trees ; it was pulled down in 1885, when the inscribed stone mentioned at Hellifield Peel was found in one of the walls. The " Old Hall " still rears its massive walls by the grassy roadway, and has a curiously large and lofty porch, with heavy oaken door well studded with iron nails. Over the door is the date, 1657 and inscription : " May the 16, E.W. and H.W." Swinden in 1378 had a population of nine married couples with their families, of whom the principal tax-payer was one Nicholas de Horton, a wealthy cattle-dealer. There was also a Ricardus Mareschall, a smith, besides eight unmarried females and three unmarried males, who contributed to the remarkable tax for carrying on the wars with France.

We now go under the railway viaduct and cross the beck in Swinden Gill, where flowering rushes and various marsh-loving plants, along with fine examples of the bur-reed (*S. ramosum*) grow in plenty. Then ascending a short distance we have close to the left of the main road traces of another **ancient camp,** which appears to have been one of a succession of defensive earthworks extending obliquely from north-east to south-west from upper Airedale, by Otterburn and Coniston-Cold to the Forest of Bolland, the same line of apparent demarcation being interspersed with numerous isolated grave-hills and other traces of prehistoric possession. The Swinden Moor Camp commands a wonderful panorama, including the whole of Pendle, whose northern slopes rise from a hamlet and tree-dotted landscape ; Cold Weather Hill running away east of it, with the depression of Pendleton Moor intervening. Further to the west the long line and north slope of Easington Fell is observed, with other ranges of Lancashire fells to the north-west ; the huge camp-like Whelpstone Crag (so-called, perhaps, from the famous Scandinavian settler in these parts, Whelp, the son of Gamel) forming a conspicuous ridge in the middle distance. Turning north we have the characteristic top and projecting gritstone escarpment of Ingleborough, with Simon Fell and Park Fell falling away from it on the north-east. In the same direction, but nearer, we have the broken and fantastic summits of Attermire and Langcliffe Scars, and then nearer again the long sweep of fell rising from High Side to the hump-like top of Ryeloaf and Kirkby Fell. If Ryeloaf, anciently Inglehow, were a beacon it would be well within sight of the whole chain of camps above indicated. Away to the east stretches Malham Moor, with the top of the Cove visible, backed by the barren altitude of Fountains Fell. Coming south we discern the rocky top of Cracoe Fell, the peculiar " cones " of Flasby Fell,—an old war beacon in the time of the Spanish Armada,—and the round boss of Embsay Crag.

From the farm at Swinden Moor Head the road passes Stainton Pond, a quiet haunt of various water birds, and then **Stainton Hall** on the right, where the Craven Harriers are wont to meet, and which Mr. Wm. Gomersall, with the eye of a true artist as well as a practical huntsman, tells us in his entertaining little volume on *Hunting in Craven*, " is one of the prettiest spots for a meet of hounds in the whole district, and the gathering of ' horse and foot ' on the gentle slope in front of the fine mullioned-windowed old house, with a few ' scarlets ' among them, makes as pretty a picture as the heart of any follower of the chase, or lover of a pretty scene could wish." And when the hounds were off in full cry :

> What music they made as swiftly they came,
> Still nearer and nearer approaching the game ;
> And louder and louder, descending the hills,
> To waken the echoes in Swinden's deep gills !

We now go on through Little Stainton and the picturesque village of **Bank Newton**, so called from the family of Bank whose pedigree is given in Whitaker's " Craven." We cross the flower-bordered beck which murmurs through the village, where the few farmsteads lie amid tall trees, and in season beauteous Flora invites us to admire her various charms in the luxuriant lanes around.

The old Hall stands on elevated ground on the north bank of the stream, the south gable, which is the only original part of the building remaining, being conspicuous from the road. It is now a farmhouse, possessing no feature of particular interest excepting a curious recess, 21 in. by 15 in., which faces the main entrance, and displays a richly-carved oak board with central shield bearing the arms of Bank, &c. According to Dodsworth the ancient chapel of Bank Newton was declared at the suppression to be of the yearly value of 34s. 8d. The road to Gargrave is now direct (1½ m.), traversing a rich pastoral country, through the hamlet of Paradise.

LONG PRESTON CHURCH.

LONG PRESTON.

"If footsore, press not on in pain
But lounge and view the place,
For time so lost will prove a gain,—
The tortoise won the race."

ROM Hellifield to Long Preston is little more than a mile. When the turnpike from Hellifield to Settle was made in 1753 it was ordered that a toll-house be erected across the road from Henry Snell's dwelling-house at Long Preston Bridge to a little close called the Swine Garth at north-east end of bridge. The house was to be slated, the timber of the house and gate and rails to be good oak, except chamber-floor, good ash. The price £41. In 1754 it was ordered that a side-gate be erected at Chapel Lane End, or a chain hung in order to prevent travellers passing through Long Preston toll free, "as they have usually done;" but in April, 1756, we find that one John Clapham, Richard Redmayne, and Richard Clapham, of Austwick, were each fined 20s. for that "they did upon their own confession, on the 19th of April, make use of a counterfeit ticket to avoid payment of toll at Long Preston." Evading the toll was frequent at this time, and so bitter was the opposition to the new taxation in some districts that the toll-bars were wrecked and the keepers' houses burned down. At the Harewood toll-bar, for example, in 1753 the mob became so furious that a company of soldiers was called out, and after the reading of the Riot Act, the soldiers were ordered to fire, with the result that eight persons were shot dead and forty were more or less badly wounded. It appears to have been at the old *May Pole* inn at Long Preston that the turnpike meetings were held.

Some forty years ago before the new road to Settle was made, the coaches went over Long Preston Moor, and we have heard a story of how, on one occasion, now nearly fifty years ago, when the Judge of Assize was on circuit travelling from Leeds to Kendal, he passed in a huge coach through Long Preston. The event seems to have been of sufficient importance to warrant the local schoolmaster giving his youthful flock a half-holiday, saying as he did so, "Now, lads, the Judge is coming ;—go into Greengate Lane and pull off the branches of the trees that hang over, so that the coach can pass." Off they went in high glee, and in very little time the road was well nigh choked with broken boughs, while in their enthusiasm a tree of large proportions had been almost uprooted and partially obstructed the narrow way. Nearly half the village had to be called out to clear the lane of tree-wood before his lordship could pass, so thoroughly had the young miscreants done their work. This lane is now almost bare of trees, and the road from Long Preston to Rundley Bridge was originally so narrow that two carts meeting could barely pass.

The village of Long Preston has a neat and affluent aspect, most of the houses being comparatively modern and the property of their occupants. On the ample Green where the Holgate Memorial Fountain (1869) stands, it is nicely planted with trees. There are two good inns, the *Boar's Head* and the *Eagle*, a Village Institute (with library of about 3000 volumes), and several Chapels, that belonging to the Wesleyans having been rebuilt at a cost of over £3000. Some years since considerable expense was incurred by the erection of a cattle and sheep stand for the weekly market in the village, but the increased railway facilities at Hellifield having led to the establishment of the well-known Auction Mart at Hellifield, the markets at Long Preston are now held only twice yearly.

The little place has a long and interesting history. When the old Britons were subdued, or probably only partially conquered by the Anglo-Saxons in the 6th century, the latter remained in tolerably peaceable occupation until the Danish inroads of Craven in the 10th century, when Ulf, son of Thorold, a Danish prince, was established in Deira and became possessed in his own name of numerous manors in the North, East, and West Ridings. Long Preston, with lands in Stainforth, Wigglesworth, Hellifield, &c., was one of these, and in *Domesday*, A.D. 1086, it is recorded that there are three carucates to be taxed and one church, which had belonged to Ulf, and were now holden by the Norman usurpers in the name of Roger of Poictou. This mighty Dane, Ulf, who had so much property in Yorkshire, became in reality a naturalised Yorkshireman, and died in the reign of the Confessor. His pedigree is given by Poulson in the *History of Holderness*, where it is shewn that the fifth in descent from him married in 1228 the daughter of Thomas, Lord of Greystock, and the later Barons of Greystock bear the Forno and Ulf arms quarterly. Ulf's horn of ivory, though deprived of its original gold ornaments, is an interesting and well-authenticated relic, preserved in the vestry of York Minster, where it is shown to visitors.

The Amundevilles appear to have been the first grantees under Roger of Poictou, and in the first quarter of the 12th century the advowson of the church at Long Preston belonged to Walter de Amundeville, by whom it was bestowed upon the church and canons of Embsay, afterwards translated to Bolton in Wharfedale. At the Dissolution the rectory and advowson were granted by Henry VIII. to Christ Church, Oxford, and in 1536 the manor of Preston, with 31 others in Yorkshire, passed by fine to Henry Percy, the great Earl of Northumberland, who had a castle at Spofforth, in the Nidd valley, where he occasionally resided. In the vestry of Long Preston Church are some fragments of contemporary glass displaying the Percy and Lucy arms, a lion rampant quartered with three lucies or pike-fish, hauriant, a match stipulated by the marriage of Henry Percy, the first Earl of Northumberland, with the sister and heiress of Lord Lucy, in the time of Richard II.

Of the pre-Norman Church and its belongings probably nothing remains but the base of the font, which has had incised upon it a plain cross or some other simple Christian symbol. The present church dates from the time of Edward III., and comprises chancel, nave, aisles, south porch, and low western tower with three bells. The chancel was entirely rebuilt in 1868 by Messrs. Healey, of Bradford; the beautiful east window of three lights, by Capronnier, of Brussels, having been inserted in 1858. There are altogether eleven windows by this well-known firm in the church, which constitute a perfect study of their work from the year 1858 to the present time. Several of the windows, in addition to some wall-tablets, are memorials of local families. In the tower is a strong vault-like apartment which in all probability was used as a safe for the keeping of documents and valuables belonging to the parish. From indications of fire discovered in the old chancel, and the burnt bases of some of the columns in the nave, it is evident that the church has been used as a garrison in war times.

There was a chantry forming the south choir of the church, dedicated to Our Lady and St. Anne, which was founded and endowed by Sir Richard Hamerton, Kt. He bequeathed in the name of his mortuary, A.D. 1480, "his best horse with his saddle and bridle and other things pertaining, to the chantry founded there, for a priest perpetually to sing for Lawrence Hamerton, Esq., and himself, the said Sir Richard, their wives, children, and all ancestors." At the suppression this chantry was certified as of the annual value of £5 6s. 8d. The tomb of Lawrence Hamerton, father of the founder, who was the builder of Hellifield Peel, is preserved here. It bears a Latin inscription and five shields of arms : (1) Hamerton impaling Tempest, (2) Hamerton impaling Assheton, (3) Hamerton quartered with Knolle and Arches borne quarterly, (4) quarterly, Plumpton, (5) Hamerton and Radcliff of Longfield.

As appears by a charter dated 10th Henry VI. (1431), there was a private chapel dedicated to St. Michael attached to the church, and Dr. Whitaker believes it to have stood near the entrance to the churchyard, as a floor of painted tiles was met with in digging graves. Not a fragment of the building remains on the site now, but we have observed in an old wall adjoining the school premises a curiously carved stone of undoubted antiquity, which may have come from this old chapel of St. Michael. It apparently depicts the conflict of St. Michael the Archangel with the Dragon, as represented in the 12th chapter of *Revelations*, but whence the stone was brought is beyond the memory of any now living.

Healthy and salubrious as the district is now, this was not always the case when houses were low and confined and the crudest notions of sanitation prevailed. Epidemics were frequent, and Long Preston in common with other towns and villages in Yorkshire did not escape these awful visitations. One portion of the churchyard here it is said has been appropriated for the burial of those who died of a " black sickness," but no date is assigned, nor do the parish accounts or registers of the church throw any light on the subject.

The Charity Hospital on the Gisburn road, founded by Jas. Knowles in 1615, provides for ten poor persons who must be natives of the parish. The inmates now receive about 6s. a week each. The Endowed School was founded in 1819 under the will of Miss Isabella Hall, a native of Long Preston, who died in 1834, aged 77. Miss Hall, who lived in the house occupied by the present schoolmaster, Mr. Edward Burlend, possessed much property in Long Preston, the rents of which now form the endowment of the school. She is said to have been of very sparing and economical habits, and was rarely or never known to indulge in any kind of domestic luxuries. An egg. she used to say, was a most extravagant meal, being too much for one person, and too little for two !

" Long Preston Peggy " was another local celebrity, whose exploit during the 1745 Rebellion would probably have been forgotten long ere this had not the circumstance of her adventures given rise to a well-known ballad which obtained as much notoriety in Ribblesdale as the famous historical ballad, " Chevy Chase." The only two remembered verses of it are contained in Dixon's *Ballads and Songs of the Peasantry of England* (1857). The lines are these :

> " Long Preston Peg to proud Preston went,
>   To see the Scotch rebels it was her intent.
>   A noble Scotch lord, as he pass-ed by,
>   On this Yorkshire damsel did soon cast an eye.
>
>   He called to his servant, which on him did wait,—
>   ' Go down to yon girl who stands in the gate,
>   That sings with a voice so soft and so sweet,
>   And in my name do her lovingly greet.' "

*   *   *   *   *   *

The late Mr. Abraham Holroyd, of Eldwick, near Bingley, supplemented the lost verses with a ballad of his own composition, in which he follows, with admirable spirit, the story to its completion. The ballad contains a score verses in all, but a few of the stanzas must suffice :

" When thus commanded the messenger went
And brought the young damsel up into the tent,
And there was Prince Charlie—before whom she did kneel,—
And the brave young Lovat, and the daring Lochiel.

*   *   *   *   *   *

Then up spake Lord Murray : ' Of thee I would speer,
Whence comest thou, lassie, and what dost thou here ?
Art thou for us or not, I pray thee relate ?
And what was the song thou didst sing in the gate ? '

' You shall know what you wish, if you list to my tale :
I come from Long Preston, by sweet Ribblesdale ;
A milk-maid I am, Peg Rathmell by name,
And to see bonnie Prince Charlie hither I came.

Arthur o'Bradley was the song that I sung,—
A song of two lovers who wedded when young,
And it tells of old customs, which still do prevail.
In Craven, in Yorkshire, and sweet Ribblesdale.' "*

Long Preston to Settle by Wigglesworth, 8 m. To Wigglesworth by Cow Bridge, 2 m. The most notable edifice at **Wigglesworth** is the old Hall, which was the residence of the Hamertons. owners of Hellifield Peel, &c., from the marriage of Adam de Hamerton with the heiress of De Knolle, *temp.* Edward III., to the attainder of Sir Stephen Hamerton in 1537. After his execution the manor was granted to Sir Thomas Holcroft, and subsequently passed to the family of Sherburne of Stonyhurst, Lancashire. The house has long been occupied as a farm, and little remains to tell of its former grandeur or of its architectural pretensions and the once extensive deer park that surrounded it. What is left of the original premises consists chiefly of portions of an ancient gateway, and at the east end of the buildings, a low rubble-built edifice (now used as a lumber-room) which has evidently been the domestic chapel of the family, and is probably, from the appearance of two pointed arch-ways, as old as the first Hamerton of Wigglesworth.

The ancient soke-mill stood at an angle of the beck not far from the front side of the Hall, but allowed to go to ruin it was demolished about 1860 and the stones used for building purposes. The large old tithe-barn is however standing here yet, and is spoken of by Thoresby

* See *Leeds Mercury Weekly Supplement,* (Local Notes and Queries), October 27th, 1888.

in his *Diary*, September 18th, 1694, as "the finest barn possibly in England, measured by our servant to be 22 yards wide and 46 yards long, of stone," &c. In the village of Wigglesworth itself there is little of interest, but the place is healthy and pleasant, and many years ago a project was set afoot to popularise it, as the old Sulphur Spa here was said to possess virtues equal to the water at Harrogate, and at one time had a more than local repute. It has now fallen into disuse but may be seen near the beck below the Hall House farm enclosed with a quaint stone canopy dated 1666, coupled with the initials of Sir Richard Sherburne and Isabella, his wife, whose "pious memory" is commemorated in Mitton Church.

From Wigglesworth Hall to Rathmell is 1½ m. by a pleasant road, commanding a capital view of Penyghent and the country northwards to Ingleborough. After crossing the Hollow Gill Wood Beck, which divides the parishes of Long Preston and Giggleswick, the farm of **Far Capelside** is passed and a little beyond is Capelside House. In this vicinity was found some thirty years ago a very fine bronze paalstave, or winged celt, measuring 5 inches in length and 2¾ inches across the edge, its weight being 15 ounces. Also close to the drive leading to Capelside a pair of ancient stag's horns, in excellent condition. was unearthed, a relic no doubt of the time when native deer roamed through the glades and fells of our Craven Highlands.

Rathmell (derived probably from the Celt. *radh* and *maol*, meaning an eminence cleared of growing wood) is a very old settlement, and like Settle over the water, and Giggleswick, has preserved evidences of occupation in the first Celtic era. A variant of the ancient Celtic numerals was until recently used in counting cattle here and also formerly by women in counting stitches when knitting, &c. The numbers ran, (1) aen, (2) taen, (3) tethera, (4) fethera, (5) phubs, &c., in pentads or sets of five, an arrangement obviously referable to the primitive method of counting upon the fingers. There are a number of **prehistoric burial mounds,** probably of Celtic origin, although the enclosure in which they are situate bears a Danish name, viz., Coney Garth. The mounds are all square with one exception, which is of the long type. They have been partially examined with the result that several pieces of charcoal, small flint scrapers and flint chippings were found. In the largest of the square mounds (B) fragments of a broken urn were come upon. It was of coarse unglazed pottery, ornamented with straight lines, and burnt and black inside, as if once filled with charcoal. The surface of the earth in the centre of the mound (H) was hard and black and full of cracks as if it had been subjected to intense heat. It would therefore appear that the funeral pyre had been kindled in the central space and the urn placed in it, a practice that carries us back to the time of the Druids, who we are told killed the victims of their sacrifices with flint knives. Above Cleatop Farm on the opposite side of the valley, there are we may here observe, distinct remains of a **Druid's Circle,** about 60 feet in diameter.

In 1842 Rathmell, which had hitherto been an appurtenance of the parish of Giggleswick, was made a separate chapelry and a neat

G

church was erected. It contains some choice memorial glass to the Brown and other families, besides a rather curiously inscribed font. The view from the church-yard, taking Penyghent as the centre of vision, is very beautiful. There were two **old tithe barns** here, one of them having been built into the present Wesleyan Chapel, but the other is still used as a barn and stands on the Wigglesworth

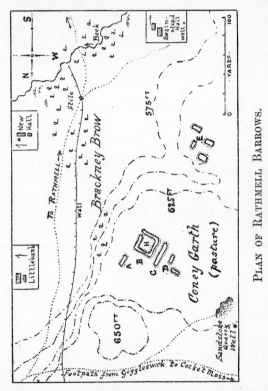

PLAN OF RATHMELL BARROWS.

road about ¼-m. from the village. The tithes were collected by the holders of three farms, viz., Capelside, the *Cross Keys* inn, and the Green or Huggan House, and when the sheaves had been gathered into hattocks—ten sheaves forming a hattock—the tithe was drawn out of every tenth hattock, and then taken to the barn to be thrashed, after which an equal division took place by the three claimants.

It was at Rathmell that the celebrated Rev. Richard Frankland founded the **first Nonconformist College** ever established in England. Mr. Frankland was born here in the year 1630 and opened his academy about 1670. During his lifetime he educated and trained no fewer than 304 students for the dissenting ministry, but the violent persecutions of the period obliged him frequently to change his residence. For a time the school was conducted at Calton Hall (the home of the Republican Lamberts) and afterwards at Natland near Kendal. Frankland died in 1698 and was buried at Giggleswick, where a tablet, recording in Latin his great virtues and learning, is to be seen in the church. The old college building at Rathmell has been turned into four cottages, which occupy an enclosure still known as College Fold. At the back of the buildings there is an inscribed stone, F. R. E., 1686.

About midway between Rathmell and Giggleswick, at a point of the Ribble called **Long Streams,** there is an old ford, which is supposed to be coeval and continuous with an old British road that runs north of Hollin Hall and by Scoutber End westwards across the moors. Formerly this part of the valley was much subject to floods, and the overflowing waters have been known to make a lake nearly three miles long and one mile wide, and in places from six to ten feet deep. It is in fact only about twenty years ago that some members of the Preston family, of Merebeck, rowed across the valley in order to attend service at Rathmell Church ! During one of these floods, in the days before railways, when the dalesfolk rarely left their homes, it is said that a farmer had fallen asleep on a hay-stack in Rathmell Ings, and was unaware of what had happened until he awoke and found himself, to his great consternation, gently floating down stream in the direction of Long Preston. A man on the bank some distance away, observed the floating stack with the captive farmer upon it and called out to him in the vernacular : " Eh, mon, whar are ta fra ?"

The farmer being scarcely yet aroused to the consciousness of his position, and quite ignorant of his whereabouts, cried out, " Whar am aw ? Whar am aw ?" " Whar are ta fra ?" again shouted the man on the bank. " *Ra'mill i' England,*" came the reply at last, the unfortunate fellow believing that he had reached some foreign shore made it quite plain that he was from " England " ; and " Rathmell, England," became a bye-word of oral and literary precision in matters local for a long time afterwards.

Long Preston to Settle by Scaleber Force, 5 m. This is a roughish tramp over Wild Share to the Malham and Settle road described on p. 44, and should not be taken after a flood when the streams are swollen. Go up Greengate Lane round by the *Eagle* inn, and when near the top a capital prospect is obtained of the country southwards, including Pendle and the surrounding fells, Rathmell, Wigglesworth, and the big tithe barn, &c. From this point is also had the best view of Long Preston. When the open moor is reached at a barn, you leave the main road (which is the old coach route, before mentioned, to Settle) and branch to the right by a track alongside the wall. This runs through the "**Beacon Coppy**" where is the site of old-beacon fires, and last used at the celebration of Her Majesty's Jubilee in 1887. The lonely Bookilber Farm,—perhaps the most solitary house in Craven,—is seen some way off to the right, backed by the frowning heights of Kirkby Fell and Ryeloaf. The path goes straight on about ½-m. to a moor gate just above Long Preston Beck, and from this gate you have a good view of the splintered rocks of Attermire, but the entrance to Attermire Cave is not seen, only the "slits" of the Horse Shoe Caves being visible in the lofty scar opposite. A zig-zag track leads down to the romantic little glen traversed by the **Long Preston Beck**, which is crossed by stepping-stones, whence the track continues with the stream on the left. In less than ½-m. you go over the crest of the hill on the right and enter Longber Lane within ½-m. of Scaleber Bridge, where is the famous **waterfall**. This ridge marks the boundary of the **South Craven Fault**, having a westward downthrow, with the limestone on the north side and the grits on the south. The more adventurous tourist will follow the beck up to where the wooded dingle divides, and taking the one sharp to the right he will reach in ¼-m. the foot of the waterfall, which with a moderate flow of water is one of the most beautiful in Craven (*see* p. 44).

A surer way from Long Preston to Scaleber (3½ m.) than either of the above routes is to take the lane opposite the School and follow the track up with Long Preston Beck on the left. This passes a little to the north of Bookilber Farm and enters Longber Lane, whence you have a straight road to Scaleber Bridge and by the Roman Camp (*see* p. 44) down to Settle. The Stockdale Beck, we may add, which enters the Scaleber Beck a little above the Force, is on the watershed of England, itself draining into the Ribble and the Irish Sea, while the streams just beyond, to the east, drain into the German Ocean.

SETTLE IN 1822.

SETTLE.

Though sluggards deem it but a foolish chase,
  And marvel men should quit their easy chair,
The toilsome way, and long, long leagues to trace,—
  Oh, there is sweetness in the mountain air,
  And life that bloated ease can never hope to share !
BYRON.

 HE line of lofty limestone scars, fretted with fissure and cavern, and extending northwards from Settle to Stainforth (where they are cut off by the upcropping Silurians) and eastwards to the Black Hills and Attermire, includes a circuit of about seven miles and attains an altitude above mean sea level of about 1400 feet. This area and elevation are exactly identical with the rocky, cave-pierced island of Gibraltar, the "key to the Mediterranean," while the romantic little town of Settle itself, nestling at the foot of its grand, beetling rock, Castleberg—with its traces of ancient forts—may not inappropriately be designated the Gibraltar of Craven. But unlike the famous Mediterranean fortress, Settle is no longer a sea-coast town, although we have evidence of the Ribble in its vicinity having been a tidal river at no very remote period, as geological reckonings go, while various maritime plants still flourish in the pure air of the surrounding hills.

Settle likewise may be said to be the key to the 'straits' of Ribblesdale, and in ancient times must have commanded the advance of any hostile tribes moving northwards or southwards through the dale. This restricted passage continues for several miles until the open territory about Horton and Penyghent is reached, and if we might venture a derivation of the name of this well-known mountain we should say that it is found in the old Cymric-Celtic *pen*, a head, or hill summit, and *gwent* (pron. *gooent*), a fair, wide or open region, an exceedingly appropriate appellation given by the ancient Britons, who, after penetrating the Settle pass, reached the open country below Horton. That the neighbourhood of Settle has been occupied at a very remote era is abundantly testified in the numerous prehistoric relics found in the caverns of the district, in the existence of the "Druid's Circle" at Cleatop; in the discovery of cinerary urns at Anley, and in the digging up of the rare and interesting old British fishing-boat in the bed of the dried-up Giggleswick Tarn, which is now in the Museum at Leeds, but whose proper home we think should be in the Museum at Giggleswick.

Although Settle is the market and post-town of the parish it has always been an appendage ecclesiastically of Giggleswick, on the opposite side of the river. The ancient parish of Giggleswick, which includes an area of about 18,500 acres, comprises the townships of Giggleswick, Settle, Stainforth, Langcliffe, and Rathmell. Langcliffe was made a separate ecclesiastical parish some time before the death of the Rev. W. H. Coulthurst, vicar of Giggleswick, in 1892, when Settle, Rathmell, and Stainforth were constituted separate ecclesiastical parishes.

Before the Domesday Survey was made in 1086 the manor of Giggleswick was held by one Fech and had 17 carucates to be taxed; while the manor of Settle, with Anley, was held by Burun, an ancestor of the poet Lord Byron, and had six carucates to be taxed. On the failure of the line of De Burun the bulk of the estates belonging to this family were granted by Henry II. to Ranulph, Earl of Chester, who married Maud, daughter of Robert, Earl of Gloucester, and whose arms, five chevrons, *or* and *gules*, may be seen upon a quarry of very old glass in Long Preston Church.

The aspects of Settle have very much altered since the poet Gray visited the town over a century ago. He describes it as "standing directly under a rocky fell; there are not a dozen good looking houses in it," he says, "the rest are old and low, with little wooden porticos in front." The last of these wooden porticos disappeared about sixty years ago, when the Town Hall was built. The latter handsome building stands on the site of the "Old Toll Booth." In this mediæval institution, always near the market place for the convenience of the lords' toll-gatherers', the law documents were kept, courts were held, and other official business of the parish transacted. Here dwelt the town watchman, and here too was the old Lock-up or Prison, with its Black-hole or underground dungeon, a dismal and unwholesome cavity, probably as old as the Norman centuries, when

> " Silent on the pavement stone
> A warder knelt and placed thereon
> Coarse fare and scant, a meal austere,
> Though meet for a doomed prisoner ;
> No word nor sign betwixt them passed,
> Each deeming word or sign but waste."

Near it stood the Market Cross, which now forms the top of the Fountain, only a few yards from the original site of the cross. The markets date from the 33rd Henry III., (A.D. 1248). Among the many curious exactions of tolls and stallage here was a long-established one of a claim of one halfpenny for every new hat worn on market days, a demand that has probably something to do with a statute passed in the time of Queen Elizabeth, by which every person above six years of age (ladies and nobles excepted) was obliged to wear, on Sundays and Holy Days, a cap of English-knit wool on pain of 3s 4d. fine for each day's transgression. These so-called " statute caps " are frequently alluded to by the early dramatists. Around the Market Place are several old inns, one of which exhibits a stone figure of a naked man holding a shield inscribed I. C., 1663, such signs having originated as a satire upon the whims of our ancestors in the matter of dress :

> " So fickle is the English nation
> I would be clothed if I knew the fashion."

At Langcliffe, near Settle, there was also an inn called the *Naked Woman*, the stone effigy of which still remains in front of the house. Of other notable buildings still happily remaining to remind us of ancient Settle, may be mentioned the Shambles, with its quaint arched front and stone balcony, facing the Market Place, and the house known as the Folly, with its handsome façade in the domestic style of the Stuart period. This conspicuous mansion was built by a person named Preston, but not having the means to complete it in the style in which it was begun, the old house carries a tell-tale name. In Upper Settle may still be seen the old Cattle Pound, a relic of the times when roads and fences were not so abundant as they are now, and cattle and sheep went often astray.

The lofty crag of **Castleberg**, above mentioned, which hangs over the town, may be conveniently ascended. It is nicely planted, and laid out and provided with walks, seats, swings, &c., and from the top commands an excellent view of the town and surrounding country. A small charge is made for admission.

MARKET PLACE, SETTLE.

Settle is well provided with hotel and house accommodation for visitors intending any length of stay. There is the *Ashfield*, the largest hotel in Craven, the *Golden Lion*, the old coaching house, Hayton's temperance hotel, and a number of others, public and private, where comfortable lodgings may be had. There is a station close to the town on the romantic Carlisle line, and another about a mile distant at Giggleswick on the Lancaster line, both of which afford a convenient means of making day-excursions to places of interest. There is a post office (with, on week-days, three deliveries daily) and a telegraph office, both open from 8 a.m. to 8 p.m. on week-days and on Sundays from 8 to 10 a.m. The Settle Literary Society possesses one of the oldest provincial circulating libraries which contains about 10,000 volumes. There is ample church and chapel accommodation ; the Church of England, the Roman Catholics, the Society of Friends, the Wesleyans, Congregationalists, and Primitive Methodists all having their own places of worship, at which strangers are always welcome. The population of the township is a little under 2400, but in the summer months this number is greatly increased by the influx of visitors.

Before we enter upon a description of the numerous walks, drives, and diverse attractions of the neighbourhood, let us cross the Ribble for a peep at the adjacent picturesque old-world village of

GIGGLESWICK.

From the bridge over the Ribble there is a capital view of the huge round bulk of Penyghent, which the celebrated Archdeacon Paley, when once viewing it from this spot, said looked very much like a raised pie ! In descending Bell Hill to the village you will pass the house (to the left of the road) in which the family of Archdeacon Paley lived. His father, the Rev. Wm. Paley, was for 54 years Master of the Giggleswick School, and died in 1799, aged 88. His distinguished son died in 1805, aged 62, having been brought to Giggleswick when a child from Peterborough, where his father was a Minor Canon in the Cathedral. Many amusing anecdotes are told of the Archdeacon, who though of a quiet and meditative turn possessed a fund of dry humour. But his satire occasionally was much too pungent, and there is a passage in his chapter on " Property " (*vide Moral and Political Philosophy*, Book III.) which is said to have lost him the chance of a Bishopric. He loved indeed the hills and scars of this romantic neighbourhood, which he regarded almost as his native haunts, and like Wordsworth in his constant rambles drew inspiration and knowledge from the mystic lore which Nature always dispenses to those who love her.

But now we are in Giggleswick, a name, says Dr. Whitaker, with his aristocratic fondness for rich and noble rulers, that

GIGGLESWICK.

means the *wick* or village belonging to one Gikel, but in the absence of historic proof of the existence of this local 'monarch,' we beg leave to seek another interpretation in the Anglo-Saxon word *gugglian*, to bubble up, in allusion to the famous Ebbing and Flowing Well here. In various early charters the name is suggestively written Gugleswic, Guckilswic, Gukleswic, and the like, while in Saxony and Bavaria and other parts of Germany and Austria there are scores of place-names compounded with Kick, Kickl, Gigg, Gigl, &c., which have unquestionable reference to their situation beside some notable spring or flowing-well. And assuredly there could be no more remarkable or peculiar feature by which this locality might be identified than by a name derived from the almost unique and mysterious spring at Giggleswick, in the immediate vicinity of which the houses or huts of the primitive inhabitants were collected long before the foundation of the parish church.

The earliest discoverable reference about a church at Giggleswick is contained in an attestation of one "Laurentius, Persona de Guckilswic," to a charter of William de Percy, in the reign of King Stephen. Subsequently the ecclesiastical authority, with all its profits, was conferred by the Pudsays on the Benedictine Priory of Finchale, and the Prior and Convent of Durham, as patrons of that monastery, held the presentation to the vicarage of Giggleswick up to the dissolution of religious houses in 1538, when the patronage fell to the Crown. About the year 1600 the advowson was granted out, and the living is now in the alternate presentation of the Hartley and Coulthurst families.

The present spacious and substantial fabric, dedicated to St. Alkelda, belongs to the great church building era of the time of Henry VII. The building has recently undergone a very thorough and efficient restoration at considerable cost ; the whole roof among other necessary work having been taken off, and the old oak rafters replaced with solid timbers of new oak. The nave is of four bays with clerestory, and there are north and south aisles to both nave and chancel. The chancel, which had formerly a rather poor window of six lights, has now a handsome six-light stained glass window representing the Crucifixion and Ascension ; this beautiful addition being the gift of John Hartley, Esq., of Clapham, in memory of " John and Esther Hartley, of Catteral Hall." A noteworthy object in the church is the fine old oak pulpit (with sounding board) and reading desk. The panels are

very ably carved with the names and badges of the Twelve
Tribes of Israel, viz. :

REUBIN, *waves* ("unstable as water"), SIM, *sword* ("instruments
of cruelty"), LEV., *a scroll,* GAD, *flag of battle* ("He shall overcome"),
NAPH, *a hind let loose,* ASH, *cup* ("royal dainties"), JUDAH, *a
rampant lion,* ZEB., *a ship,* ISAAC, *an ass,* DAN, *a coiled serpent,*
JOSEPH, *an ox,* BEN., *a horse with cloven foot.*

In front of the reading desk is cut, "HEAR IS THE
STANDARDES OF THE ISRAELITES WHEN THE TO CANAN CAM
AGENEST THE CANANITES," and on the sides are the initials
of the churchwardens for the year 1680, along with their
badge, a carved representation of three collecting-boxes.
Observe also the carved alms-box bearing the quaint inscription : "1684, Remember the Pore."

There were three chantry-chapels formerly attached to the
church. (1) the Stainford Chantry, situated where the organ
is now placed, founded by Robert Stainford (*ob.* 1391), and
at the suppression stated to be of the yearly value of £4 ;
(2) the Chantry of the Rood on the south side of the chapel,
of the foundation of James Carr, priest, of the yearly value
of £6 1s. 8d. ; (3) the Tempest Chantry, on the north side,
where the vestry now is, founded by Sir Richard Tempest, Kt.,
and of the yearly value of £4 13s. 4d.

During the recent restoration a cumbent statue of Sir
Richard Tempest, of Stainforth, was found buried face
downwards, along with portions of two other stone effigies.
Sir Richard was born about 1425, and was knighted by Lord
Clifford at the battle of Wakefield, in 1460. He was a great
soldier and a prominent figure on the Lancastrian side in the
unhappy broil between the Houses of York and Lancaster
during the Wars of the Roses. A very unusual discovery
was made at the time these effigies were found, namely of the
skull of the knight's favourite war-horse buried close beside
its long-deceased master. The animal had probably saved
its owner in many a bloody fray, and must have been regarded
with a special tenderness to have found so honourable and
exceptional a resting-place. The Knight's statue, which is
six feet in length, is represented clad in the armour of the
period, with the head reclining upon a goat's head. The
other 15th century effigies, which have been unfortunately
much mutilated and broken, are of Dames Sibill, daughter

of Sir Richard Hoghton, and Mabel, daughter of Sir Walter Strickland, being respectively the first and second wives of the same Sir Richard Tempest. Both figures are sculptured in the garb of the Guild of Corpus Christi of York, and it is said are the only ones known to exist in this costume. Under the careful supervision of Mr. Thomas Brayshaw, the indefatigable hon. secretary of the Restoration Committee, these statues, with various other relics, including some early Norman carved stones, have been cleaned and restored for permanent preservation in the church.

In the churchyard is a stone coffin, and in the pavement just outside the porch is an old tombstone incised with a double cross and sword. The churchyard is entered by a lych-gate, erected about fifty years ago, and opposite it is an ancient upright stone cross raised on three steps, and close to this are the remains of the old parish stocks. The original purpose of the cross seems never clearly to have been ascertained, but as the Settle Markets originated by charter in the time of Henry III., and as the design of this cross is precisely of that era, there is just a suspicion that it came from there. A writer in the *Gentleman's Magazine* for 1784, in giving some account of the cross, remarks, "Tradition, through the channel of the inhabitants of Settle, informs us that some of the Giggleswick residents stole it from the base of the old cross at Settle in order to prejudice the trial concerning the antiquity of the market, but this is partial, and as it is an interested tale the inhabitants of Giggleswick deny the assertion." Yet it is not improbable that markets were held at Settle soon after their institution by Alfred the Great, and the discovery last century of a supposed Saxon medal at the base of the old Settle Cross strengthens this conclusion. The Giggleswick Cross may therefore be a relic of an earlier church than that now existing, and was presumably a Weeping Cross. When England was Catholic, weeping and praying for the dead at such crosses was an universal practice, and bodies on their way for burial would be rested at these places for a few minutes. prior to their being carried into the church or churchyard for interment. After the Reformation it was ordered that there "be no praying for the dead at crosses, or places where crosses have beene in the waye to the church."

A short stroll along the banks of the Tems—a little stream with a big name—brings us to the famous Grammar School at Giggleswick, one of the oldest as well as one of the most opulent institutions of the kind in England. A few years ago the Governors of the School expended a sum of about £30,000 in building a large boarding-house or hostel, in providing masters' houses, school-rooms, laboratories, &c. The handsome range of buildings occupies a fine and healthy site with a principal frontage to the grand line of scars on the west. The School was founded by James Carr in 1507, and some forty-five years later was endowed with lands, &c., on petition of the Rev. John Nowell, vicar of Giggleswick, who was at that time chaplain to King Edward VI. The revenues, which at the foundation were valued at £23 3s., amounted in 1844 to £1071 14s. 4d., and have since considerably increased.

Among names of distinction associated with the old school and neighbourhood may be mentioned the Paleys, of whom mention is made above ; the Shutes, eminent divines, one of whom, the Rev. Christopher Shute, D.D., was vicar of Giggleswick, and master of the Grammar School from 1615 to 1619 ; the Very Rev. John S. Howson, D.D., Dean of Chester, born 1816, died 1885 ; Dr. George Birkbeck, founder of Mechanics' Institutes, who died in 1841, and whose monument, with an inscription by his friend Lord Brougham, is now in the restored church at Giggleswick ; Thomas Proctor, the celebrated sculptor, born in 1753 in a house in Kirkgate, Settle ; Abraham Sutcliffe, a famous medical practitioner, born in 1710 at Halifax, and his son William Sutcliffe, of Settle, physician and botanist ; Dr. Lettsom, F.R.S., born in 1744, a pupil of Dr. Abraham Sutcliffe at Settle. He removed to London and founded the Medical Society of London, was exceedingly benevolent, and "although he made as much as £12,000 a year, he gave it away as freely to charitable institutions of all kinds." In 1782 he persuaded the great botanist Curtis to visit Settle (at his expense) and prepare a list of local plants. He was specially interested in botany, and is credited with having introduced that useful root, Mangel-wurzel, into this country, the seed of which he sent all over the world. Dr. Lettsom

died in 1815,—an able, genial, and sturdy sort of man,
about whom the following amusing epigram was current in
last century :

> Whenever patients come to I,
> I physics, bleeds, and sweats 'em :
> If after that they choose to die,
> Why ! what care I ?—I LETTSOM.

The Museum at Giggleswick (the key of which is kept
by Mr. Brown, whose house adjoins the school) contains a
valuable collection of local relics and other objects of interest.
The doorway of the building, which forms part of the old
school premises, was erected by Dean Howson and his
brothers to the memory of their mother. The following is
an epitome of the contents of the Museum :

Collection presented by the Victoria Cave Committee, 1869—78.
Stones introduced by Man, and many of them used by him as whet-
stones and hammer stones. and for grinding and polishing. Pottery,
Bronze and Silver Coins of the Roman occupation. Worked bones
and ivory, forming pins, needles, spoon-brooches, sword and dagger
handles, &c., some with incised patterns. Beads and fragments of
ancient glass.

Animal remains from the Victoria Cave, which include remarkably
fine skulls of male and female Grisly Bears, Ulna of Cave Bear,
Radius of Stag, bones of Deer, Reindeer, Bison, Woolly Rhinoceros,
Hippopotamus, and Hyenæ ; milk-teeth of young Elephas Antiquus ;
a hamperful of complete skeleton water-rats ; a cast of the "Bone of
Contention." or Human Fibula, (conjectured) supposed pre-glacial.

Ancient Stone Celt found in a rabbit-hole at Neal Ing. Several
glaciated stones. Burial Urn found near Hellifield. Old Quern and
Armour presented by W. Morrison, Esq., J.P. Collection of beautifully-
mounted local and other birds, presented by T. R. Clapham. Esq., of
Austwick Hall.

Case of Carboniferous fossils from Settle, Malham Moor, Clitheroe
&c., including *Buccinium imbricat, Eunomplatus Dionysi, Pleuroto-
maria oridea, Orthoceras undulata, Goniatites mutabilis, Productus,*
(several good species), *Ctenodonta, Cladodus, Helodus, Amplexus,
Syringopora,* etc.

With respect to the supposed fibula found in the Victoria
Cave it is now generally conceded by biologists to belong to
one of the lower animals, possibly an ape. The absence of
implements or indications of human presence in the stratum
where found is insufficient to prove the existence of pre-glacial
man in this neighbourhood. There has however been much
wrangling over the subject, which puts us in mind of a story
we heard of a gentleman who visited the Museum with his

young son.   Said the boy, pointing to this particular object,
" Pa, what is the bone of contention ?"   " The bone of
contention, my boy," said papa solemnly, "'is the jawbone—
the jawbone."

Now for our " tramps and drives."

GIGGLESWICK SCARS.

**Settle or Giggleswick to the Scars and Ebbing and
Flowing Well,** 1¼ m.   One great source of pleasure is variety.
Uniformity, said the great Dr. Johnson, must tire at last, though it
be uniformity of excellence.   Now one great charm of this locality

Speight's "Tramps and Drives in the Craven Highlands."

is its diversity of scenery ; hill and plain, crag and dell, darksome cave, sunny mount and woodland glade, are here mingled in bountiful variety, and in viewing these with their multitude of curiosities, we shall surely find much knowledge and interest—

—Tongues in trees,
Books in the running brooks, sermons in stones,
And good in everything.

From Settle cross the Ribble Bridge and along the Clapham road˙ From Giggleswick pass Catteral Hall to the Clapham road. Coming from Giggleswick Station, you may notice (about 50 yards from the station) a large roughly-squared block of sandstone built into the wall on the right. It has a shallow cavity in the centre. Tradition affirms this to be a **Plague Stone**, and to have been used during the plagues which ravaged Craven, and Yorkshire generally, in the 16th and 17th centuries. The inhabitants of infected villages were forbidden, under heavy penalties, to pass beyond these plague-stones, and orders for goods and provisions were communicated by written requests deposited on these stones with the money in payment. The recipients took the money out of the basin or cavity in the stone, usually containing lime water or vinegar, and the goods were deposited in exchange.

Entering upon the Clapham highway under the splendid range of caverned scars which extends for nearly a mile, you are in presence of one of the grandest geological phenomenas in England. These scars of picturesquely-broken limestone are the direct result of what is known as the **Great Craven Fault,** a fracture in the crust of the earth by which the strata have been vertically disturbed to the extent in some places, as at Ingleton, of about 3000 feet. Here on our right-hand we have the massive lofty scars of mountain limestone, while below us on our left we have the millstone grits of much later date, the highway doubtless marking the line of fault. The fault, as will be observed, has been a downthrow to the west, and the throw or subsidence has been about 1000 feet. The scars are picturesquely wooded and present a rich undergrowth of shrubs, mosses, and wild flowers ; among the latter are many interesting and uncommon species, such as the helleborine, fragrant orchis, blood-cranesbill, &c.* On warm summer nights the bright phosphoresence of the rare glow-worm may also be occasionally seen shining among the rank grass near the Ebbing and Flowing Well. These tiny creatures, says the famous pastor of Selborne, usually put out their lamps, like most well-regulated families do, before midnight and are seen no more for the rest of the night. How delightful is a saunter under these flower-spangled cliffs on a calm summer's eve ! A couple of " spoons " were once walking along this road ; the young lady had been talking about the old heroism of Swiss youths climbing the dangerous Alps for the edelweiss, by which to win their lady-loves. Then stopping and looking pensively up at the most awkward and precipitous part

* For List of Local Plants *see* APPENDIX.

H

of the scars, said as if in challenge to her companion, "But men never do brave deeds now-a-days to show their love for women!" "But don't they just," came the sharp and cruel answer, "*Don't they marry them?*" That young man deserved to remain a bachelor.

Now we are at the **Ebbing and Flowing Well**, which greatly puzzled "Drunken Barnaby" and the wits of his day,—

> "Neither know the learned that travel,
> What procures it, salt or gravel."

many supposing the peculiar motion of the well due to some mysterious action of the sea. But the accompanying diagram affords perhaps the best explanation of the phenomenon : The large upper cavity (A) is probably connected with a lower and smaller one (C) by several inclined channels (FG). The centre channel (B) is curved in the

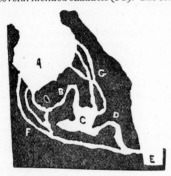

manner of a syphon towards the lower basin (C) and from the latter a second and larger syphon (D) runs downwards to the well (E). In ordinary weather when there is a medium supply of rain the water gradually fills the lower basin, and when it has reached the summit of the lower syphon, the latter being of larger dimensions than the upper one, quickly draws off the water before the narrower upper channel has time to re-fill the basin. Ordinarily the water will rise and fall 6 to 8 inches in a few minutes, but in a time of flood or of drought the ebb and flow obviously cannot take place. Sometimes what is known as the "silver cord," a thin current of air extending through the length of the well, may be seen and it is considered an omen of good luck to those who witness it. On Easter Sunday troops of children visit the well, and taking bottles with them make "Spanish-juice" of its ice-cold waters, this being doubtless a survival of some form of ancient well-worship.

Old Drayton in his *Polyolbion*, published in 1612, tells us of a tradition that prevailed in his day regarding the cause of this wonderful ebbing and flowing. He says that

> —in the mountains high
> Of Craven, whose blue heads for caps put on the sky,

there dwelt a most beautiful but very shy nymph. She was in truth so beautiful that she hardly dare show herself, lest some wicked god should want to win her to himself, much to her distrust and discomfort. But one fine day she ventured rather further from her home than was her wont, and was soon spied by a sneaking old satyr. Then there was a run. The nymph fled in the direction of Giggleswick Scars, and was being hotly pursued by the fearful being at her back who was quickly gaining upon her. At last, terribly alarmed and growing "wondrous scant of breath," she prayed the gods to turn her into a spring, and this they did to her intense relief, just as the horrid satyr was about to seize her "flowing silver hair." Thus she gained immortality in that the ebb and flow of the water where the transformation took place is thought by the faithful to be the visible panting of the sylph's heart!

In the low ground on the left of the road below the Well was formerly an extensive sheet of water known as **Giggleswick Tarn.** It was drained in 1837 and some time afterwards an ancient whole tree-boat was discovered embedded in the soil near the present barn at the southern extremity of the lake. The boat was of the primitive Celtic type, hollowed out of the trunk of a single oak, and measured 8 feet 2 inches long, 21 inches broad, and 14 inches inside depth. No doubt it had been used for fishing purposes by the original settlers in the vicinity of the tarn 2000 or more years ago. This interesting relic is now in the Leeds Museum.

Before the present coach-road was made in the middle of last century an old lane passed a little distance below the Well. The latter emptied itself by two streams into the Tarn, and at this point had to be forded,—a rather awkward spot in wet weather. Our view of the aspects of the Well at that time is from an old engraving by Buck and Feary done in 1778. The horse-in-steps at the Well, as well as those near Crow Nest, about two miles further north, were placed there in 1760, when the road was completed. Some distance above the Well is a gap in the Scar called **Nevison's Nick,** which according to local tradition, was a passage by which the great highwayman managed on horseback to evade his pursuers. From the "spirit of the well," saith the legend, he obtained the magic bridle that enabled him to perform this wonderful feat. Not far from this point are a couple of caverns high up in the scar, called **Staircase** and **Dangerous Caves.** The former can be seen from the highroad about 100 yards before the well is reached. Neither of them are of any particular extent, and have been robbed of their pendant lustres. The Scar Top can be ascended by the depression between the Well and the Staircase Cave, and a fine view obtained. Here is a lofty cairn of stones called the **Schoolboys' Tower,** built up by an old custom at Giggleswick School of every new scholar climbing up here and adding one stone to the cairn. The "tower" is visible many miles off, and must represent a goodly school-roll.

Giggleswick or Settle to Stackhouse and back by Langcliffe, 2¾m. From Giggleswick ascend Bell Hill to Stackhouse Lane. This rustic road was formerly called Lobley Lane, and when the Keighley and Kendal turnpike was made in the middle of last century had a toll-bar at the end, " 200 yards west of Settle Bridge." From the bridge a field-path keeps the west side of the river, and emerges into the lane near **Stackhouse.** This snug little hamlet was anciently a possession of Furness Abbey, and for very many

EBBING AND FLOWING WELL (OLD ASPECTS).

generations was the seat of two old and respectable Craven families, the Carrs and Brayshaws, whose picturesque homesteads still remain here. The owner of the pretty ivy-grown mansion we perceive on entering the place is evidently proud of his possession. In summer the garden is a perfect Paradise of bright-hued flowers, rustic arbours and clean-shaven lawns ; the house and grounds being wrapped in a cloak of forest green which gives an agreeable shelter and completeness to the site.

A lane shortly diverges to the right and crosses a long plank-bridge to the hamlet of Locks. Or if time permit the walk from Stackhouse may be extended by the road direct to Stainforth (1¼m.) for a view of the fine **Falls of the Ribble,** and thence back by Langcliffe. The village of **Langcliffe** was razed to the ground during the Scottish raids into Craven after Bannockburn in 1314, and is said to have formerly occupied a site a little to the north, in a field called Pesbers leading to Winskill and Catterick Force. The parents of Archdeacon Paley (see p. 93) resided at Langcliffe in a house still standing and which faces the green. They had a small estate here, which is still in the possession of the family. Langcliffe Hall, formerly a possession of the Swales and Dawsons, is now the residence of the Misses Perfect. About thirty years ago the late Miss Dawson, of Settle, enlarged the house and improved and remodelled the grounds, and upon her decease the property was bequeathed to her relative, Mr. W. Mosley Perfect. Here resided Christopher Dawson, who married a daughter of Sir Thomas Craven of Appletrewick, who died in 1682. He was a son of Robert Craven, first-cousin of the famous Sir Wm. Craven, who from the condition of a poor farm-lad at Burnsall rose to be Lord Mayor of London, and was father of the celebrated Earl of Craven, who married a sister of King Charles the First. Thus in two short generations this remarkable family rose from poverty and obscurity to the very steps of the throne ! William Dawson, son of the above Christopher, married in 1705 the heiress of the Pudsays of Bolton-by-Bolland, descendants of the old lords of Giggleswick. He was a Major of the Militia, and a man of high classical attainments. It is averred that he was one of the very few persons living at that time who could comprehend Sir Isaac Newton's *Principia Philosophiæ*, an erudite and once much-talked-of work, published in 1687. The great philosopher is said to have been an occasional visitor of Major Dawson at Langcliffe, and before the rearrangement of the gardens Newton's Arbour is believed to have stood at a corner of a small orchard, where the kitchen garden is now, on the north side of the house. Here are two old apple-trees which are reputed to have sprung from cuttings derived from an old tree planted by the Major to commemorate the philosopher's great discovery of the law of gravitation, from the well-known story of his watching an apple fall while meditating in his garden at Woolsthorpe. No memorial of Sir Isaac is preserved in the house. A portrait of the Major hangs in the hall, which is also finely adorned with old black oak. Over the west or original main entrance there is a shield of arms with initials and date 1602.

CELTIC WALL, NEAR SMEARSIDE.

From Langcliffe to Settle is 1 m. A short distance above the lodge entrance to Langcliffe Place (H. Christie, Esq., J.P.) the road divides, the lower one emerging near Settle Bridge, and the upper one at the Market Place, Settle.

Settle by the Celtic Wall to Smearside and back by Stainforth, 6 m. This is a rugged but exhilarating hill-walk of no great distance. From Giggleswick by Stackhouse Lane and from Settle by the field-path to Stackhouse, as described in the last route. Where the road divides, just beyond Mr. Waugh's pretty house, you wind beneath the wood behind Scale House to a gate and stile on the left. Here ascend the field between two large trees, and at the top mount the stile, whence a path leads up the field a good half-mile to a gate, which opens into a **prehistoric burial-ground.** There are several barrows of varying dimensions within this elevated and rocky enclosure. The largest of them lies to the left of the grassy cart-road as you proceed. It is described at length by a writer in the *Gentleman's Magazine* for 1784 and 1785, and locally was known (like many other such heaps) as the "Apronful of Stones." In form circular and composed of earth and stones, it measured (when opened in 1784) 210 feet in circumference at the base, the height being about 30 feet, and the diameter of the summit 45 feet. In the centre of the mound was a cavity containing a chest composed of four upright stones and a lid 6¾ feet long and 3 feet broad. The chest was in partitions, in the edges of which was a kind of hole with a rude mould. There was found a well-preserved human skeleton and several other human bones, including part of a jaw and several teeth, along with a small circular piece of ivory and the tusk of an unknown beast, probably a boar (a symbol of hunting), but no ashes or implements were discovered. From this imperfect description we are left to infer that this was the mausoleum of some famous Neolithic hunter, identical with the gallery-tombs of Sweden, and fashioned like the rude dwellings of the Esquimaux in Greenland. The latter believing that the departed will continue after death the same activity which marked their life, build the same kind of dwellings for the dead as for the living, and place them in the grave in the same crouched position as they were accustomed to in life, along with the heirloom by which they were known, or some particular emblem of their prowess. Does not this old hero's cairn of piled-up stones remind us of what we read in the poems of Ossian,—of Oscar, the warrior, crying in his last moments :

> Ossian, carry me to my hills !
> Place the horn of a deer,
> Place the sword by my side,
> Raise the stones of my renown,
> And they shall speak to other years !

Following the grassy cart-road mentioned to the gate, you turn left about 30 yards to another gate, which opens into a field, whence at a distance of about 300 yards an old lime-kiln will be observed at the foot of the scar. Having shut the gates you ascend the scar on the left of the kiln and climb the wall at the top, whence a turn is made to the left to a conspicuous gap. Proceeding northwards some distance you will come to the remains of two conspicuous (supposed) **Celtic Walls** occupying an extensive area of open, broken ground. These fragments of what appear to have been protective enclosures either for people or for cattle are exceedingly interesting, and are probably unique in England. They occupy a site about 1000 feet above present sea level, and are of such proportions and strength as to be altogether beyond the requirements of a civilised age. Of the larger wall there remains a length of 66 feet, which is 4½ to 5 feet thick at the base, 3½ to 4 feet at the top, and 5½ feet high. The stones are laid wedge-fashion, some being of exceptionally large size, measuring at a yard or more from the ground 2 to 4 feet long and a foot in thickness. The stones at the north end are built transversely to the length of the wall, shewing this to have been an entrance-way The other wall is of like thickness, but neither so long nor so high, only about 15 yards remaining. They may be as old as the Roman invasion of Craven, when the native tribes as we have elsewhere pointed out, were driven to the hills by stress of conquest. They would probably be enclosures used for the double purpose of securing their cattle, sheep, or goats from the predatory attacks of invading enemies, and at nights the herds would be collected here out of harm's way of the wild bears and wolves then infesting these highlands.

The rocky summit of **Smearside** (1192 feet) is now seen directly before you, a short distance to the north, and the hollow ground below the Celtic Walls must be crossed in order to gain the highest or easternmost peak. Smearside (*pron.* Smearset) is to Craven what Great Gable is to the Lake District, perhaps the most central view-point for obtaining the best idea of the surrounding dales and scars. From some places Smearside looks like a huge cone, its northern face going down with a long, even surface into the valley, as if it had been planed or smoothed by the passage of ice. There are indeed many erratic boulders lying about, and there can be no doubt that the whole mountain from base to summit has been glacier-ridden. Upon the summit there were formerly very distinct indications of an ancient watch-tower, which may have been as old as the Romans, as on the flat below there are appearances of a Roman camping-ground, and such a central point as Smearside would be a useful look-out post secured by the great Roman strategists, who occupied all the best positions during their exploiting conquests.

The view from Smearside embraces the whole of the Ingleborough range on the west, and the whole of Penyghent, with Fountains Fell on the east, while to the north rise the mural scars of Moughton, and southwards the Lancashire moors, with the massive outline of Pendle conspicuous on the horizon. Many lesser hills and dales, hamlets and tree-shaded farms fill up the intervening landscape, making this as we have said one of the best viewing points in the Scar Country.

A descent may be made in a south-easterly direction to the hollow across which extend the earthworks of the **Roman Camp** above mentioned. It would not appear to have been a regular camp, but used only as a temporary halting-place by troops while on march.

The defences are meagre and comprise a number of rectangular fortifications, the largest of which is about 80 yards long and 50 wide, divided into three portions, and separated from two other smaller earthen ramparts on the north by a long open space, which may have been the *principia*, or division of the general's from the soldiers' camp.

Make for a conspicuous barn near some large trees, whence a narrow lane leads into the main road a half-mile from Little Stainforth for Settle or Giggleswick. Or from Smearside a descent can be made direct to Little Stainforth, or to Feizor for Austwick or Giggleswick, as next route.

Settle to Feizor by the Celtic Walls to Stainforth Force and Settle, 8 m. This is a capital round for a fine half-day. Follow the Clapham road past the Ebbing and Flowing Well and keep straight on to the top of **Buckhaw Brow** (815 feet). This is the highest point of the old coach-road between the eastern and western seas. In the **Kelcowe Scar** there is a small **cave**, in which various Roman fibulæ, and coins of the reign of Vespasian have been found. At the road top a small gate leads between two bastion-like walls of solid limestone, and the path then holds due north through fields to **Feizor** (3½ m.) Brunton House, the property and summer residence of the Rev. A. Holden Byles, is passed a little to the left, whence the retired hamlet of Feizor appears like a lonely raven's nest built against the picturesque crumbling scars of Smearside on our right. What an out-of-the-way spot this is now, and yet it has a history of no small importance ! There was land here belonging to Fountains Abbey, and in a *Compotus* of Sallay Abbey for A.D. 1381, is an entry of 43s. 8d. paid to Jo'. Fesar, a master carpenter in the employ of that monastery. The old Hall has no doubt a long history, but of this little is known. The building stands east and west, and at the east end is a small round-headed window in an upper chamber, a huge, projecting chimney-stack at the west end, and curiously carved door head with c ᴺ ᴇ 1699 over the entrance. At the head of the village is a picturesque two-storey dwelling-house, which the late Mr. William Byles, proprietor of the *Bradford Observer*, made his summer home for several years up to his death in 1891. A branch of the family of Clapham, of Clapham, was seated here for upwards of two centuries, and is now represented by T. R. Clapham, Esq., F.R.A.S., of Austwick Hall, who owns the old family estate at Feizor.

The district is a very interesting one to the botanist, and it may be as well to place on record the discovery here in May, 1894, by Mr. John Wilman, of the rare plant, *Asarum Europæum*, which is described in Dr. Lee's *Flora of West Yorkshire*, as an extinct alien.

From Feizor it is a nice walk of 1¼ m. to Austwick, but our present route is in an opposite direction, so going up the lane past Feizor Hall we enter the field gate on our right (please shut the gate) and follow the rough track up the gap to a stile in the wall on the right. Keep forward up the hollow betwixt the scars. Looking backward you have a fine view of Ingleborough. Presently an isolated sheep-fold is seen in the bottom of the hollow, and about 30 yards above it is a step-stile and opposite it is another, whence an obvious track goes over the " tops " in a south-easterly direction for Stainforth.

Try the echoes here. **Smearside** rises on the left and may be conveniently ascended (*see* p. 108). From the sheep-fold above mentioned, a few minutes' scramble up the hill on the right will bring you to the remarkable **Celtic Walls** (*see* p. 108). Come down the

STAINFORTH FORCE.

hollow to the stile in the wall facing you and so by the path over the "tops," as described, which leads to another stile, whence the path goes down hill to a gate near four ash trees. Here a rustic lane leads quickly down to Little Stainforth.

There are only a few houses at **Little Stainforth.** The oldest bears the initials and date, C. D., 1649. The old Hall has been rebuilt and is a plain Georgian building, with many voided windows, telling of the obnoxious window-tax, when the very light and air— two great essentials to human health and happiness—were taxed. " Where the sun never enters the doctor must," is the best retort to this deleterious impost. In front of the house is a sun-dial dated 1724. About 200 yards below Stainforth Hall is the celebrated **Stainforth Force,** the finest water-scene on the whole course of the Ribble. From the picturesque old stone bridge a path on the right leads to the fall, where the scene after a moderate fresh is remarkably grand. The water does not fall from a height, but makes rather a series of shelving descents down its broad and mossy bed, bordered with rich masses of impending foliage. Beautiful indeed at any season, but especially so in Spring, when wild flowers are awakening on the banks, the birds enliven the river and coppices with their active and graceful movements and happy songs, and the clear blue sky canopies the rich scene. It is then, as the poet of Winskill truly says :

> Such scenes as these, when seen in Spring,
> Wad mak a Quaker dance and sing,
> An' mak a clown turn poet !

The broken river-bed is due probably to the fault which brings up the older Silurian rocks against the Carboniferous limestone on the south. The limestone over which the river flows is much "pot-holed" by the grinding action of pebbles in the water.

Regaining the bridge, the tourist may wind forward to the village of **Great Stainforth,** (inn) ½ m., and thence by the road direct to Settle (2½ m.), or return through Little Stainforth and Stackhouse (*see* p. 103) to Giggleswick (2 m.) or Settle (2½ m.)

Settle to Catterick Force and back by Stainforth (7 m.) This is an upland tramp to the finest waterfall in Craven—the " Gem of the Highlands" we might call it. In dry weather the Catterick Glen is always pleasing, but the waterfalls (there are several) are the great charm of the place, and after a moderate spate present a spectacle of romantic beauty probably unmatched. But unfortunately there is no proper road to the immediate vicinity of the falls, and there has been much (not undeserved) complaint of breaking down walls in the haste to reach them. A proper entrance and a notice board directing the way would greatly facilitate matters, and thus provide a fund of innocent pleasure to visitors who often come long distances to view this charming scene.

The road to Langcliffe (1 m.) is direct (*see* p. 105). Turn round by the vicarage and follow the lane which leads into the fields and then right before you ascend the rugged steeps called the Cat Steps. Looking backward you have a fine prospect of wild and lonely Ribblesdale. At the top bear a little to the left and the solitary farm-house at **Winskill** will be noticed. This was the early home of Tom Twisleton, the well-known Craven poet, and author of *Splinters struck off Winskill Rock,* first published in 1867. The **Catterick Glen** lies deep down on your left, and the highest and grandest of

the waterfalls is situated some little distance above the Winskill
farm. The water comes down a lofty ravine, thickly clothed with
trees and flowering shrubs, (amongst the latter the giant rose-bay in
August makes an effective show), and falls in two magnificent leaps
into a shadowy pool below, running then onward among immense
boulders to fall again and again in lesser but still beautiful cascades.
In a time of flood we have seen the ravine literally choked with foam
and seething mist ascending like steam from a cauldron ; the water
boiling and churning, not like the sharp rattle of musketry—as
stones and boulders were completely smothered—but like the roll
and roar of heavy guns. It is not however during a monster flood
that the scene makes the liveliest picture and creates the happiest
impression, but when there is a moderate supply of water in keeping
with the beautiful framework of rock and trees. At all seasons,
indeed, it is a charming spectacle, as sings Mr. H. L. Twisleton, a
local poet :

> I ween, wild scene, thy summer splendour
>   Brings praise to every wanderer's lip ;
> Praise still, when autumn trees surrender
>   Their verdure to the Ice-king's grip ;
> Or in the spring's sweet, brooding noon,
> By morning light, or midnight moon.

The enterprising tourist out for a brisk "spin" may cross the
stream above the highest fall and step on to the heather, when the
commanding form of **Penyghent** will be seen some 4 miles off to
the north. It is a rough, but for the most part a comparatively level
tramp to the mountain, and a good pedestrian might leave Settle,
visit Catterick Force, cross the moor to the Silverdale Road, up
Penyghent, and down to Horton-in-Ribblesdale within the time
allowed by an afternoon excursion-train,—a round, stout walk of
about 12 mountain miles.

Returning from Catterick, cross the beck to the north side and
follow it down a rough mile to the fields, when the path improves
into the lane for **Stainforth**. This little village became part of the
possessions of Sallay Abbey soon after the foundation of that house.
It was the seat of an ancient and honourable family that took its
name from the place far back in the turbulent Norman times. A
famous knight was Robert de Stainford, who contributed the large
sum of 20s. towards the tax levied by King Richard II. (1378-9) for
carrying on the French wars and maintaining Calais as an English
port. Other householders at Stainford then paid 4d. and two paid
6d. each to this impost. Robert de Stainford died in 1391, and
founded the chantry in Giggleswick Church, elsewhere mentioned,
where he was buried. There is now a neat church at Stainforth, and
the village wears a clean and inviting aspect.

A half-mile walk behind the village and across the railway brings
the visitor to the picturesque Ribble bridge and **Stainforth Force**
(see p. 111). The bridge is of high antiquity and seems to have been
on a Roman road from the Camp under Smearside (see p. 108) over
Malham Moor by the Streets into Wharfedale.

CATTERICK FORCE.

Settle to the Victoria Cave and back by Attermire, 5 m.
If we were asked which were the **seven greatest natural
wonders of Craven** we should say (1) the Victoria Cave, (2) the
Ebbing and Flowing Well, (3) Alum Pot, (4) Ling Gill, (5) Malham
Cove, (6) Gordale Scar, (7) Kilnsey Crag. It will be noticed that
all, except Alum Pot and Ling Gill, are on the line of the Great
Craven Fault. Gaping Gill and the wonderful Ingleborough or
Clapham Cave are just beyond the Craven boundary.

The Victoria Cave does not differ in its formation from other
caverns in the district, but as a natural store-house of prehistoric
lore, that has kept secret to the dawn of an enlightened Age the
unequivocal testimony of the presence of Life, existing period by
period from the remote Glacial Submergence to the Roman occupation
of Britain, it is indeed a great and well-merited wonder. Our route
is through Langcliffe and up the Malham Tarn road a good mile
until the level is reached, where is a branch road on the left leading
to Winskill Farm, mentioned in the last route. Close to this by-road
is a huge gritstone boulder called **Samson's Toe**, an exceptionally
fine glacial relic, proving by its large size (about ten feet by six feet)
the immensity of the frozen mass in this upland valley during the
great Ice Age. Regaining the main road you are in front of a range
of magnificent limestone scars, which forms one of the escarpments
of the Great Craven Fault. A track runs south close to the foot of
the scars, and by following this about half-a-mile you arrive at the
famous **Victoria Cave**, situate at an elevation of 1450 feet above
the sea. Access to it is up a steep slope of clay and limestone debris,
partly natural and partly artificial caused by excavations. The cave
was discovered in the year of Her Majesty's Accession (1837) and
hence its name. The discovery was somewhat strange. Mr. Joseph
Jackson, of Settle, was out walking with his dog, when the animal
disappeared behind the rock and then barking disclosed the existence
of the cavern. Mr. Jackson removed the debris which almost obscured
the entrance, and eventually was able by lying down to get in. He
found the interior beautifully hung with stalactites, white as snow.
Unfortunately these adornments have now entirely disappeared.

The existing entrance (which is shewn in the centre of our
illustration) is about 100 feet wide and 32 feet high. Before the cave
was opened out in 1870, under the auspices of the British Association,
the entrance was by a crevice on the left of the present opening, but
at a much higher level. There are three main chambers accessible by
different galleries or passages, but as the cave is usually very wet and
dirty, explorers should don an old suit and go well provided with
candles. Upon a vertical excavation of the largest or main opening,
discoveries were made of a very astonishing and valuable character.
In the uppermost bed of cave-earth an old floor was come upon about
two feet from the surface. Here were evidences of charcoal fires, also
burnt bones of domestic animals, and of the smaller rodentia and
carnivora, broken pottery, Roman-Celtic coins, a Roman key, bone
pins, amber and glass beads, silver and gold-plated bronze brooches,
finger rings, and other ornaments of great beauty, all proving the

cave to have been occupied during the Roman Conquest. The coins date from the reign of Trajan in the first century of the Christian era to that of Constans in the fourth, and are rude imitations of current Roman coins, probably made by those warlike Britons who, while beholden to, were unwilling to submit to the yoke of the conquerors.

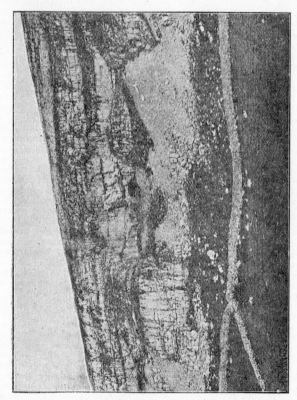

ENTRANCE TO THE VICTORIA CAVE.

Four feet lower again splendid evidence of a still earlier race was disclosed. These relics included rude flint-flakes, a perfect stone bead, and a curious fish-harpoon, four inches long, with two barbs on each side, of a type never before observed. Likewise a small adze of melaphyre, identical in form, size, and material with those in use in the Polynesian Islands, and of which no other example is known to have been found in Europe. How this unique object was imported to Settle at that day it is now difficult to tell. There were also bones of the brown bear, stag, horse, dog, and Celtic shorthorn. These all proclaim the cave to have been the shelter or habitation of man 4-5000 years ago, and the various bones indicate the kind of animals he had in his service or had to contend with. With his rude weapons of flint and stone, the half-savage lords of the soil fought the huge bears that roamed the deserts of Ribblesdale, and some of these, to judge from the skulls now in the Giggleswick Museum, must have been of prodigious size and strength.

Lower again, sealed beneath a thickness of broken stalactite and cave-debris, was revealed plainly as if written on parchment roll the story of life here in the Ice Age. Although there was no evidence of man, there were traces in plenty of animals of an arctic or inter-arctic character, such as the grizzly-bear, bison, fox, reindeer, and arctic hare. But below these, in the very lowest stratum of cave-earth, was discovered a supposed human fibula,—the well-known "bone of contention," (see p. 99), along with numerous remains of tropical or sub-tropical animals, such as the hyæna, hippopotamus, elephant, and mammoth. From the characteristic manner in which most of these bones were cracked and gnawed it is conjectured that they were the remains of prey brought into the cave by the hyænas. It is, however, not altogether compatible with modern belief that man was contemporary in this locality with this last named set of creatures. It is an open question whether they are to be referred to a strictly definable ante-glacial epoch, or whether their presence here is due to seasonal migration, consequent upon the intermittent warmth occurring on the retreat of the ice. Such a sluggish animal as the hippopotamus cannot, however, be supposed to have travelled very far. That man existed here at the time the reindeer and other arctic or sub-arctic animals infested these highlands is highly probable, although no positive trace of him is yielded in local contemporary deposits. But that he lived with the reindeer and the mammoth in these latitudes is sufficiently testified by the discoveries in English and Continental caverns, of bones and tusks scratched with rude outlines of these animals, shewing clearly that the originals were familiar to the eyes of the artists. Just like the Esquimaux in Lapland at the present day his life passed in the frozen world about here ; accustomed only to the use of such tools and weapons as enabled him to maintain himself under these climatic conditions, he would follow the ice and the reindeer as they gradually retreated to the far north.

The "history" revealed by this truly royal cavern is indeed a long and noble one, probably of its kind unique in the world. What pictures does it not conjure up of that vastly remote epoch—the very twilight of human Life—when the laughter-like cries of hyænas and the growlings of cave-bears echoed in the fastnesses of these Craven hills ; when our first known "tramps," the monster mammoth and the crashing elephant roamed through our highland forests, until long, long afterwards—far down the "avenues of Time," came the measured tramp of the Roman legions, who, regardless of the laws of climate and race, vainly endeavoured to sow the seeds of a gentler civilisation in the stony soil of this unyielding Land of Crags. Yea, the barbarous native highland-men, though accustomed to hardships and privations, disdained to forfeit their independence, and like their four-footed predecessors, the wild denizens of the forest, have left the story of their existence and fate in this wonderful cave!

But "tramps" of another species now claim our attention, so we must move on. Keeping alongside the wall, which runs down between the cliffs, with the rifle-butts some distance on the right, you have then the **Attermire Scars** before you, a majestic pile of fantastically formed summits, looking like the shattered bastions of some giant's citadel. The time-worn crevices and ledges of these rocks are adorned with rare and choice plants, while among the rarer birds of these noble cliffs, says Mr. Peake, may occasionally be seen the mountain-loving raven, with beak and talons strong almost as a bird of prey, and whose loud croaking may be heard echoing among the scars.

Attermire Cave is another of those prehistoric abodes already described. It is rather bad of access up a long slope of debris, at a distance of about 300 yards east of the rifle-targets.

[As rifle-practice usually takes place on Saturdays it may be advisable to caution the tourist, who must keep wide of the red flags conspicuously displayed.]

The cave may be explored for a considerable distance, but the passage is in some places narrow and dirty and necessitates creeping. Some thirty to forty yards from the entrance is a spacious grotto about 50 feet high, once beautifully adorned with stalactites. Roman coins, a carved bead, and a single adult skeleton have been found in the cave. At the very summit of the cliff is another opening, the **Horse Shoe Cave**, but it is not penetrable very far. Another cave, in King's Scar, which was investigated in 1871 and found to contain bones of the Celtic shorthorn, goat, horse, stag, &c., along with a rude flint scraper and a whetstone, is situated about 500 yards north-west of Victoria Cave. Near here, at the summit-edge, is a heap of stones forming a rude enclosure, supposed to have been a Watch or "Look-out" for the primitive inhabitants of the caves.

From Attermire the scars may be descended as described in the next route, or you may cross the flat open land between the cliffs on the left and the targets on the right, and in half-a-mile you reach the Stockdale Lane, and winding along it to the right you are soon in the Kirkby Malham and Settle road, 1 m. from Settle and not very far from the romantic Scaleber Force (*see* p. 44).

Settle to Scaleber Force, and Attermire and back by the Scars, 3½ m. This, like the preceding, is a bracing hill-walk, and on a summer's day under a clear sky the return walk by the Scars is like a peep into Switzerland. Leave Settle by the Roman Catholic Church and ascend to the junction of the roads (1 m.). Take the one *r.* leading to Kirkby Malham and a short walk brings you to the **Scaleber Bridge** which the road crosses. After viewing the **Force** (*see* p. 44) return to the road. Here is a small quarry in the limestone abounding in fossils, chiefly of the genus *Brachiopoda*. The beck may be followed up a good half-mile until the Malham bridle road is reached (*see* p. 68). It is a roughish scramble between broken crags, starred with pretty saxifrages and other mountain wildings. The grand range of **Attermire Scars** towers in front, but the entrance to the cave is not seen, as it is situate in an angle of the cliff high upon the right. Now cross the open fields, straight for the rifle-targets ; by keeping well to the left you will find stiles in the walls leading direct to the targets. [Hence you can reach the Victoria Cave, Catterick Force, &c., as described in the two previous routes.] The entrance to Attermire Cave is now seen on *r.* (*see* p. 116). From the stile at the notice-board near the targets a path leads *l.* under the Scars, and after going over several stiles, in about ¾ m. a glorious view of Ribblesdale bursts upon the vision. Country town and hamlet, scar and field, and lonely hill and dale appearing under diverse accompaniments of light and shade, make up a truly enchanting scene. The white, climbing road up Buckhaw Brow stands out prominently, with the volcanic-like top of Smearside, partly in shadow, rising above the white road to Stainforth, while Ingleborough, the "mammoth" of the western hills, fills up the distant background. Giggleswick, with its extensive Grammar School buildings, is visible beyond a grove of trees, relieving the wide expanse of field and moor behind. Well may we say with Cowper :

> The achievements of art may amuse,
> May even our wonder excite,
> But groves, hills, and valleys diffuse
> A lasting, a sacred delight.

We now drop sharply down into Settle. On a bright warm day our descent is like that of some sunny alp in Switzerland ; the *jodel* of cow-boys being only required to complete the illusion.

Settle to Lawkland and Cross Streets and back by Giggleswick Scars, 8½ m. This is a lowland walk through flowery lanes and by rustic homesteads. Go through Giggleswick, past the entrance to the **Grammar School**, and forward up the green lane with the School cricket-field on the left. From a gate at the first ascent a charming view of the long line of **Scars** is obtained with the Schoolboys' Tower conspicuous on the top, and an extensive view eastwards of the hills beyond Settle. Proceeding to the summit of the **Ridge** a very wide prospect of the valley of the Lune is now had, with the Ingleborough range towering away to the north. Our route is through a perfect wild-garden of various shrubs and flowers ; in summer the "wild-rose tiptoe upon hawthorn stocks" mingles its beauty and fragrance with the delicious honeysuckle and a thick undergrowth of living colour, and in autumn the road is lush with the fruit of rose and bramble.

This rustic lane was formerly the coach-road between Settle,

I

Lancaster and Kendal, before the broad highroad under Giggleswick Scars and past the Ebbing and Flowing Well was completed about 1760. It was a very **old pack-horse route**, and at one time the only practicable thoroughfare to Lancaster, Kendal, and the north, being doubtless upon an unrecorded Roman vicinary way from Lancaster to the Roman Camp above Settle, whence it crossed High Side into Airedale, and passing perhaps near to the well-known Roman Villa at Gargrave. When the first stage-coaches ran this way we do not know, but as there were only four coaches running in the whole of England in the time of Charles II., it would probably be about the middle of last century. The mail-coach from Kendal to London did not, however, commence running till 1786.

Descending by High Paley Green to the cross-roads (Settle, 2 m., Lancaster, 21 m.) we turn *r.* and a pleasant walk soon brings us to **Lawkland,** a scattered and very quiet little place. Lawkland Green, is the first house passed on the right, and is approached by two noble willow-trees. A curious ivy-grown arch is a noticeable feature at the north side of the house. A little beyond, on the opposite side of the way, stands Lawkland Hall, a stately old mansion picturesquely embosomed in trees. The manor of Lawkland, for three centuries, has belonged to the family of Ingleby,—a branch of the Inglebys of Ripley Castle, in the Nidd valley,—and the hall here was their continuous residence up to about thirty years ago. It is now let to the Rev. B. E. Watkins, M.A. The mansion has an imposing and lofty frontage in the Elizabethan style, with small square windows, and a massive central square tower, erected before the main building or probably early in the 16th century. In several of the windows are pieces of stained glass with armorial bearings. In the east wing is the old chapel in which services were held up to the time of erecting the Roman Catholic Chapel in the village about a century ago, when the Inglebys "went over" to the Protestants.

A short distance beyond the Hall and we pass the diminutive **Catholic Chapel** just mentioned. The neat little building measures 20 feet by 19 feet, and has seat-room for about 50 worshippers. In the smallness of its dimensions it almost vies with the famous little edifices at Lullington in Sussex, which is the smallest church in England, being about 16 feet square, and St. Lawrence's in the Isle of Wight, which is 30 feet by 12 feet. Instead of keeping straight on to Cross Streets, a good mile is saved by turning from the white farm-house near the chapel up a path by a barn, and into a lane leading into the main road near Crow Nest, whence it is a straight walk of $\frac{3}{4}$-m to Feizor (*see* p. 109.)

At **Cross Streets** (inn) we are at the junction of roads to Austwick (1 m.), Clapham (2 m.). and Settle (4 m.) This point was at the divergence of two Roman military ways from the east and south, continuing westwards to Clapham and Ingleton, and joining other military ways which passed Wennington to Overborough and Lancaster. Far up the dale, northwards, we can descry the lonely **Crummack Farm,** whose only sight of a human dwelling is the single house where we now stand. Turning now in the direction of Settle we pass by **Cave Ha' Wood,** and in the scar on the left of the road is seen an ancient **ossiferous cavern,** which has yielded many relics of its occupation by man and animals at a remote age. Various implements and flakes of chert and flint were found in it along with other ancient remains in stone and iron. Lower down, beneath a bed of undisturbed cave debris, remains of goat or sheep, dog, and cave-bear were turned up, similar to those found in the Victoria Cave. The cave has long been the haunt of a colony of jackdaws and on this account has earned its present local sobriquet of Jackdaw Hole.

Our road hence is under Giggleswick Scars and past the Ebbing and Flowing Well (*see* p. 102) to Giggleswick or Settle.

Settle by Eldroth to Clapham Station (7 m.) Through Giggleswick, past the School, and along the road to Lawkland, as described in the last route. At the four-lane ends (2 m.) take the Lancaster road which crosses the railway on to the road *l.* to **Eldroth** (4 m.)

Visitors wishing to include Lawkland (*see* p. 118) in this round may take the path on the north side of the Hall and at the first stile past the barn the path divides. Take the low one which at field end turns sharp *l.* and over stiles by wall side and over the hill into the main road to Eldroth.

The stream which flows through Eldroth joins the Fen Beck lower down, and these waters uniting with the Austwick and Clapham Becks about a mile to the east of Clapham station form the Wenning, which flows westward to the Lune. Consequently Eldroth is just within the Lune watershed, while the country to the east of it lies within the Ribble drainage area. The old road crosses the beck by a bridge south of Eldroth Hall ; the bridge is not arched but quite flat and was built early this century. Before then the beck, which was once fully 40 feet across, was forded, and it is not improbable that the conjunction of this ancient road over the shallow stream gave the place its name, *i.e.,* Celt. *ald,* a stream, and *rhydd* (pron. *rith*) a ford.

Some have supposed that Eldroth is the Heldetune of *Domesday*, which with Austwick formed one of the 12 manors belonging to Torfin, a Dane. Heldetune is however now ascertained to have been Killington (3 miles west of Sedbergh) in Westmorland, at that time in the great diocese of York, which with these manors formed part of the ancient honour of Lancaster, held by Roger of Poictou who was dispossessed. Little is known of the history of Eldroth, and not much remains to be seen now. The old Hall (now a farm house) is a 17th century building, but has been much modernised. Some of the old voided windows have been opened out since the abolition of the Window Tax. In the parlour is an oaken recess bearing the initials of the Moore family and date 1698. The Moores were Quakers, and the sect appears to have had a Meeting House and place of sepulture here. On the west side of the beck is an old Quaker burial-ground, but now not recognizable as such. No stone or memorial of any kind is visible, and who may sleep there we know not. The simple, holy

plot serves but to remind us of our brief mortality and of the
helplessness and strangeness of human life :

> Take them, O great Eternity !
> Our little life is but a gust,
> That bends the branches of thy tree,
> And trails its blossoms in the dust.

The grave-yard has been an enclosure about forty feet square, now
walled on three sides only, and on the east bounded by an old barn.
In the Hall kitchen was formerly to be seen one of the old-fashioned
beef-lofts similar to that in the Bridge House (Mr. William Dawson)
here.

We now continue our journey to Clapham (3 m.) ; the road
ascending and descending and revealing wide and lovely views over
the Scar country, with mighty Ingleborough, Norber, Moughton, and
the Settle hills grouped in most picturesque array. Beautiful it is
on a calm summer evening, or in the early autumn when the sunsets
create grander effects, to watch the rosy clouds gather about the
dusky head of the Yorkshire Giant, wrapping the huge mountain in
fleecy folds ; to observe the shimmering and ever-changing light on
the far-reaching landscape, with the play of flaming sunset on the
climbing woods and fields and terraced scars, transforming the endless
limestone walls into great chains of knotted gold, and covering the
eastern hills with a warm magical glow. What a glorious extent of
country this is to behold, with its grand scenery and wealth of ancient
traditions ! Indeed in point of expansive grandeur and in scenic
effect, the confined valleys of the Lake District can afford no
parallel !

Settle to Horton, 6 m. This is a romantic walk, drive, or
railway-trip. The Midland line from Settle to Carlisle which was
opened for passenger traffic on May 1st, 1876, traverses the wilds of
Ribblesdale, and reaches in Blea Moor tunnel an altitude of 1151 feet
above sea-level. With the single exception of the Tebay and Barnard
Castle line between Barras and Bowes, this is the **highest point at
which railway metals** have been laid for passenger traffic in
England. The line is 72½ miles in length, and took 5¾ years to
complete, involving an expenditure of £2,700,000. It is essentially
a line of through traffic ; there being only two or three trains daily
that stop at all stations. The visitor should take a note of these,
as they will no doubt be useful.

The road follows the east side of the valley by the prominent
Winskill Rock, where are extensive quarries worked by the
Craven Lime Co., Limited. They were first opened in 1873. About
1 m. further is **Great Stainforth** (*see* p. 112) where the effects of
the disruption of the strata by the **Craven Fault** are seen in the
presence of cliffs of limestone on the south side and the Silurian grit
land on the north. Passengers by the railway cannot fail to notice
the passage from one strata to the other in the cutting at Stainforth.
The principal fault here is about fifty feet wide, and is filled in with
fragments of limestone and clay and a large amount of quartz. Our

road up the valley is laid in the tough grits and slates of this old Silurian band, which is estimated to be here nearly two miles in thickness. The series are covered by thick beds of glacial drift, through which the river has cut its way, having dislodged and ground down numerous boulders that were formerly embedded in the soil. Various travelled boulders will be noticed in the valley, either loose or partly concealed in the drift. On the opposite side of the valley the **Moughton Fell** quarries will be observed, where the horizontal beds of limestone, resting upon the inclined Silurian slates, display one of the finest and most remarkable geological phenomena to be seen anywhere in Yorkshire.

Ascending Sherwood Brow a descent is soon made to **Helwith Bridge**, where are several cross-roads. One strikes westward over Swarth Moor to Feizor (2 m.) (*see* p. 109) ; another eastward by Sannat Hall to Malham. This is the centre of a wild, moorland country, where villages and houses are few and far between, and where often the only things of life one sees are the distant unheard railway-trains speeding through the lonely valley between Settle and Carlisle. Presently we come to the hamlet of **Studfold**, picturesquely sheltered beneath a wooded ridge of dark Silurian rock. Here is an old flag quarry in the lower division of the Coniston Flags, abounding in various fossils, chiefly of the genus *Orthoceratites*.

In the railway cutting between here and Horton there is a fine exhibition of **glacial ice-polishing**, the upper rock-surfaces about 500 to 600 yards south of the station being beautifully smoothed. The metals are laid for a distance of 250 yards between a boulder-clay ridge or drumlin, at its deepest part being about forty feet. Similar ridges occur both to the north and south of Horton, which gave the railway contractors some tough work during the construction of the line.

HORTON-IN-RIBBLESDALE.

"If thou art worn and hard beset
  With sorrows that thou would'st forget,
  If thou would'st read a lesson that will keep
  Thy heart from fainting, and thy soul from sleep,
  Go to the woods and hills !   No tears
  Dim the sweet look which Nature wears."—*Longfellow*.

E ARE now in the midst of a grand mountainous country where three sovereign heights, Whernside, Ingleborough, and Penyghent, rear their massive temples skywards from the confines of this place.

My altars are the mountains and the ocean,
  Earth, air, stars,—all that springs from the great Whole,
  Who hath produced, and will receive the soul.

exclaims Byron, who might have drawn his inspiration from the mountain-encumbered solitudes of the upper Ribble.

The parish of Horton includes an area of about 27 square miles (17,260 acres) and a population of 666, or an average of 26 acres for every inhabitant, obviously plenty of elbow room for everybody. In Leeds and Bradford this is reversed, the density in the former town being 16 inhabitants for every acre and in the latter 28 inhabitants per acre. What happiness and what freedom to the town-dweller is there not felt to escape for however brief a spell to such airy and health-giving regions as these, where nature is free and omnipotent and man has asserted but little of his power :

"On the mountain is freedom ! the breath of decay
  Never sullies the fresh-flowing air ;
  Oh ! Nature is perfect wherever we stray ;
  'Tis man that deforms her with care !"

Of Horton itself little need be said, and there is little of interest to the visitor save the Church, an ancient and notable fabric, whose dark weathered stones and sturdy square tower seem in perfect keeping with the wild, heathy moors that surround it. The whole parish appears at one time to have been monastic property, belonging chiefly to the two wealthy convents of Jervaulx and Fountains. In 1315 the Abbot of Jervaulx was returned as lord of the manor. After the Reformation the manor was granted to Matthew, Earl of Lennox, and disposed of by him in 1569—70 to John Lennard, Esq., Ralph Scrope, Esq., and others. At that time there were within the manor 50 messuages, 60 cottages, and a mill. Subsequently, in the reign of Charles II., the manor was sold by Sir Leonard Bosville, of Bradburne, Kent, and Lady Anne, his wife, to Messrs. Lawrence Burton, Richard Wiglesworth, and Francis Howson, in trust for the proprietors of lands therein.

The Church (dedicated to St. Oswald) dates from the 12th century. The existing nave is apparently of this date, all the pillars, with one exception, being cylindrical, and ornamented with emblems of the Virgin and the Holy Trinity. The chancel is of more recent date than the body of the church—probably of the time of Henry VIII. About 1825, when the church was restored, the roof was raised, and the projecting corbels shew the original height of the roof. The building underwent a further restoration in 1880 when a stain-glass window was inserted to the memory of the late John Wm. Foster, Esq., of Horton. Previously the east window was of plain glass, with the exception of a small fragment (now high up in the west window of the church) depicting a mitred head of Thomas à Becket, similar to that in the chapel of Holy Trinity in Canterbury Cathedral. Beneath the painting are the words "Thomas Canttuar." This ancient and interesting relic is all that remains of a large coloured window erected probably by the Bosvilles or Lennards, old Kent families, who as above related held the manor of Horton in the 16th and 17th centuries. The font, of freestone, is early Norman and ornamented with the chevron or zig-zag lines. The south doorway is also Norman and exhibits a similar design. It is often stated that the chevron ornament is a purely Norman characteristic, but this is not correct. The device can be traced back to the cities of the ancient Aryans, and is found on the most ancient buildings of the East as well as among the primitive ruins of America, proving therefore that it was but the survival of the decorative art of the original Celtic migrants to this country, of the people, in fact, who once dwelt here, and who have left such wonderful relic-testimony of their presence in the Craven caves.

In the church are tablets to the families of Proctor and Hesleden, and also one in memory of the Rev. George Holden, LL.D., who died in 1820, and was 40 years master of the Free Grammar School at Horton, as well as minister of the parish. He was a man of wide culture, and possessed a large and valuable collection of books, which he bequeathed to the Diocesan Library at Ripon.

The old Free School, which formerly stood at the north-east corner of the churchyard, near the present post-office, was founded by will of John Armitstead, gent., who died in 1726, and is buried on the south side of the churchyard. The endowment now amounts to about £320 per annum. New and more commodious buildings were erected some years ago, and organised under the Endowed Schools Act. Near the School are the old parish stocks. Mention may also be made of a useful Reading and Recreation Room which was opened in September, 1890.

The district is a fertile one to the naturalist, and the botanist and ornithologist especially will find much to attract notice. According to Mr. E. Peake birds exist in great variety, but the grain-eating kinds seem to have decreased in numbers within the memory of man. The goldfinch used to occur but is not found now. The bullfinch, redpoll, and twite still occur, and a colony of the latter birds exists near Horton, where also the sedge warbler (the local 'nightingale') is common. Among migrants are the spotted flycatcher, ring-ouzel, cuckoo, yellow wagtail, wheatear, landrail, sandpiper, &c. Several rarer species fortunately are strictly preserved by Mr. John Foster, who has some interesting local birds in his house, including honey-buzzard, Sclavonian grebe, great grey shrike, &c. On the moors, the golden plover, curlew, red grouse, and snipe are seen. The more rocky parts supply the kestrel and stockdove; while the water-courses yield dipper, mallard, waterhen, coot, and little grebe.

Mr. John Foster states that the badger was killed here in 1892, but the polecat, which was formerly to be found in the district, does not now occur. The otter and fox are common, as are also the hedgehog, mole, weazel, and stoat. Many of the smaller mammals and bats no doubt are to be met with, but they have hitherto received little attention.

Douk Gill, which is reached by a short walk on Horton Beck side, is a very pleasant and picturesque spot. The little glen is circumscribed at the head with a fine, lofty scar,—a miniature Malham Cove—beautifully fringed with shrubs and ferns, and nicely wooded,

> "A sylvan, shady and secluded dell,
> Where herb and leaf put on a chaster green,
> And free-winged choristers in concert dwell;
> Where daisies and the king-cup's golden bell
> Smile like noon-day starlight on the ground."

The noisy stream runs out at the foot of the sylvan scar, and forms a series of shelving cascades among huge boulders of limestone, which in past ages have become detached from the surrounding cliffs. The long cave of debouchment of the stream may be traversed a distance of about 80 feet, but the attempt should not be made except in very low water.

From Douk Gill a path may be ascended on the left, and the cart-road entered which leads up to Horton Moor Gate for Penyghent, hereafter described.

There is a peculiarity about one of the Horton streams,—the Bransgill Beck, which enters the Ribble at New Inn. This stream literally "smokes" in winter and cold weather, so much so that under certain conditions of the atmosphere a film of "cloud" or thick steam may be seen floating above it a long way up. The phenomenon is explained by the fact of the stream issuing from a great depth, and its temperature being higher than that of the outer air, produces the evaporation on contact. The stream flows underground about a mile, passing through Thund or Hunt Pot, and crosses at some part of its course, at another and probably lower stratum, the Douk Gill stream flowing through Thirl or Hull Pot, *without mixing their waters*, a circumstance first discovered by the muddy water, after a sheep-washing, going down the one passage and husks of oats down the other.

On the Horton Beck the Manchester Angling Association have an interesting trout-hatchery, established in 1884. The hatching-trough is divided into three parts, in each of which there are three trays fitted with glass rods. On these the ova are placed in regular rows. About 25,000 ova are hatched out annually, with a loss of under 2 per cent., and nearly 5000 yearlings are reared every season. It is a curious and interesting sight.

Horton to the top of Penyghent, (2273 ft.) 3 m. Now for the ascent of the big Ben ! *Ben* and *Pen*, by the way are synonymous, the former being a Scotch term for a mountain (from the Gael. *beinn*)

and the latter (from the Cym. Celt. *pen*) is used in England and
Wales. The meaning of Pen-y-ghent is explained on page 89. The
mountain forms a characteristic feature of the view in the railway
ride between Settle and Ribblehead, and from Horton station its
whole compass is well seen. The tourist alighting here should quit

PENYGHENT FROM HORTON STATION.

the main road about midway between New Inn and Horton, and go
up the long grassy lane by the Vicarage, which winds to the left a
good 1¼ miles, until the Moor Gate is reached. Hence by keeping
northwards along the low ground in the hollow, 220 yards, to the
wall in front, you will come somewhat suddenly on **Thirl** or **Hull
Pot**. It is a huge chasm in the limestone, probably seated on a line

of fracture, though no actual displacement is observable. It is about 180 feet long, 50 feet wide, and nearly 60 feet deep. The Pot is ordinarily dry, but in times of severe flood has been known to boil over and rush furiously down the glen into Douk Gill. Passing through a gate a little east of the chasm, and striking across the heather to the right about 400 yards, is a smaller but perilously deep abyss, called **Thund** or **Hunt Pot**. It should be approached cautiously. It is but 60 feet across at its widest part, the gap tapering at each end, and is only 20 feet long. It has been descended to a depth of 100 feet, but owing to the contraction of the cavity it was not possible to explore it further. It was then plumbed an additional 100 feet, when the rift apparently branched westward, in the direction of the main outlet of the stream at Bransgill Head.

Penyghent may now be ascended from Thund Pot, which lies directly under the middle of the " saddle," and within half-an-hour's steady climb of the top. This north-western flank is in winter much exposed to the fury of snow-storms, and in 1886 the snow accumulated to a depth of nearly 20 feet, and over 60 sheep perished in the drift. The mountain is built up of Scar Limestone (which is here about 600 feet thick, and attains an altitude of about 1400 feet) with some 500 feet of superincumbent shales, limestones and sandstones, embracing the Yoredale measures, and a capping of 378 feet of Millstone Grit. From the latter series coal was formerly obtained for domestic use and afterwards only for burning lime, but the workings are now altogether abandoned. In wild flowers and other forms of vegetable life the mountain abounds in many curious and interesting species. Amongst these may be mentioned the exquisite Alpine Saxifrage (*S. oppositifolia*), which flowers in Spring, and is an especially rare and characteristic plant of the western scars of Ingleborough, being doubtless a relic of the age when these mountains were mere islands in a network of crumbling glaciers. On the summit grows the Cloudberry (*Rubus chamæmorus*) which bears a rather large and solitary white flower, and in August a delicious fruit resembling somewhat a small strawberry. The plant was once so plentiful that its fruit used to be sold in quantities in the market-place at Settle.

The **View** embraces a wide sweep of mountain, moor, and fell, reaching northwards to Wold Fell and the Forest of Mallerstang, where the eastern scarp of Wild Boar Fell stands out sharply in a summer sunset. Beyond it the loftier summit of Helvellyn, 45 miles distant, may sometimes be descried. Westward we see the whole of the Ingleborough range, while to the south are the broken crags of Attermire, the round top of Ryeloaf, Kirkby Fell, Pendle Hill, and south-east the mile-long barren ridge of Fountains Fell. The east is bounded by the spreading summits of Cray Moss, Yockenthwaite Moor, and Great Whernside, and close below us runs the wild mountain-road by Rainscar and the Giants' Graves to Halton Gill and Littondale.

The " Penyghent Beagles " occasionally hunt these expansive altitudes, and a fine sight it is to see the fleet little game hounds scouring hill and crag in full cry. The pack, which consists of about a dozen couples, was established about 1882 by Mr. Foster of Douk Gill.

Should the tourist desire to reach **Littondale** he may descend the eastern spur of Penyghent to Penyghent House, a lonely farmstead at the foot of the mountain, and near the head of Hesleden Gill. Near this house are the so-called **Giants' Graves.** They consist of several mounds of earth, the largest being about 28 feet by 25 feet. To the north is an oblong excavation or trench, seven feet wide and nearly thirty feet long, in which several bodies or coffins may have been laid. Dr. Whitaker says the bodies have been enclosed in rude stone chests or kist-vaens, consisting of limestones pitched on edge, within which they appear to have been artificially embedded in peat earth. It is said that when found the bodies were completely skeletonised. The probability is that they have been interred in whole-wood coffins, in all respects similar to the ancient form of tree-burial prevalent in Denmark, and that they are relics of the Danish occupation of Craven. Such tree-coffins have been turned up elsewhere in Craven. The main road now skirts the northern flanks of Fountains Fell, and in 2 m. makes a rapid descent to Litton, whence it is 2 m. to Arncliffe and 7 m. by road to Kettlewell.

Horton to Alum Pot, 3½ m. Follow the direct road up the valley to Selside (3 m.). About midway, close to the east side of the road, there was formerly a very large **cairn,** computed by a writer in the *Gentleman's Magazine* for 1761, to contain 400 cart-loads of stones. Whether anything was ever found in it we have no knowledge. It may have been raised to commemorate some conflict between the Romans and the native hill-tribes. There was a Roman Camp some few miles lower down the valley under Smearside, and a Watch and huts of the period on the top of Ingleborough, three miles to the west.

Half-a-mile west of Selside, situate on the east flank of Simon Fell, and near Mr. Wilcock's farm, is **Alum Pot,** the most extra-ordinary of all the Yorkshire ground-chasms. This ancient and formidable-looking pot-hole has been variously spelt Alumn, Alum, Allen, Hellen, Helln, and Hell. The oldest forms are the first-named, and the local pronunciation has been always Alum Pot. As to the application of the word " Pot " to these wonderful natural cavities in the limestone various explanations have been given. It is not likely from their often great and profound depths that they were so called from comparison with the ordinary pot, a vessel. Howson's opinion, and the one which is generally accepted, is that the name has come from the Anglo-Saxon *botin*, a bottom or lowest depth. We think, however, a better interpretation is to be found in the A.S. *beot* or *peot* (the labials *b* and *p* being interchangeable), meaning a *peril* or *danger*. Before the Norman Conquest, when cattle and sheep were put on these hills, the land was not enclosed with stone walls like it is now, and these holes would be known to the dwellers here, to their cost, as " perils " and " dangers," a characteristic which has survived in our use of the word " Pot " at the present day. Alum Pot is now protected by a strong wall.

The appearance of the Pot at the huge mouth must fill the spectator with awe and astonishment. In shape an ellipse it measures 130 feet by 40 feet, and has a perpendicular depth of about 200 feet. It is without doubt the most terrific natural opening in the ground (a thick mass of limestone) that is known in Britain, and we have classed it among our " Seven Wonders of Craven." The first reported attempt to explore the cave was made in 1847 by a party of ten persons led by Mr. Birkbeck of Anley, and Mr. Metcalfe of Weathercote. They entered the gulf by way of Long Churn and Diccan Pot, these being respectively the upper and lower portions of a subterraneous water-passage—doubtless at one time one continuous cave—which terminates eastwards in about 150 yards, at a depth of nearly 90 feet from the surface, and discharges its volume in one unbroken cascade to the bottom of the abyss. Fatigue and wet prevented the party from doing more than reaching the bottom, but next year the same adventurous spirits descended from the summit of the Pot by means of a windlass fixed on two baulks of timber laid across the chasm. A bucket covered with a shield and lowered by two guiding-ropes to prevent whirling, enabled two persons to descend at a time. The quantity of water in the chasm, however, prevented a satisfactory exploration being made, and it was not until the Spring of 1870 that this was accomplished. The party included Mr. Birkbeck, Mr. Metcalfe, Prof. Boyd Dawkins, and three ladies, in all 13 persons went down. They were provided with ropes, ladders, and every convenience for the proper exploration of the cave. Prof. Dawkins states the actual vertical descent measured on this occasion was 198 feet, and that the Pot gradually narrowing, was at the bottom not more than 10 feet wide. They traced the stream downwards through a large cave 70 feet high, and through pools and rapids to a waterfall of about 20 feet. Thence the passage went downwards through smaller waterfalls and rapids until a descent was made into a chamber, where the roar of water was deafening. Here they stood on the lowest accessible point of the cave, about 300 feet from the surface. A powerful stream poured out of a cave too high up for the torches to penetrate the darkness, and fell into a deep pool in the middle of the floor, causing such a powerful current of air that all the torches but one were blown out. The two streams eventually united and disappeared in a small black circling pool, which completely barred further ingress. The party then returned to the summit, after about five hours' work in the cave, wet to the skin.

Various descents have been made since then. Intending explorers should not hazard a descent except in settled dry weather. The Spring months are the best. The party should consist of at least three persons, who should be well provided with ropes, also a rope ladder (of wire is the best) at least 40 feet long, plenty of candles and matches, and (wise precaution!) a little brandy, plaister, and bandages, in case of accident. It is also desirable that some person (or some indication) be left at the top to warn visitors from throwing stones down. From the neglect of this precaution a Bradford party who made a recent descent of the Pot, had a narrow escape of being killed by several boulders thrown in at sharp intervals, which luckily just missed the heads of the adventurous cave-hunters.

From Alum Pot the summit of **Ingleborough** can be reached by a rough tramp of 1½ m. in a south-west direction over the south shoulder of Simon Fell. From Selside a foot-path skirts the northern slopes of Park Fell into **Chapel-le-dale** for Ingleton (8 m.), passing Weathercote Cave (3½ m.) From Alum Pot over Ingleborough to Ingleton it is 5½ miles.

Horton by Birkwith and Ling Gill to Ribblehead, 8½ m. This tract of country was the uppermost portion of the old Percy Fee, where it joined that of Mowbray on Cam and the water-shed of Langstrothdale. It is now largely cultivated and contains many good and extensive farms. But in the Norman centuries it was little better than one vast moor, indented with numerous well-wooded ravines, the haunt of the wild-boar, stag or red deer, and savage wolf. The bear probably lingered here as late as the Roman occupation. It may be noted that as appears by a rent-roll of the time of Henry II., the whole of the Percy Fee, extending from Sallay Abbey on the south to Penyghent on the north, and including an area exceeding 100,000 statute acres, produced an annual revenue of less than £100, not the rent now of a single moderate-sized farm ! Subsequently under the fostering care of the monasteries the region of the upper Ribble was much improved, and immense numbers of sheep roamed the fells. From sheep's milk the monks made annually large quantities of butter and cheese, which met with a ready sale among the labouring and poorer classes.

Leaving New Inn by a broad grassy lane to the left of the *Crown* inn, you ascend along the west of Horton Moor (1200 ft.) Hence is a good view. In the hollow below the road leading to New Houses is **Horton Tarn,** now preserved by the Manchester Angling Association. Between the Tarn and the Ribble is **Turn Dub,** a churn-like chasm, about 30 feet across, of unknown depth. The water from Alum Pot is supposed to enter it from under the Ribble, as when the marble quarries above the Pot were worked, the dirty water flowing through it had the same murky colour in the Dub. The latter discharges its surface waters into the Ribble.

Proceeding, the road crosses the **Sel Gill** burn and bridges here a narrow chasm descending by a narrowing channel probably into the valley. It has been examined for about 40 yards. On passing through a gate the road runs along a verdant level about half-a-mile, when a cluster of ash and fir-trees will be observed on the left. Here is another peculiar opening called **Jackdaw Hole.** Though of no particular depth it is a formidable looking place, and is walled off. It is 70 feet long, 40 feet broad, and at one point 45 feet deep. On the north side a wide natural arch opens into a low cave. The scars below may be descended to the Tops farm, and the road followed down to New Houses and Horton. Ferns and wild flowers fringe the craggy slopes, and amongst them may be found the pretty sea-thrift. But to keep along the road in about a mile we come to the farmhouse of **High Birkwith,** now a quiet and out-of-the-way place enough, but in former days it was on a busy thoroughfare, and this was a hostelry, where the packmen and waggoners rested on their rough journeys between Settle and Hawes. Anciently the two farms of High and Low Birkwith belonged to Jervaulx Abbey. Fountains Abbey had also a small property here, and the monks of Furness likewise owned an extensive estate about Ribblehead. At the Dissolution they had possessions at Birkwith and Ling Gill valued at £6 19s. yearly.

Near Birkwith there is a **Cave**, which has been penetrated a distance of about 600 yards, but it is low and wet, and usually difficult of access. Below **Low Birkwith**, at the junction of the Cam Beck with the Ribble, is a peculiarly-formed Pot called **Nanny Car Hole.** It was formerly a rather spacious cavity, having a plentiful supply of running water, and during the construction of the Settle and Carlisle railway was used by the workmen for bathing purposes. A mile beyond High Birkwith the road crosses an old pack-horse bridge at the head of **Ling Gill.** The romantic Gill may be descended southwards from here and Ribblehead Station reached by way of Ingman Lodge (3 m.), *see* p. 137. The road now goes over Deer Bank on Cam Fell End (1432 ft.) with a wild outlook of moor and sedgy hill on all hands. A mile from Ling Gill Bridge there are divergences of the road to Hawes (9 m.), Bainbridge (11 m.), and Ribblehead (2½ m.) Taking the last named a tramp of about a mile brings the tourist to the main carriage road (Ingleton and Hawes) near the inn at Gearstones, 1½ m. from the station at Ribblehead, and 7½ m. from Ingleton.

Horton over Moughton Fell to Austwick, 4½ m. Leaving Horton Station by the wicket-gate on the west or up-side, you pass over a large drift-hill to the retired farm-house at **Beecroft.** This was formerly a fine old hall, and the chief residence of the ancient manor of Beecroft, which in Elizabethan days comprised about a score tenements, with lands belonging thereto. The Hall for some time was the seat of the Wilson family, and here resided the celebrated Dr. Thos. Wilson, afterwards Dean of Carlisle, who died in 1778. On leaving the Hall the tourist turns southwards and commences a steady pull up on to the fell. Hundreds of ice-transported sandstone boulders lie scattered about the weathered limestone and on the patches of denuded boulder-clay. Ferns and plants of various kinds grow about the much-broken limestone and springy green turf of this vast breezy upland, while here and there in the hollows of glacial drift are gay spreads of scented heather. The eye wanders over an immense tract of hill and fell and wooded gill, hiding many a sweet and beauteous scene, while the invigorated tourist, striding along in the bracing and unconfined air of this wild highland tract, will feel inclined to exclaim with the poet,—

> In glens which resound to the waterfall's song,
> My spirit shall play the wild echoes among ;
> And the keen winds that harp on the heathery lea,
> Shall sing the grand anthem of freedom to me.

When the end of the fell is reached, where are the extensive quarries and workmen's cottages, you veer to the right, or westwards, when

presently you come to the edge of the lonely Crummack valley, and
a gingerly descent must be made to the romantic hamlet of **Wharfe**.
It will be better to proceed northwards some little distance along the
edge of Moughton before descending, as the south end is very
precipitous.

If time permit the tourist should descend to the **Moughton
slate quarries** [beware of the blasts!] in order to obtain a near
view of the wonderful geological phenomenon of the horizontal beds
of Carboniferous limestone, resting upon the inclined slates of
Silurian age. These old Silurian strata, extending eastward from
near Kirkby Lonsdale, attain their highest elevation (1166 ft.) here
on the south side of Moughton Fell. The section has been often
photographed and engraved and makes an interesting picture. Near
the foot of the cliff, and now only accessible by a ladder, is a small
cave, in which bones of a few small animals, such as foxes and rats,
were found when it was first opened some 28 years ago. From the
quarries you may reach the valley at once and proceed westward by
the road to Wharfe (1 m.), or southwards to Feizor (1½ m.). The
descent of **Crummack Dale** to Wharfe is however very fine and
an agreeable change from the characteristic limestone scenery. Here
the slates form grand and precipitous heights, clothed with trees,
heather and fern, while the beck in the bottom foams noisily over
beds of the same rock. It is like a peep into North Wales. **Wharfe
Gill** is also nicely wooded, and contains a picturesque waterfall.
From Wharfe there is a good road through Austwick to Clapham
(2 m.), and under Giggleswick Scars to Settle (5 m.).

LING GILL.

RIBBLEHEAD.

SETTLE, 12 m. LANCASTER, 23 m. INGLETON, 6 m. HAWES, 11 m.
RICHMOND, 35 m.

HE sky, unlike man, is most cheerful when the *bluest*, and you really need a blue sky, not to mention a cheerful temper, in order to tackle the wild country that surrounds you at this point. Standing on the platform of Ribblehead station (1080 feet) you are in the midst of a grand wilderness of caverned hills and wide-reaching moors, encompassed by three of the highest mountains in Yorkshire—Whernside, Ingleborough, and Penyghent, where those, forsooth, who are fond of wild prospects may get their hearts' fill. An old couplet runs :

> Whernside, Ingleborough, and Penyghent,
> Are the three highest hills between Scotland and Trent.

Indeed at one time it was thought that this Yorkshire trio exceeded Snowdon in altitude, or even Ben Nevis. Hurtley, a century ago, gave the height of Ingleborough as 5280 feet, and so it appears marked on old maps. Mickle Fell (2591 feet) is now ascertained to be the highest land in Yorkshire, and it is 980 feet lower than Snowdon. "While Mickle Fell," observes Professor Phillips, "reigns supreme over the solitary wastes in the North of Yorkshire, Whernside, Ingleboro', and Penyghent shine with milder glories over magnificent scars of limestone, penetrated by numerous and beautiful caverns, and give birth to sparkling waters which enliven the greenest of valleys. They are all easy of access from a country full of comforts, amongst which pedestrians and equestrians will not overlook the establishments for feeding and resting man and horse ; yet how few of those Yorkshiremen who glory in their county, have set foot on the rocky summit of Ingleborough ! "

K

Ingleborough is accessible either from Ribblehead by a rather tedious four mile tramp over Park Fell and Simon Fell, or from Weathercote Cave (two miles from Ribblehead) up Southerscales Fell. It is however more easily ascended from Ingleton or Clapham. Penyghent is also best reached from Horton. Whernside may be ascended from Chapel-le-dale or Ribblehead and a descent made into Deepdale (for Dent) or to Dee Side for Dent Head or Hawes.

At Ribblehead, near the station, there is a convenient inn with limited night accommodation. It is now kept by old John Kilburn, who was 35 years master of the little school in Chapel-le-Dale, and for six years a shepherd on Ingleborough. At Gearstones, one mile on the Hawes road, there is also a good and comfortable inn, (usually full in the shooting season), and at Hill Top, two miles on the Ingleton road, is another house of accommodation. The latter is kept by Mr. Joseph Dean, who is well acquainted with the caves and curiosities of the district. He has been down Alum Pot.

Having referred to the prominent natural features about Ribblehead, let us say a word about the most striking work of man to be seen here. This is the immense railway viaduct constructed by the Midland Railway Company for the passage of trains between Settle and Carlisle. It crosses Batty Moss, and gave the contractors some trouble before solid and durable foundations could be obtained. Nearly all the piers rest on a bed of concrete six feet thick, laid upon the solid rock. The length of the viaduct is 1328 feet, composed of 24 arches of an average span of 45 feet, and the height of the loftiest from the parapet to the foundations is 165 feet. It contains 34,000 cubic yards of masonry, besides 6000 feet of concrete. About a mile to the north of it (between Ribblehead and Dent) is the famous Blea Moor tunnel, one of the longest in England, being 2640 yards in length and 500 feet below the outer surface at the deepest part. The metals in the tunnel attain an altitude of 1151 feet. Blea Moor and Wold Fell being on the watershed of England, the streams on the latter, descending westward, drain into the Irish Sea, and eastward into the German Ocean.

The usually accepted **source of the Ribble,** or Ribble Head, is reached from the road going up to *Gearstones* inn, through a field on the right and below a barn, near two thorn trees. The water flows into the Gale Beck just below. This beck comes down from Newby Head (1400 feet) three miles north, and is really the furthest tributary of the Ribble. The Cam Beck, to the east, which rises within a mile of the source of the Wharfe, on the opposite watershed, joins the Gale Beck a half-mile north of Selside, and the two streams united form the Ribble proper.

Ascent of Whernside (2414 ft.). As stated above, the Chapel-le-Dale road may be followed 2 m. from Ribblehead Station to Weathercote Cave, and after viewing that great curiosity and the neighbouring Gingle and Hurtle Pots, the south or lower end of the mountain may be attacked and the 'roof' then ascended by a long and gradual pull of 2 m. to the northern extremity, where are three small tarns. Or from Ribblehead by taking the road under the railway-viaduct and crossing the Dale Beck by a wooden bridge, a field-path runs between the farm of Gunnerfleet and the white house at Winterscales, direct to **Ivescar House.** Here are several **caves** which are described in the walk from Ingleton to Ribblehead. The middle buttress of Whernside is now close at hand, and the top can soon be gained, Ivescar House standing at about half the altitude of Whernside.

The **rock structure** of Whernside is similar to that of Ingleborough on the opposite side of the valley. There is, however, a lesser thickness of gritstone at the top, but the Yoredale beds are in greater evidence, thinning away eastward. On Whernside they are upwards of 900 feet in thickness, and on Ingleborough about 800 feet, consisting of limestones, sandstones and shales, resting on the thick compact mass of the Great Scar Limestone. The Main Limestone (the topmost bed of the Yoredales) and the Underset Limestone next below it (which is entirely missing on Ingleborough) stand out on Whernside boldly, immediately below the capping of Millstone Grit. There are some peculiar **moraine-like ridges** near the summit of the mountain, but according to the Government Surveyors' report, they are not in such places as would have been occupied by a glacier. The ridges start from some great piles of slipped shale and sandstone just below the highest point of the hill, and curve round to the north on a platform of shale supported by the Main Limestone. They run for about 800 yards nearly parallel to the steep face from which they start, at a distance of about 300 yards from it, so as to enclose a large hollow with two little **tarns,** and known as Greensett Moss. They are in all probability due to avalanches of snow rolling down the steep slopes, rather than to deposits from a glacier.

In tramping about these wild, bare hills one frequently comes across certain **plants** and floral wildings that seem strangely out of place here now. The adaptability of some of these plants to survive under altered conditions amid the pure air and accommodating soil of our Craven Highlands, is indeed one of the most striking phenomena of the district. Such, for example, are the primrose, foxglove, globe-flower. some of the cranesbills and the melancholy-thistle, all woodland types, which we may find growing sometimes in very high and exposed places. Apart from their natural interest they serve to remind us of that remote era when these spreading barren hills and climbing scars were clothed with wood, and the whole region in fact was a wild and tangled forest, the haunt of the bison, bear, wolf, and other strange and formidable creatures. Evidences of ancient birch-woods occur in Greensett Moss (1950 ft.) to the east of Whernside, and the mountain is also noted for its long-continued maintenance of the smallest of living trees. This is the *Salix herbacea*, a very tiny willow, whose habitat we dare not proclaim, but which has been known on Whernside for over 200 years. Well do we remember finding the little rarity away in wild Caledonia while creeping against a wind-blast on the rocky summit of Ben Lawers. "*Salix herbacea floreat*" is the motto of the Scottish Alpine Club, and may the wee plant too, still long flourish in our Yorkshire Highlands !

The **view** from Whernside. though not so interesting as that from Ingleborough, embraces a very wide circuit, reaching from the hills of Wensleydale and Upper Wharfedale northwards and eastwards, and over the fells of Lancashire and Lune Forest to the abrupt heights of the Howgills southwards and westwards. The summit, unlike that of its neighbour Ingleborough, does not appear at any time to have been used as a beacon or look-out post. Ingleborough, from its isolated and more commanding position, has the appearance of being higher than Whernside, and was always regarded as the higher hill even down to modern times.

Ribblehead by Gearstones to Thorns Gill, 1½ m. Just below the station houses and close to the road was a deep chasm called **Batty Wife Hole**, which was filled up when the railway was made. Of the Pot nothing remains but two low-arched holes, about 14 feet apart, the water running down that on the left with a peculiar rumbling noise, and then curving back into the other, reappears at the bottom of the road near the finger-post. On the rocky common called **Rainscar**, to the left of the road, are three other cave-holes, all within about 30 yards of each other. The middle one is perhaps the easiest of access, and its entrance is close to a conspicuous thorn-tree, among a lot of tumbled rocks.

At **Gearstones** up to about 20 years ago, there was a **market** for corn and oatmeal, held from time immemorial every Wednesday. As many as 20 to 30 waggons laden with oatmeal used to come out of Wensleydale, which went to supply all the farm-houses for a good many miles round. When the market originated is not known, but probably in monastic times when Gearstones, as part of the ancient manor of Newby, to which it still belongs, was a possession of Furness Abbey.

Thorns Gill may be entered by a footpath descending behind the inn to a wooden bridge that spans the gill head. The little glen may be traversed on either side, and is very prettily wooded, while the sounding stream below plunges and eddies in a succession of miniature cascades. About 200 yards down, on the east or left bank of the stream, is a cavern called **Katnot Hole**. It has a rather low opening, but on descending within it attains a convenient height, although the passage is but narrow. In about 40 yards from the mouth a spacious grotto is entered, whence the fissure suddenly bends to the east, and continues at a moderate elevation for a distance of over 400 yards. The passage can only be penetrated in single file and frequently contains an inconvenient amount of water. The cave has been denuded of its crystals, although a century ago, according to Hutton, "spar and petrifactions abounded in every part." Ling Gill is situated across the open pastures about a mile to the east, but from this point there is no direct path.

Ribblehead to Ling Gill and back by Ingman Lodge, 7 m. Follow the road to beyond Gearstones inn (as above) and thence turn right over the moor by the old pack-horse road over Cam End to **Ling Gill bridge** (2 m. from Gearstones inn). There is an old milestone at the junction of the roads marked " To Settle XII." The ancient bridge at Ling Gill Head appears to have been rebuilt soon after the new turnpike roads through Craven were completed by Act of Parliament, obtained in the middle of last century, and when in 1761 it was ordained " that the several surveyors get their roads measured and a stone fixed at the end of each mile." The interesting old structure bears the following inscription : " This bridge was repayred at the Charge of the whole West Rideing, anno 1765."

Ling Gill, which is on the Cam Beck, is unquestionably one of the finest and wildest ravines in Yorkshire. The erosive action of the mountain torrent—anciently a much more formidable stream than it is now—has carved out a deep channel in the Great Scar Limestone. This, in the upper part of the glen, forms grand, beetling walls nearly 300 feet high, rivalling the scars of Gordale in altitude, and clothed with the most luxuriant vegetation. As an extraordinary specimen of a sub-alpine glen, it is, we think, unmatched in Yorkshire, and will bear favourable comparison with the best scenes of the kind to be found in the Jurassic Alps of Switzerland. The approaches to it are unfortunately rough, and a scramble up or down the glen is one not to be attempted in patent-leather boots. The tourist indeed tramping these wild hills and glens requires to be well shod and amply provided against the wonders of meteorology ! There is no doubt that the glen has been partly excavated and its walls and rocks smoothed by the passage of an immense glacier downwards from the snow-fields of Cam Fell, and **ice-groovings** trending S.S.W. have been observed on solid rock east of Ling Gill, near the Hawes and Settle road. On the melting of the ice-sheet the quantity of water coming through this gill, caused by the sudden floods of summer, must have been prodigious, and from the size of many recently-rolled boulders in the stream-bed, we may see even yet what a great flood can do. The Alpine Scurvy-grass (a medicinal plant that used to be much eaten in Polar expeditions) fringes the beck and running pools, while many another native of the frozen North still clings to the surrounding scars. A great variety of trees, shrubs, mosses. and flowering plants adorn the various parts of the Gill, among which may be mentioned the Tea-leaved willow (*S. phylicifolia*), the Red-berry laurel (*D. mezereum*), and the London Pride (*S. umbrosa*), one of the few localities in Yorkshire where they are truly wild ; Field-gentian (*G. campestris*), a common flower in sub-alpine pastures of the Jura mountains. Small-scabious (*S. columbaria*), Bird's-eye primrose (*P. farinosa*), &c.

But the most notable plant of the upper Ribble area is the now famous **Gothland sandwort** (*Arenaria gothica*) discovered by Mr. Lister Rotheray, of Skipton, in 1889. It is a small plant, with a perennial root, and bears 1—4 pure snow-white blossoms on a stem. It has been found nowhere else in the British Islands and only in one or two places on the Continent, and consequently for the safety of the plant we refrain from defining its habitat. The fact, however, of its discovery here is interesting, and yields one more instance of the survival of Glacial plants in primitive and unmolested tracts of these unpolluted highlands. The writer, however, may observe that being with the discoverer on one occasion the plant was found growing in some profusion among loose stones of the road, close to the railway-station. Subsequently, when the writer visited the spot the road had been raked and repaired and not a plant was to be seen !

Ling Gill and the neighbouring ravines probably gave cover to wolves and other now extinct animals long after the time of John of Gaunt, who is credited with having slain the last wild wolf in Yorkshire, near Woodlesford, about A.D. 1380. Wolves, we know, lingered in Scotland until near the end of the 17th century. The old Mowbray Fee, which included a vast expanse of country, extending eastwards as far as Ribblehead, or in the terms of a contemporary survey, from "Gemesike to Caldkeld super Camb, and from Caldkeld sup. Camb to the top of Penyghent," where it joined the territory of the Percys, abounded in wolves and stags, for in a fine of the time of King John, between William de Mowbray and Adam de Staveley, particular reference is made to these animals, with respect to concessions of free chase. In the time of the monasteries the wolves were hunted with a powerful breed of mastiffs, and rewards were given by the monks for ridding their land of these blood-thirsty marauders. Ling Gill anciently was the property of Furness Abbey, and the monks may have introduced the cray-fish into the stream. They are, however, thought to have been imported from Semer Water.

At the foot of the gill the farm-house of Nether Lodge will be seen, whence a path goes over the hill and across the Ribble by a wooden bridge to Ingman Lodge, whence the road to Ribblehead (1 m.) is direct. A short distance to the east of Nether Lodge (or reached from Ling Gill bridge by a half-mile walk along the east or

Settle road to a barn, whence descend right about 50 yards) is **Brow Gill Cave,** which can be penetrated for a considerable distance. The mouth is about 20 feet high and as many wide, and upon entering the floor of the cave is found to be curiously fluted in a succession of razor-like edges of limestone, like frozen waves, running parallel with the direction of the stream. These are probably due to the swift flow of water along natural joints being unaffected by any side currents. In places the roof is very low, and the passage by creeping a little difficult. But it opens out in a lofty fissure, whence after more creeping there is a waterfall, beyond which the cave is barely accessible. The stream descending through the cave rises on Green Haw Moor. about 1½ miles to the north-east of Brow Gill.

Ingman Lodge, above mentioned, has been a fine old mansion, and was once the property of the monks of Furness. A clump of trees near the house is said to mark the site of an ancient burial-ground. In the 17th century, the house was in possession of the family of Weatherhead, and initials C.W. and date 1687 appear over the canopied portal. Two large battle-axes are cut in stone on the sides of the doorway.

Ribblehead to Dent Head over Gale Moor, 7 m. This is a wild tramp and in places rather swampy. After wet weather it is preferable to take the main road until within a ¼ m. of the Newby Head inn, whence a lane branches to the left down to Dee Side. It is unnecessary to describe specially the main route from Ribblehead to **Hawes** (11 m.). It is a fine, open drive or walk along the Lancaster and Richmond highway, attaining at **Newby Head** an altitude of 1421 feet. The inn at Newby Head is one of the highest situated in England, and in winter-time especially, when the hills around are covered with snow, the sturdy isolated dwelling looks singularly lonely and impressive. It may be interesting to remark that letters, &c., for Newby Head are brought up Dent Dale from Sedbergh Post Office, a distance of 13 miles.

Hawes itself is a capital stopping-place, and there are some first-rate " sights " and mountain tramps in the vicinity, not to forget the famous Hardraw Scar waterfall and the walk or drive over the Buttertubs into Swaledale.

Apart from the wildness of the scenery the route to Hawes is very interesting to the geologist. The **Great Scar Limestone,** which about Ingleborough has a visible thickness of not less than 600 feet, dips northwards and forms the floor of the river in Dent Dale nearly to its source. It may also be seen at Low Brig beyond Gearstones (1080 feet), near to which above Intack and in Gate Gill the overlying shales crop out, and limestone is seen over these shales at Low Gale and at Winshaw. The shales overlying this limestone appear in Hazel Gill and over them a sandstone. Over the sandstone comes the Simonstone Limestone, which was quarried in Short Gill for the building-stone of the Dent Head viaduct. It is a black and homogeneous rock, and has been quarried in Oliver Gill for " black marble." It is seen in Hazel and Gate Gills and in the neighbouring gills. The overlying shales are well exposed in the same gills, as also in Ouster Gill, where a thin limestone, three feet thick, lying on sandstone, appears in these shales. This thin limestone is again visible in the main beck below Newby Head, not far from the 27th mile-stone. Over these shales comes the Middle Limestone, which crops out above the limekiln on Black Rake, and in Gate and Winshaw Gills. Over it are alternations of sandstone and shale in the same gills and also in Dry Gill (*see Memoirs of the Geological Survey*).

About 200 yards past the **Gearstones*** inn you come to a barn and some trees. Here you leave the main road and take the cart-road over the moor westwards, which soon veers left to the keeper's house at **Winshaw,** where are the kennels belonging to Sir George Pilkington. But the moor, as stated, forms part of the ancient manor of Newby, near Clapham, and belongs to Mr. Farrer, of Ingleborough. The road goes through the gate between the kennels and the dwelling-house, and thence straight on over a rushing torrent to a farm house at **High Gale.** What more appropriate name could be given to this extensive and bleak moorland which is exposed to every "gale" that blows! There is hardly a tree visible now, though doubtless at one time it was a thick forest. Decayed roots are occasionally dug up in the moss, and woodland plants such as the melancholy-thistle, may be seen about the open lands as you go along. Wild moor and in its season purple heath limit the prospect. The long range of high moor which you have away on your right is Cam End, and a grand sight it is to watch in stormy weather the gusty clouds and mists playing "bowls" along the desolate tops!

Leaving the **High Gale** farm the tourist crosses the beck at a barn above an old limekiln, and skirts the Gale Moor side for about a mile (the Hawes turnpike running almost parallel some distance below), when the walled road is entered at the Moss Head Beck. Turning left on the road the beck deepens as you descend to the Dent Head railway-viaduct. This beck is the farthest tributary of the turbulent Dee, and joins the Hazel Gill Beck below the viaduct, whence it becomes a broad and rapid stream, known thenceforward as the Dee, flowing through Dent Dale to the Lune.

A more striking contrast with the wild bare hills left behind could not be imagined than that which greets the tourist in descending from the **Dent Head** viaduct. The beautiful and romantic dale, extending for many miles, is richly wooded, fresh and verdant pastures dotted with wild flowers, reminding one of the flower-enamelled alps of Switzerland, rise steeply on either hand. Rustic cot and quiet farmstead peep from their umbrage of trees, and many a swift and noisy waterfall leaps down from its moorland home through the sunless gills. Hazel Gill, the deep ravine on our left seems almost impenetrable through the density of foliage, and in its abrupt crumbling walls the Yoredale series of rocks, above described,

---

* The name Gearstones is probably derived from the A.S. *gerœstan,* to rest, from the circumstance of there having been a hostelry or resting-place on this ancient highway in Anglo-Saxon times. The land about here was certainly cultivated at a very early date, and the origin of the name may perhaps be discoverable in the A.S. *gœrst,* meaning green like grass.

are fully displayed. The first inhabited house we pass is at **Bridge End**, where the Yoredale shales again crop out by the stream side above the Scar Limestone. Down below the cross-jointed limestone is very curiously furrowed by the action of the flowing water, and appears in transverse sections or squares like a great chess-board, with blocks of black limestone stranded upon them, brought down by floods. We now pass the picturesque Dee Side **Shooting Lodge** belonging to Lord Bective, and a little further on is **Scoo** or **Scow Farm**, at a point of the glen where doubtless it has always been well wooded. The name comes from the Danish *scua* (a wood), and has survived, with many names of like origin in Dent Dale, from the time when the old piratical Vikings were victoriously settled here. During the construction of the Carlisle railway the Scow Farm was a " public " known as the *Wonder* inn, but the house has since been rebuilt.

We now pass on the left the romantic **Blake Gill**, a wooded ravine which contains a very fine and lofty **waterfall,** not unlike the cascade at Hardraw Scar. The swift-descending stream has cut deep down into the Yoredales and then tumbles over a solid marble ledge of Hardraw Scar Limestone. The great Arten Gill viaduct on the opposite side of the valley is built on a foundation of the same rock. At the foot of Arten Gill are the **Dent Marble Works,** (Messrs. Blackburn & Co.), where a variety of fossil and plain marbles obtained from the neighbouring Yoredales are worked up into chimney-pieces, grave-stones, and slabs of every description. The firm also imports various foreign marbles which are wrought in a similar manner ; all the stone being cut and polished by machinery driven by a large water-wheel, the power for which is derived from the Arten Gill Beck. The works are interesting and by the courtesy of the proprietors are shewn to visitors, who have the option of purchasing any article from a small paper-weight of local marble to a handsome Italian mantel-shelf.

We now cross the Dee by a substantial stone bridge, and passing the *Sportsman* inn the scenery continues picturesque on to Lea Gate, (locally Lea Yat), 1 m. from the Marble Works. Hence we may follow the romantic valley downwards to Dent (4 m.) or climb the hill to the railway station.

DENT HEAD STATION TO DENT.

ENTDALE has been praised in prose and verse, and it must be confessed that it has few, if any rivals in picturesque interest in the Yorkshire valleys. Watered by the lively Dee, a rapid mountain torrent rising in the wild wastes of Blea Moor, the whole course of the stream from Dent Head to Sedbergh (10 miles) is replete with interest. Day and half-day excursions are frequently run to Dent Head, and given a fine day it is a most enjoyable trip of eight miles out and home from the little Alpine station at Dent Head to the romantic village of Dent, where there are several inns and tea-rooms.

From the station a rapid descent is made to **Lea Gate** (or Yat) by the side of the rugged Monkey Beck, which enters the Dee a little below. This acclivitous and exposed nook is one of the worst spots in Yorkshire for floods and " gill-bracks " or avalanches. Some burial entries of victims of a fearful avalanche that occurred here on January 31st, 1752, may be seen in the parish registers at Dent. Floods have been not infrequent, the most memorable being that which occurred on July 9th, 1870, during the construction of the railway, when a waterspout fell on Whernside and Blea Moor tunnel was choked to the roof. Two lives were lost and many suffered narrow escapes, while the loss at the railway works and by the washing away of bridges, cattle, &c., throughout the valley was very considerable.*

At Lea Gate there is an old **Quaker Chapel** (with burial-ground) which owes its origin to the visits and ministrations of George Fox in the neighbourhood. Passing the beautifully-placed Vicarage, and the National School, we are soon at the picturesque little **Cowgill Church,** a

---

* For detailed notices of these floods see the author's larger work, *The Craven and North-West Yorkshire Highlands.*

chapel-of-ease to Dent. The foundation-stone was laid in
1837 by Professor Adam Sedgwick, and in 1875 the building
underwent a thorough restoration at the sole expense of the
Misses Elam, of Thorns Hall, Sedbergh. The outside of the
sacred edifice is partially concealed with luxuriant ivy, and

IBBY PERIL.

its aspect along with the adjoining burial-yard, enclosed with
mossy and fern-clad walls, and the prattling beck below, is
one of quiet rustic beauty and seclusion. An old county
bridge close by informs us by its inscription that it was
repaired in 1702.

Following the flower-banked river downwards you come to an old (hosiery) mill. It was of the scenery hereabout that Mary Howitt, the Quaker poetess, who was a frequent visitor to Dentdale, wrote some beautiful lines, which may be found in her collected poems. During the construction of the Dent Head railway the old mill was put in repair and temporarily occupied as a store and brew-house. A little below the mill the river becomes contracted and forms a picturesque waterfall known as Ibby Peril, the haunt it is said of a ghostly old witch, who is particularly anxious to clutch inebriates. The little hamlet of Gibs Hall is near by, and an old house (now a shop) is a prominent object in Mary Howitt's pathetic story of *Hope on, hope ever*, or a *Peep into Dent*. Here the famous authoress used to visit her Quaker friends, and here it was, in the words of the story, that Andrew Law, the schoolmaster at Dent, removed with his child after the death of his beloved wife Dorothea. Gibs' Ha' fireside then became the most popular one in the dale, for it was soon discovered that the "maister's books were worth a' the knitting-sangs as iver were made." At one time the house was in possession of the Sedgwicks, who had some profitable tanning-pits here.

At Gibs Hall a small charge is made for crossing the land to see a dark, deep pool on the river called Hell's Cauldron. The rocks rise precipitously on three sides of the chasm, and some caution is necessary in approaching the abrupt edges, especially after rain. A cascade plunges violently down into the eddying pool, and during a flood the water has been known to cover the high funnel-shaped rock called the Devil's Pulpit, on the north side of the cauldron. A little higher up the stream is a low opening in the limestone known as Hackergill Cave. It is ordinarily the channel of a good current of water, but in dry weather it may be penetrated about 100 yards, when "daylight" is seen. Formerly about the mouth of the cave the pretty lily-of-the-valley grew in some profusion.

Approaching Dent the valley expands, and the Dee receives a copious tributary stream from Deepdale, (the road through the Vikings' Dale to Ingleton, and in later days a pack-horse route of the woollen traders between

Dentdale and the manufacturing districts in the south), *see* " Ingleton to Dent."

Dent Town, as the natives still speak of their remote little village, is the Dentone of Domesday, and was a Norse or Danish settlement held before the Norman conquest by one Torfin, a Dane. Native curtness of speech has apparently shortened the name to Dent, in the same way that it has shortened the name of Sedbergh to Sedber or Sebber, and Garsdale to Gastil, &c. The " town " is romantically placed in the lap of rugged hills and dark, towering rocks, still the haunt of the black and boding ravens which were brought hither on the Scandinavian irruption. As the eagle was the ensign of Rome, so the raven was of the Vikings, and large numbers of this now rare bird were brought over seas by the old pirates, which by and bye established themselves in likely spots in free company with the warlike usurpers. The raven figured on the mighty and invincible battle-flag of Odin, which was long the famous flag of the ancient Danes, and borne before the advancing armies it was for ages the terror of these northern wilds. Their oft-repeated prayer,—which might almost suit the spirit of our own time,—may be freely translated thus : " Merciful gods, we do not ask for wealth : only that we might be placed *within arm's length of some man who has it.*" But the old marauding Vikings have long gone, yet the sable arbiter of their voyages remains with us, and may it long wave its glossy pennons over the cliffs and winding scars of Dentdale,—a living symbol of the old Norseman's cunning and prowess !

Dent, though deprived of the curious architectural charm that belonged to it a generation or so ago, still possesses a rugged, quaint look in its one long, winding thoroughfare. Formerly many of the houses were approached by flights of steps on the outside, and their pent-up upper rooms and open galleries (similar to those one sees in old towns in Normandy and Western France) projected so far into the narrow street that they almost shut out the sight of the sky, and rendered it difficult for any vehicle of more than ordinary size to pass. The street was doubtless built on the old Danish and Norman lines, before wheeled traffic was thought of. In the little " square " is a useful drinking-fountain, erected a few years

ago, as a memorial to **Professor Sedgwick**, the
eminent geologist.   It is appropriately formed of a large
block of unhewn Shap granite.   Professor Sedgwick, or
" Adam o' th' Parsons " as he used in his early days to be
familiarly called, was the son of the Rev. Richard Sedgwick,
incumbent of Dent, and was born at the old parsonage
March 22nd, 1785, and died at Cambridge January 27th,
1873, aged 87.   There is a lengthily-inscribed tablet to his
memory in the church.

The old Norman **Church** (St. Andrew's) was rebuilt in
1417, and after undergoing various renovations since that
time, was in 1889-90 thoroughly restored at a cost of about
£3000, raised by public subscription.   Some of the Norman
piers remain in the nave, and the foundations of the tower
are apparently of like age.   The floor of the chancel is of
Dent marble, bordered with limestone-marble obtained from
Barrow.   The font, which is octagonal, is also of Barrow
marble.   The carved oak pulpit is inscribed M.T., 1614, and
many of the old oak pews have been retained, and bear dates
and initials of their former owners.   The church contains
many memorial tablets to local families, and two stained glass
windows commemorative of the Sedgwick family's long
connection with Dent.   The **Grammar School**,
founded by charter in 1603-4, adjoins the church on the
north-west.

In the vicinity of Dent are many places and objects of
interest.   **Flintergill** rises just behind the village and
in dry weather a walk up its rocky and tree-shaded pavement
may be enjoyed, while to the geologist, the various sections
above the Scar Limestone afford a rich treat.   **Helen Gill,
Dove Cote Gill** (with its small cave), **Pease Gill,
Oliver Gill,** and **High Gill,** are also ravines of great
beauty and scientific attraction.   To the angler likewise, the
Dee and its tributaries yield plenty of trout, eels, &c., and
salmon also ascend the river for spawning purposes to a little
above Dent town.

CLAPHAM.

CLAPHAM.

"A breath of unadulterate air,—
The glimpse of a green pasture, —how they cheer
The citizen, and brace his languid frame."—*Cowper*.

E HAVE described the fine walk or drive from Settle to Clapham (6 miles) under Giggleswick Scars and by Cross Streets in our tours from the former place. Now we are at Clapham, perchance on a bright and sunny day in genial spring-time or summer, —the long white roads are dry and firm, the air crisp and clear, the mountains have donned their blue caps, bird-music in many keys awakens sympathetic chords in human hearts, while rushing rills sing songs of freshness and welcome to the town-jaded visitor,—

The flowers, the leaves, the river on its way
Blue skies, and silver clouds, and gentle winds,—
The swelling upland, where the sidelong sun
Aslant the wooded slope—

and high, grey scars, proclaim 'tis Nature's carnival ! And quiet Clapham, ever inviting by its rustic seclusion, is now our halting-place and verily we think it one of the pleasantest and prettiest spots in our many-acred shire. Let us see it at its best, — not when the storm-cloud lowers, and misty Ingleborough, sire of all, in whose great lap the village lies, wings desolation over hill and plain, but come when " woods are green and winds are soft and low," and we warrant you shall not be disappointed. True the place is small, but such as it is, it captivates by its retired and sylvan aspects, its trim gardens and neat, well-to-do appearance. A grey stone bridge spans the prattling trout beck opposite the only inn in the village, and a little above the bridge we spy a lovely cascade descending from the Ingleborough Hall grounds beneath a picturesque ivy-clad arch into the rocky stream bed. Close beside the stream stands the remains of an ancient market cross, left here to tell of the time when King John, in the third year of his reign (A.D. 1201), gave his written assent to Squire William de Clapham to hold a market here every Thursday, and four fairs annually. The weekly markets were long ago discontinued, and the fairs are now held on September 27th and October 2nd yearly for cattle and sheep.

The manor of Clapham was granted by Roger de Mowbray in the time of Henry II. to the above William de Clapham. With this family it remained some centuries, until in 1572 it was purchased by John Ingleby, of Acomb Grange, son of Sir Wm. Ingleby, Kt., of Ripley Castle. John Ingleby had lately purchased (and removed to) Lawkland Hall, and left Clapham and Lawkland to his son Thomas, who died in 1622. Arthur Ingleby, his son, sold the manor of Clapham to Josiah Morley of Scale House, Rylstone. who died in 1731. The property descended through the female line of this family until 1856, when it was bought by James W. Farrer, Esq., J.P., one of the Masters in Chancery, who died in 1863 in his 79th year. The Farrers have been resident in the neighbourhood of Clapham about two centuries. Richard Farrer married at Clapham in 1686, Elizabeth, daughter and heiress of Oliver Guy of Lanshaw, a farm in the parish of Clapham. James Farrer, who married in 1782 Frances, only daughter of Wm. Loxham, Esq., of Woodford, Essex, built Ingleborough Hall, the present family seat at Clapham. The present lord of the manor and occupant of the Hall is James Anson Farrer, Esq., J.P., son of the Rev. M. T. Farrer, M.A., and a gentleman well and favourably known in the world of letters. He is author of several volumes and treatises dealing principally with social and political subjects. His *Military Manners and Customs*, and pamphlet on *War*, including *The Laws of War*, *War and Christianity*, and *The Limits of Military Duty*, have been widely read. In 1880 Mr. Farrer wrote for Mr. Ivan Muller's edition of *English Philosophers*, a volume on Adam Smith, virtually an abbreviated edition of that writer's *Theory of Moral Sentiments*, with the story of his life.

The old Manor House is passed on the way from the bridge to the church. At one time doubtless, it would be thought a grand and ample residence, but compared with the present manorial seat, it is a very small place indeed. Over the main doorway are the initials of the Inglebys and date 1701. For many years the house was neglected and one portion of it was used for a stable and lumber-room. But in 1890 Mr. Farrer had it carefully restored and fitted up as a reading and recreation room. The building has provision for meeting and class rooms and also a savings bank. There is likewise attached an excellent village library containing about 2000 volumes.

A little beyond stands the picturesquely-seated Church, around whose familiar walls cluster memories of love, and joy, and sorrow, of hopes unfulfilled, of designs incompleted,— the story of our lives as the ceaseless ages roll !

> Alas ! the world is full of peril !
> The path that runs through the fairest meads
> On the sunniest side of the valley, leads
> Into a region bleak and sterile !

The church has a history which carries us back to the Norman era, but of the original building nothing is now left but the low embattled western tower. The rest of the fabric dates only from the year 1814. It consists of chancel, nave, of five bays and aisles, with accommodation for about 700 persons. The clock in the tower was inserted in 1885. Soon after its foundation the church formed part of the numerous endowments of the Benedictine Abbey of St. Mary's, York. On the creation of the See of Chester in 1542, the benefice, with patronage, was given with other possessions of the Archdeaconry of Richmond, to the Bishop of Chester. The ancient parsonage at Clapham was for many generations the occasional residence of the church dignitaries from Richmond, and its site on the south-east side of the church is identified by the name of Archdeacon's Croft, which from the discovery of human bones within it, appears to have been taken out of the old church-yard. The living is now in the gift of the Bishop of Ripon.

Among the epitaphs is a remarkable one to the memory of a family named Balderston, of Sedbusk. The father and mother died in 1814 within six weeks of each other, and the

L

whole of their family of ten died within eight years, between 1810 and 1818.   The pathetic record is inscribed :

> We're here to day, to-morrow yield our breath,
> O reader, tremble and prepare for death.

Another old "poetical" epitaph reads :

> Here Richard Balderston lies down
> In peace we may hope,
> In life and conversation was to Heaven his full scope.
> His time was nothing as some have been,
> His age was thirty-two.
> On the eleventh of May he took his way
> To Heaven as all should do,
> In seventeen hundred and forty-two.

Among the more notable families connected with the vicinity of Clapham were the ancestors of the distinguished scientist Professor Michael Faraday, LL.D., F.R.S., &c.   He was the son of James Faraday, the "village blacksmith," of a family long resident at Keasden, near Clapham.   Though not a native of these parts (he was born at Newington, in Surrey, in 1791) his family ties with this parish make his name and fame dear to us in a very particular manner.   We could indeed wish that some memorial of his parentage and life might be permanently established here, where his father lived and toiled.   Dr. Faraday was a prince among British scientists, and well has he earned the approbation and benefactions of his countrymen.   Thrice he received the degree of Doctor ; Oxford making him a D.C.L., Prague a Ph. D., and Cambridge an LL.D.   He was altogether decorated with no fewer than 95 titles and marks of merit, including the blue ribbon of science, for in 1844 he was chosen one of the eight foreign associates of the French Academy.   Proud the father of such a son, who could lay down his hammer after a heavy day's work at the village forge, and list to the story of his boy's ascension to honour and wealth,—

> Thus at the flaming forge of life
> Our fortunes must be wrought ;
> Thus on its sounding anvil shaped
> Each burning deed and thought.

In the old coaching days Clapham was a busy place, for it lay on the main road from Leeds to Kendal. The mail from Lancaster also arrived every morning (Sundays excepted) and returned in the evening. There were at that time four inns in the village.

Clapham to Clapham (Ingleborough) Cave, 1½ m. As this is, out of all comparison, the finest and most extensive cavern in the north of England, it is well worth a special visit. Parties should write to Mr. Henry Coates at the *Flying Horse Shoe* hotel, Clapham station, who is the lessee of the Cave, or tourists may apply to Harrison, the guide, who lives near the *New* inn in the village. The charge for admission is 2s. 6d. for one or two persons, and 1s. each when there are three or more.

The guide has permission to conduct visitors through the extensive grounds of **Ingleborough Hall.** This is a very pleasant route to the cave, the path going through a narrow and picturesque gorge, the bottom of which is occupied with a long, winding lake, very naturally and skilfully formed by embanking the Clapdale Beck. It covers about 8 acres and is beautifully environed with wood. The Hall was erected about a century ago, and is a substantial and spacious building of stone, with a handsome arcaded portico of the Corinthian order.

Arrived at the **Cave** the visitor will be struck with the romantic entrance at the foot of an umbrageous cliff. The mouth is 56 feet wide and 15½ feet high, and narrows in for about twelve yards to a well-weathered iron grating and gate, preventing further progress without the "open sesame" key of the guide. The first portion extends for nearly 60 yards, is 18 yards wide, and 3 yards in height. This is denominated the **Old Cave,** and has been known from the earliest times. It was once richly adorned with crystal petrifactions, but unfortunately as there was no "magic key" to prevent the incursion of the "forty thieves" the sparry jewellery was long ago carried off.

Nothing was known of the extensive ramifications beyond until 1837 (or about the same time that the Victoria Cave near Settle was discovered) when a thick barrier or curtain of stalagmite was removed, and the stream of water which had been observed to flow along one of its sides, and gave indications of a continuation of the cave, was diverted, and access obtained to hitherto untraversed galleries beyond. Harrison, the old guide, was the first person who entered these lonesome vaults, but the work of exploration was subsequently undertaken with considerable spirit and admirable management by the brothers Mr. James and Mr. Matthew Farrer, along with Lord Encombe, afterwards Lord Eldon, who was on a visit to Ingleborough Hall at the time.

More than half-a-mile, or about 1000 yards, has been explored, although the actual penetrable length of the cavern is little more than 700 yards. Over this length a path has been laid and other conveniences constructed for the easy and safe passage of visitors.

The cavern extends first to the north, then to the north-west, then north and north-east, and finally to the east. Through most of the route the elevations are such as to admit of persons walking erect, but in one or two places the height is reduced to about four or five feet and necessitates stooping. Commendable care has been taken of the natural decorations within the cavern, and these include an innumerable variety of curious and exquisite transparencies, some having the appearance of half-finished statuary, or of wrought marble or ivory, and bearing more or less resemblance to familiar objects. The first great chamber of the new cave is called **Eldon Hall** in honour of the original explorer, Lord Eldon, mentioned above. Hence the rich and fairy-like **Stalactite Gallery** is entered, and in this the impending stalactites and encrustations display a rare and remarkable array of beautiful and fantastic designs. Some of these bear names such as the Turkey's Head, Jew's Ear, Fleece, Glacier, Bee Hive, Belfry, Flitch of Bacon, Jockey Cap, &c. The latter is a singularly-formed mass of stalagmite, 10 feet 8 inches in circumference, and maximum height 30 inches. Having been watched it is calculated to be made up of the accumulated droppings of 308 years (1895). There is no doubt that floods must have ravaged the cave along channels that have for ages been deserted, and thus prevented the accumulation of calcareous deposit in places where it is now forming. The stream which now flows through the cave at a lower level and issues beside the main entrance is the same undoubtedly that falls into Gaping Gill on the east side of Ingleborough.

Leaving the wonderful **Jockey Cap** we proceed through the **Pillar Hall** and presently the silvery tones of a small cascade arrest our attention. In the words of Robert Story,—

> What song shall reflect it ? A gem-studded ceiling,
> On columns of crystal appearing to lean ;
> Sides flashing with brilliants ; the wide floor revealing
> A pure water-mirror that doubles the scene.

About a hundred yards further on, passing the **Lake** to the end of the Long Gallery, is the **First Gothic Arch,** and to the right is a huge boss of stalagmite called the **Ladies' Cushion.** A fluted coating of tufa, partly detached from the left wall, emits when gently struck a variety of musical sounds, to which the name **Ring of Bells** has been given. Beyond is the long, low aisle called the **Cellar Gallery,** and the **Second Bells,** followed by a number of cross vaults or fissures in the rock designated **Arches.** This part of the cave is subject to big floods, and on several occasions it has been nearly filled with mud and sand, rendering its clearance a matter of some difficulty. At the end is the **Second Gothic Arch** and so-called **Giant's Hall,** a lofty irregular chamber, reaching upwards of sixty feet. This terminates the accessible portion of the cave, but there is on the right a small orifice leading down to a shallow water-course, which is supposed to continue northwards to Gaping Gill. This passage, which in places contains deep water, was first explored by the late Mr. James Farrer, who, with a candle in his cap and a rope round his body, managed by crawling and swimming to penetrate it for a good distance. No large chambers, or anything particularly noteworthy, was however discovered. It may be noted that at a certain distance in the temperature is never found to vary, whatever may be the intensity of the heat or cold outside. It has been tested well at all seasons, and found to maintain a uniform temperature of 48°.

Clapham to the Cave and Trow Gill to Gaping Gill and up Ingleborough (2373 ft.) down to Ingleton, 8 m. We gather from Montague's book of *Gleanings in Craven* that he found it necessary to carry pistols when travelling through this district sixty years ago, and that at Clapham, he tells us, he slept with a brace of pistols on his bed ! We do not know whether he met with any rough usage on the way ; we think not. At any rate the statement looks ridiculous to us in these busy get-about days, when the railways are continually bringing thousands of visitors to the district, and where the stranger will meet with as great security and as much comfort and freedom from molestation at the inns and lodging-houses, as well as in the remotest byways, as he will find about his own home. The " Nevisons " and " Turpins " have in fact found no harbour in this district for many a generation past, and the intricate caves of our Craven Highlands shelter no prowling banditti, as they still do in less-favoured lands.

If the tourist's plan is to reach Gaping Gill and the top of Ingleborough without visiting the great Cave, he should at the entrance-gate to Ingleborough Hall turn to the *left* and then very soon to the *right* up a long, winding lane, which leads in about a mile through the farm-yard of **Clapdale Hall** (where light refreshments may be had), and thence down past the entrance to the Cave. Dodsworth, the 17th century antiquary, somewhat pompously describes this house (one of the ordinary strongly-built forest-lodges, with walls in places 6-8 feet thick, and formerly roofed with lead) as " a great old castle joyning on Clapham, the antient demesne of the family of Clapham, who have lived here in good reputation till our father's days." It is supposed to date from the 12th century, and to have been built by one of the De Staveleys, from whom Roger de Mowbray purchased it, with the chace of Ingleborough. in the time of King John, and by whom it was afterwards (*temp.* Henry II.) granted to William de Clapham. The house is raised on a natural foundation of rock, and a wilder or more secluded spot for a gentleman's residence could hardly be found. But in the old days of constant war and menace such a site would be considered well-chosen. Arthur Ingleby, Esq., D.L. for Co. York, who died at Clapham in 1701, was the last of its lords who dwelt here, and since that time it has been occupied as a farm-house.

Leaving the imposing entrance to the **Ingleborough Cave** (*see* p. 151) we pursue the park-like path between cliffs of well-wooded limestone, mounting the step-stile at the lane-end in the direction of Ingleborough. Readers of Mark Twain may remember how the author ascended many of the highest Swiss mountains without the

aid of guides, ropes, or any of the paraphernalia common to an Alpine
outfit.   He simply sat at his hotel window and fixing a telescope on
a particular snow-clad peak raised it leisurely from base to summit,
and in this facile manner performed many surprising ascents !   But
in going to Ingleborough by the Cave route you cannot " do " the

GAPING GILL.

mountain in this convenient way, for the summit is not seen until
the saddle of Little Ingleborough is gained, within a few hundred
feet of the top.

From the step-stile above mentioned you pass into the short but
grand ravine of **Trow Gill**, which has been the passage of a large

stream and at its upper end of a once powerful waterfall. Ages have passed, however, since this was happening. In a limestone country we know that the streams are continually altering their courses ; swallow-holes are also formed which, as they enlarge, engulf many of the descending waters, to be borne by devious and ever-changing ways through the subterranean vaults. It seems indeed evident that the walls of the Trow Gill gorge have been hollowed out by the passage of a large body of water, before the chasm of Gaping Gill was large enough to receive the whole volume that now drains into it from the wastes of Ingleborough. The scooped-out bed of the old river-course can be followed all the way up to Gaping Gill, and there is no doubt that to the enlarged fissure of this great hiatus in the limestone is owing the extinction of the Trow Gill stream and waterfall, just, for example, as the pot-holes above Malham Cove have extinguished the lofty cascade which doubtless at the same era was precipitated from its summit in one magnificent leap.*

Climbing up the gap of this **extinct waterfall** you follow the wall side up about 600 yards to a small gate on the left. Here you will see on the left some rocks and an incipient " pot," with a few ash-trees hanging over it. Keep this on your left and follow a faint track over broken limestone, under a low, rushy hill, about 150 yards, when the track veers to the right another 200 yards, and you will see the broad, turfy gill which carries the Fell Beck directly into the huge rift of **Gaping Gill**. Owing to the wide and open character of the moor the chasm is not good to find, but by following the above directions you cannot get wrong. In wet weather, or in Spring, after frost, when the peat is loose and breaks from the feet, great care should be taken in approaching the opening (which is unprotected), and especially the lower ledges, as these, even if dry, are slippery with the continued plash of the water. The altitude of this wild spot is about 1380 feet above the sea, and 1000 feet below the summit of Ingleborough. The hole is funnel-shaped, 8 feet wide and about 20 feet long. The side opposite to that on which the stream enters is very much broken and battered with rocks brought against it by floods. Several attempts have been made to descend the chasm, but owing to its contraction only about half its actual depth has been explored. It has, however, been plumbed and found to be 356 feet deep, or measured from the top of the steep bank above the hole 385 feet. The stream that enters it flows as before explained through Ingleborough Cave and emerges near the mouth.

From Gaping Gill you now steer north-west over the open fell—a long and stiffish pull—up to Little Ingleborough, as the southern buttress of the burly mountain is called, when the summit (2373 ft.) will be seen ahead. A track runs along the east side of the fell, which presently bends northward up the side of **Ingleborough** to its

---

* It has been suggested to make up the fissures of the Malham Tarn stream, so that the water might fall as of old in one grand sheet from the top of the Cove. Ordinarily a mere spout, it would, however, become during a spate undoubtedly the sublimest single waterfall in the British Islands.

flat and spacious top. By this route you traverse a thick and unusual
tract of hill-peat, which in some places covers the flats of limestone,
and has generally been formed in such situations where a sandy and
thin drift has been deposited in the depressions, being doubtless in
some cases the dried-up beds of small tarns. Here and there erratic
blocks of gritstone are seen stranded on the crumbling limestone,
the work of the last great ice-flow.

As Ingleborough is more conveniently and most frequently
ascended from Ingleton we describe it in that section of our work.
The tourist alighting at Clapham, however, may find an agreeable
diversion from the Trow Gill route in ascending Ingleborough by
following the *old* road to Ingleton as far as **Newby Cote** (1¼ m.).
Going up the wall side by the houses, when at the top keep slightly
to the right and the Knowe Gap stream (which is a good guide to the
summit) will be encountered coming down southwards from the
mountain. This route is shorter and less of a climb than that from
either Ingleton or Trow Gill.

**Clapham to the Long Kin Holes and Alum Pot to
Horton,** 8 m. This is a rough tramp along the eastern declivities of
Ingleborough and Simon Fell. Pass the Church and under the long
tunnels of Ingleborough Park, ascending the road about ¾ m. Here
a lane branches *r.* to Austwick, but do not turn ; open the gate and
keep straight on, descending across the depression of the North
Craven Fault, with the fine scars in front, and on the left the deep,
narrow valley of Clapdale. You can see the mouth of the great
Ingleborough Cave, with the Clapdale "castle" high above.
This scene, viewed under the warm glow of a bright Autumn noon,
amid the various tints of the trees, and the decaying brackens and
shrubs upon the scars, reminds us not a little of Shelley's lines :

> The noonday sun
> Now shone upon the forest, one vast mass
> Of mingling shade, whose brown magnificence
> A narrow vale embosoms—

Passing shortly through a second gate, or rather the *third* from
Clapham, you emerge on the wild open fell with the wooded **Trow
Gill** some distance on the left. The long lane you have come up
runs about north-east by south-west, and by crossing the hollow
northwards from here, and then walking up with the gully on our
right, we shall arrive at a gate in the wall which crosses our route.

From this gate by following the wall downwards 600 yards to
another gate (*see* p. 155) **Gaping Gill** can be visited. This wall is
continuous northwards with another, which separates the west fell
from the large allotments on the east, and runs all the way up the
south slope of Simon Fell (2125 feet). Marching up with this long
allotment wall on the left about 400 yards you enter a hollow of bare
limestone, to the left of which are two deep rifts known as the
Long Kin Holes. They are about 1000 yards to the east of Gaping
Gill. The deepest is that to the north which has been plumbed to
a depth of over 200 feet, but it is too narrow to admit of anyone
descending it. The southern hole is more open and longer but its

depth is only about 100 feet. Following the hollow upwards you come to a point where the stream has, for a length of nearly 50 feet, cut through the thick turf to the rock below, and here the torrent goes down a succession of ledges into the **Long Kin Cave.** The entrance is about 12 feet high and a yard wide. To penetrate this chasm requires caution, as the descent in some places is very rough and rapid, and should not be attempted except in settled weather, as a sudden rising in the water on the fell above would speedily submerge the cave and render the explorer's escape almost impossible. Soon after getting in the passage branches suddenly to the left, and may thence be penetrated for a distance of nearly 250 yards.

A little to the north-west of the cave, and close under the allotment wall mentioned, is **Marble Pot,** so called from the fine polish of the rock out of which it is formed. The water is carried to the mouth of a hole nearly 50 feet in depth, over which the torrent leaps in one unbroken cascade. This "pot" sometimes fills up and "boils" over About ½-m. north-east of this cavity is another large rift in the limestone called **Juniper Gulf.** The water descends the contracted chasm a vertical depth of about 80 feet, and must then fall more or less rapidly to the south, perhaps joining the underground stream of Long Kin. That interesting shrub the juniper, with its narrow, sharp-pointed leaves (one of the few plants found in the deserts of Arabia) flourishes on the brink of this chasm. In the next field to the east are two other small caves of engulfment.

Crossing the heathery waste about a mile to the north you will come to **Alum Pot,** the site of which may be recognised by a clump of trees, and short dipping wall enclosing it (*see* p. 128). The hamlet of Selside lies below, whence Horton-in-Ribblesdale station (the nearest) 2½ miles distant may be reached by a good road.

Clapham to Austwick (1½ m.) **and the Norber Boulders** 3 m. Return by same route 6 m., or by Scars 4½ m. The group of erratic boulders at Norber, in point of number, situation and interest, presents a spectacle of its kind probably unrivalled in England. Going round by the *New* inn at Clapham there is a stile or gate opposite the old Market Cross, whence a foot-road runs through the park of "Ingleborough," and up through a small plantation direct to **Austwick.** The village, somewhat scattered and straggling, is picturesquely placed on the sunny side of the valley, with very sweet views of the woods and scars about Wharfe and Feizor. Smearside, like the cone of some worn-out volcano, is also conspicuous to the south. Austwick, which received its name from its position *east* of Clapham, is a very ancient and at one time an important place, being in the Norman era the head of the lordship or barony, consisting of 12 manors and 12 dependent villages. Subsequently the manor of Austwick came to the Yorkes, (now seated at Bewerley in Nidderdale), and in 1598 was sold by them to Sir Richard Shuttleworth, Kt., Chief Justice of Chester, in whose family it remained till the year 1782, when the manor was purchased by James Farrer, Esq.. of Clapham. The manor-house and demesne, however, were sold by Sir John Yorke in 1573 to the Inglebys, about the time they acquired Lawkland.

The Austwick Hall estate was bequeathed in 1846 by the late Thomas Clapham, Esq., of Stackhouse, son of the Rev. John Clapham, Vicar of Giggleswick (1782—1839) to Thomas R. Clapham, Esq., F.R.A.S., of Feizor, who is the present occupant of the Hall and one of the principal landowners. The house is a building of great antiquity, the entrance hall having been an old fortified peel or border-lodge, apparently of the 12th century. It is very strongly built, with walls 7 to 8 feet thick. At the north-west corner the house stands on a large glacial boulder of Silurian grit.

Austwick, in May, 1879. was formed out of the mother parish of Clapham into a separate parish. The Church of the Epiphany was built in 1841, and was formerly a chapel-of-ease to Clapham. In 1883 it was enlarged and consecrated. It is a neat stone building in the Early English style, and contains some beautiful stain-glass windows ; the handsome east windows being a public memorial of the Queen's Jubilee (1887). The communion table is made of oak grown in Lawkland Wood. There is also in the village a Wesleyan Chapel. a Reading Room (with library), and in an open space at the junction of the roads is the base, consisting of four tiers, of an old Village Cross. The present stone pillar was, however, set up only about fifty years ago.

Many are the tales told of the "Austwick carles" in bygone days, of their strange failings and reputed lack of common intelligence. It is said, for example, that once a man was observed to wheel repeatedly an empty barrow into a hay-loft, and when an explanation was sought, it transpired that he was wheeling sunshine into the barn to dry the hay with ! It is also related of a farmer here calling together nine of his neighbours to assist him in lifting a bull over a gate which separated one field from another. After "tewing" and struggling some time they were told by a passing traveller to open the gate and drive the bull through. Putting the animal down, and wiping their heated brows, they took the hint and were spared further exhaustion. Another story relates to the time when the thatch of Austwick Hall annually bore a good crop of grass, and on one occasion several farmers gathered together to discuss the best way of getting a cow or two on to pasture it. It was not until an outsider told them that the better way would be to cut the grass and bring it down that their difficulty was solved. Still another story carries us back to the days when umbrellas were not a very common article of personal equipment, at anyrate in the Craven Dales. An Austwick man having occasion to go to a doctor's at Settle, the latter on seeing his visitor to the door and finding that it was raining very hard, generously offered him an open umbrella, explaining as he did so its use, and saying that it would be all right if he returned it the next time he was in Settle. On reaching home, comparatively dry, the man astonished not only his wife, but a number of the inhabitants, none of whom had ever seen such an article before. After a good deal of close inspection an attempt was made to get the open umbrella through the doorway, but without avail. The people collecting, the wife grew angry and chastised her husband severely for coming home with such an awkward machine. At length a wiseacre in the crowd suggested that they should try the chamber window, which was above the ordinary size, and so the expanded umbrella was tied to a piece of cart-rope and hauled up to the second story window, but this again was not wide enough to admit of its passing into the house. The wife now became furious : "Tak her, ye cauf heead, an' tether her to't bull stoop i't pastur," and looking very sheepish he did as he was bid. A week later the man walked into Settle with the umbrella still up, although the day was gloriously fine. He explained his troubles to the doctor, who on hearing the end of the tale, gave a hearty laugh and explained the simple mechanism of its opening and shutting, much to the Austwick man's dismay.

Of course Austwick now-a-days is not behind any other village in the dales either in general intelligence or business aptitude, and many a good laugh is enjoyed by them of the many tales attributed to their erring ancestors. The village has long had a good school with an average daily attendance of over sixty. Many of the houses in the neighbourhood have begun to lay themselves out for receiving visitors and to those needing rest and complete quiet, with the tonic of pure air and inviting scenery, the place would be hard to beat. To the geologist and botanist the district is full of interest. Within a few miles' radius of Austwick, a local botanist, Mr. Wm. Handby, has collected nearly 70 species and varieties of ferns alone, including the extremely rare holly-fern (*P. lonchitis*), now almost extinct in Britain. But the "hamper men" have made sad havoc of these graceful plants, which is all the more to be regretted, as the ferns, accustomed to a pure air and congenial soil, only perish when removed to the towns where they are mostly sold.

But we must now direct our steps towards **Norber**, or the North Hill, as its name signifies. above Austwick. Going by the old Hall, before described, we follow the lane up about ¾-m. to where the roads divide. Here there is a field on the left, containing numerous large travelled boulders, which may be profitably examined and the scar ascended in front, on the top of which the black-looking, massive Silurian erratics present a strange contrast with the grey-white broken limestone on which they rest darkly against the sky ! It will however be better to go down past the plantation and follow the Crummack Lane up the dale until near its junction with the White Stone Lane, which crosses the Crummack Beck. Here you are at the foot of Norber Scars, and close to an old limekiln. Scores of **ice-borne boulders** lie scattered about the valley bottom to the south and west, and many have been broken up to build and repair the walls. Hundreds remain on the scar above, saved from destruction by reason of their peculiar and inconvenient position. They lie scattered together, mostly within a space of half-a-mile, being of every shape and size, some very curiously formed, and perched or stranded on the worn limestone, or piled one on another in the most fantastic manner. The source, whence the bulk of the boulders have been derived may be seen and studied in the vicinity of the limekiln above mentioned. It is a prominent ridge of dark bluish-grey

calcareous grit, extending across the valley, rising somewhat westward, with a rapid dip to the north-east. Fragments of all sizes, torn
from this ridge lie in its immediate vicinity, and the surface of the rock
hereabouts has been worn smooth by the passage of the ice over it.
About 150 yards north of this outcrop there is good evidence of the
direction of the glacier in the deep groovings on the rock, all pointing
directly southwards.

A curious circumstance connected with these phenomena is that
while the parent-ridge lies at about 900 feet elevation, most of the
blocks from it are found ascending to an altitude on the south and
west of nearly 1200 feet.   It is evident that they have been pushed
forward up the slope by the irresistible force of the glacier and raised
also partly by lateral pressure of the thick body of ice crammed
between the sides of the valley, the numerous boulders have been
dropped on the more elevated limestone bed. The transported stones
gradually thin away to the west and north, and do not ascend to
more than about 1200 feet, consequently we may infer that the hill,
which rises northwards about 100 feet higher, has not been crowned
with ice.   The aspect of the dark detached stones in such a wild
and lonely spot is singularly weird and impressive, and in ancient
times must have generated many strange superstitions. How the old
Ice King has graven in striæ, his presence upon the rocks, plain and
meaningful as the " Writing upon the Wall !' The many blocks stand
like pillars and tables, deserted by all but the wild winds that play
about them.   Some of them are tons in weight and poised in the
most remarkable positions.   One of the largest, resting on a narrow
limestone base, measures 49 feet in circumference and 6 feet in height.
The boulders seem but comparatively little affected by the forces of
Nature operating upon them through countless ages, while the grey
limestone pavement has almost crumbled away.   What centuries
forsooth have vanished since these time-hallowed monuments were
left here at the bidding of the unseen Power who guides and governs
all !

> O, wondrous Stones ? Grant us the Light
>   Of Ages that have gone before,—
> Ten thousand years on this bare height
> Have ye withstood the tempest's might,
>   And shall do ten thousand more ! *

At the west end of the plateau there is a fine view over Lunesdale,
and eastward of the massive grey scars of Moughton, with their long
line of screes.   Down below, in a basin-like cavity, is the site of
an ancient tarn, drained about 80 years ago.   It is called **Tarn
Thwaite** and is strewn with glacial boulders.   From this craggy
edge, called **Robin Proctor's Scar,** you can reach Clapham in
about 40 minutes by descending into the Thwaite Lane opposite,
which goes straight down under the tunnel of Ingleborough grounds
and emerges at the church.

---

* A fuller account of the Norber Boulders will be found in the writer's larger
work, *The Craven and North-West Yorkshire Highlands.*

Ingleton.

INGLETON.

Ye who love the haunts of Nature,
Love the sunshine of the meadow,
Love the shadow of the forest,
Love the wind among the branches,
And the rain-shower and the snow-storm,
And the rushing of great rivers
Through the palisades of pine trees,
And the thunder in the mountains,
Whose innumerable echoes
Flap like eagles in their eyries.

UCH is the declamation of Longfellow in the *Song of Hiawatha*, and with these words for our text we invite you to join us in our exploration of this Yorkshire Wonderland. True there are no "great rivers," except when old Ingleborough—King of the Rocky Mountains—rings his thunder-bell, and the storm-fiend whips the hill-becks into deluges of tawny foam. Then, forsooth, there is a great rush and roar worthy of the poet's theme. The mention of the eagle reminds us that that noble bird of prey has long been exterminated from our Yorkshire Highlands, although the peregrine-falcon, kite, and merlin, still build in the district. And it is devoutly to be hoped for the interest of the larger public, that anyone aware of this fact will forego the few minutes pleasure of shooting them, or indeed of molesting them in any way. They give an interest to the district far beyond their value as "stuffed specimens."

There is no doubt that most of the great birds of prey were once common in the Scar country, but like the wild beasts that dwelt here too, they have been shot and destroyed by man. We can of course well spare the bears and wolves, but let us, if possible, retain a few of the rarer birds ! At one time the whole district seems to have been a vast tangled wood of trees and scrub, with only the bare tops of the mountains peeping through the sweeps of forest. Many strange beasts, including fierce boars, the grizzly bear, skulking wolves, &c., then infested the Ingleton glens. The huge mammoth and the elephant came crashing along their accustomed tracks in the glades of Chapel-le-Dale, where now the familiar carriage runs pleasantly along an open country road. This is no mere picture of the imagination, but deductions from actual fossil remains obtained within recent years from the surrounding fissures and caves. The last of the wild animals to inhabit the district were the stag or red-deer and the wolf, both of which were in a truly wild state here probably as late as the 16th century. Special rewards were made to wolf-slayers in Craven as late as the 14th century, so that they must have been very numerous and destructive at that period. The stag, however, was in a semi-wild state on Ingleborough and Penyghent for centuries after this, and it was allowed to run wild on the fells though actually the property of the lords of the soil.

The old Celtic immigrants did not do much to clear the woods,—that was left largely to the Roman conquerors, who invaded the Craven dales in the first century A.D. The old Britons lived in summer on the top of Ingleborough, where traces of their horse-shoe shaped habitations were until recently very plain. They kindled the Beltane fires up there in honour of their gods, and also to keep the wild beasts away. They were a highly superstitious people, and some of their beliefs, in fact, have come down to our own day. At Ingleton, for example, within the last thirty years or so it was a common practice to kindle the so-called "Need-fire" by rubbing two pieces of wood briskly together, and setting ablaze a large heap of sticks and brushwood, which were dispersed, and cattle then driven through the smoking brands. This was thought to act as a charm against the spread or development of the various ailments to which cattle are liable, and the farmers seem to have had great faith in it. The custom was also rife of keeping the fires constantly burning, (the precursor of the half-burnt Yule log of our own time), exactly as they do at some places in Ireland at the present day, where certain house fires are known to have been kept perpetually burning for at least 200 years.

Ingleton, *i.e.*, fire-town, seems to have been so named from the fact of the long-continued prehistoric fires on Ingleborough beacon. In the *Domesday* survey (A.D. 1086) it is spelled Inglestune. At that era the village was a dependent of the important manor of Whittington, (now a small place two miles south of Kirkby Lonsdale), belonging to the tyrant Earl Tosti, ruler of Northumbria, and chief minister of Edward the Confessor. He was slain at Stamford Bridge in 1066, and some weeks later when his brother Harold fell on the memorable field of Hastings, William the Conqueror ascended the throne of England. Ingleton, in common with a vast territory extending from the Hambleton Hills on the east to the borders of Westmorland on the west, was bestowed by the new monarch on the powerful family of Mowbray. This wealthy house in the time of King Stephen owned 280 Knights Fees in England and Normandy, in addition to other valuable possessions. One of their castles or strongholds was at Burton-in-Lonsdale, about two miles west of Ingleton.

The manor descended through various owners to the distinguished family of Cholmondeley, who in the reign of Queen Elizabeth, leased it to the Lowthers, of Lowther Hall, Westmorland. Sir Gerard Lowther, Kt., son of Sir Richard Lowther, Kt., of Lowther Hall, was Chief Justice of Common Pleas in Ireland, and in 1654 was Lord High Chancellor of that kingdom. He was thrice married ; his first wife being Anne Welbury, widow,—daughter and co-heir of Sir Ralph Bulmer, of Wilton,—who appears to have died at Ingleton Hall, as the parish registers under date, October 13th, 1619, record the burial of Lady Anne,wife of Sir Gerard Lowther,Kt. Sir Gerard's younger brother, William Lowther, J.P., lived at Ingleton Hall and had a numerous family. His eldest son, Sir Richard Lowther, left a son Henry who resided at Ingleton and at Lowther Town, Cockermouth. He married, and leaving an only daughter the Ingleton estates were disposed of to the family of Bouch, and subsequently passed by marriage to the Parkers of Browsholme.*

* A more detailed history will be found in the writer's larger work, *The Craven and North West Yorkshire Highlands.*

Of Mr. Edward Parker, lord of the manor of Ingleton, who died in 1794, we have an interesting note from the poet Gray. Describing his journey from Poulton to Ingleton in the autumn of 1769, he remarks, "Now our road began gradually to mount towards the Apennine, the trees growing less and thinner of leaves, till we came to Ingleton. It is a pretty village, situated very high, and yet in a valley at the foot of that huge monster of nature, Ingleborough." Here, while taking refreshment at the inn, he met "Sir Bellingham Graham and Mr. Parker, lord of the manor, one of them six feet high and the other as much in breadth!"

With the exception of the Lowthers the township does not appear to have produced any family or person of particular eminence. The place, however, gave name to two Abbots of Sallay, Fr. Wm. de Ingleton, *circa* 1350, and Wm. de Ingleton instituted in 1443.

There is nothing particularly noteworthy as regards public buildings at Ingleton. It is a long straggling village climbing the road to Ingleborough, which rises just 1900 feet above it to the north. The church, however, should be noted; the date of the tower is usually assigned to the 15th century, but with this exception the fabric of the church has been since several times rebuilt. The present building was erected only about eight years ago. It contains some beautiful stain-glass windows, and a pulpit in Caen stone with Connemara marble pillars, of very neat and chaste design. On the west arch are traces of an old fresco, but the subject is much defaced. The most remarkable object within the church is the curiously-carved Norman font. It is circular in form, and around its circumference it is exquisitely sculptured in arched sections with illustrative designs from the history of Christ, including the Virgin and Child, the presentation of the Magi, the Massacre of the Innocents, &c. Portions of the carvings are unhappily disfigured, and their subjects cannot be properly identified. This beautiful relic was fortunately rescued from a sacrilegious destruction by Dr. Whitaker, the historian. He found it thickly encrusted with lime, caused by its having been used as a trough for mixing mortar, and afterwards as a whitewash bowl for "adorning" the interior of the church!

There are a few old houses in and around Ingleton. The ancient manor house, Ingleton Hall, has been rebuilt, but traces of a possible moat that enclosed the original hall, which stood a little to the west of the present building, are still apparent. One of the oldest existing dwellings is the Cross Farm, for nearly two centuries used as the parish workhouse. Another is the Blue Hall (date, 1668) opposite the National School, and another near the church, formerly an inn called the *Black Bull*, has the lintel over the door inscribed 1710. But the oldest is probably that known as the *Cock* inn, on the Ingleton Hall road, below the railway-bridge. It was formerly a well-known trysting-place of cock-fighters, and it is said that more than one dark deed of crime has been perpetrated within its rooms. One of its floors showed many ominous blood-stains which no amount of scrubbing could remove. The house, of three gables, was probably built in the time of James I., but it has been much altered and improved since.

In addition to the "noble" sport of cock-fighting there was also the old-time sport of bull-baiting indulged in at Ingleton in the open space near the centre of the village. The old bull-ring is still here, fixed to a stone in the ground. We mentioned the bull-baiting at Skipton (page 7), where according to the parish accounts the last entry for a "bull-rope" occurs in October. 1786, and happily these brutal pastimes were probably discontinued at Ingleton about the same time.

Since the formation of the "Improvement Association," ten years ago, the place has become extremely popular as a health and pleasure resort, and there has been a considerable increase of building operations in the neighbourhood. When the scenery was first opened out the people who came here might have been counted in hundreds, but these rapidly increased, and in 1893 the maximum inrush was reached, when it was estimated that at least 100,000 persons visited the place in the course of the season. Formerly it lay on the old coach route from Kendal to Leeds, and from 1807 to 1823 the coaches came past the Broadwood toll-bar and down the main street. The village is now approached by two branch lines of railway, the Midland, and London and North

M

Western ; their stations, a few hundred yards apart, being
separated by the southern embouchure of the deep, romantic
glen formed by the Greta, above which Ingleton stands, and
which is spanned by a lofty viaduct of eleven arches. It is
distant 52 m. from Leeds, 42 m. from Bradford, 18 m. from
Lancaster, and 10 m. from Settle. Cheap excursion tickets
are issued from the principal towns.

There are several good large hotels and temperance inns,
besides innumerable private houses where ample accommodation for day-visitors or families prolonging their stay can be
obtained. The mansion of Moorgarth, erected by the late
A. S. Kirk, Esq., has lately been converted into a hydropathic
establishment. Carriages, post-horses, and guides (if required)
can be obtained at the inns. There is a post-office and
telegraph-office : address, Ingleton, Kirkby Lonsdale.

**Ingleton up the Twiss to Thornton Force and back
by Beasley Falls through the Dale Glen,** 4 m. This is,
perhaps, the most romantic four miles of glen and mountain scenery
to be found in our broad-acred county. From end to end it is a
succession of natural surprises. The route may be reversed but we
prefer the one to be described, as the more expansive Twiss or
Kingsdale Glen is viewed and appreciated better, we think, before the
wild and contracted ravine of the Dale Beck is approached. The
round is only accessible on foot, and three to four hours should be
allowed for it. **Refreshments** can be obtained above the Pecca Falls,
and at the Twisleton Hall farm at the head of the glen. After heavy
rain, when there is a fresh from the mountains, the numerous waterfalls present a grand spectacle ; care, however, should always be
exercised as the paths in places are slippery and precipitous, and more
than one life has been lost. The "Improvement Committee" have,
however, done wonders in opening out the two glens, in clearing a
road, and in laying down paths and constructing "staircases" and
bridges for their safe and easy exploration. The cost of making and
maintaining these paths, &c., necessitates a small charge being levied
on all persons visiting the glens.

Going down by some cottages below the *Ingleborough* hotel (or
from the station in walking towards the village, descend the first
road on the left) you will soon cross the bridge and must then enter
a stile on the right, which opens into **Broad Wood,** an extensive
verdant expanse, though somewhat spoiled by large hoardings. Here
is the ticket-box, where you have to "stand and deliver." Proceeding
you enter the ravine of **Creeping Steads,** where a path has been
constructed along the shelving wooded bank, and presently descends
by means of a ladder into a narrow defile below. Here the scene is
wonderfully grand. The river in its contracted bed tumbles among

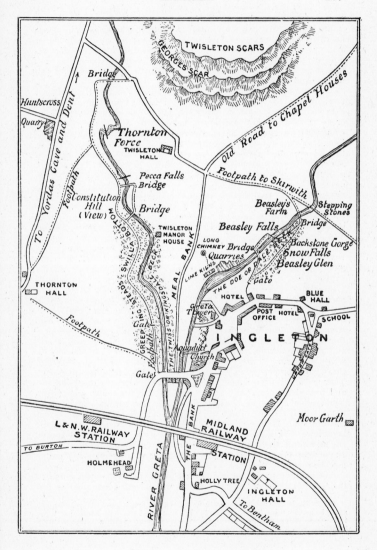

moss-grown boulders, and the precipitous banks on each side are richly clothed with vegetable life. Opposite, towering to an immense height, are huge walls or ramparts of wood-crowned rock, their ledges and crannies and steep-rifted declivities affording a precarious root-hold for a perfect forest of native growth, amongst which the dark foliage of the yews contrasts finely with the tender green of the birches and other trees.

Proceeding now through the delightful glades of **Swilla Bottom** you come to the Lovers' Seat (where it is said much nonsense has been enacted) and soon you have the option of two ways : either to cross the bridge and walk up the east bank of the stream—a comparatively tame and level stretch—to Pecca Falls, or mount the long, winding staircase of **Constitution Hill**—the name you will think is well deserved—for the sake of the fine view from its summit. Here the lowest waterfall, gleaming white in the distant ravine amid a setting of wooded rock and fell, looks very effective. You now descend by a mere ribbon of a road continuing along the declivitous side of the hill, past an old lead-boring and thence to the old Pecca slate quarry, which has not been worked these forty years. These slates are accounted the equivalents of the green slates and porphyries of Borrowdale in the Lake District. Here are the famous **Pecca Waterfalls,** a series of seven or eight beautiful and plentiful cascades, which if Southey, the poet-laureate, who was no stranger to Ingleton, had celebrated by such a poem as he wrote on Lodore, he would surely have merited greater approbation in the choice of his subject than he has done. The ordinary waterflow at the famous Cumberland rock-scene is a mere driblet by comparison. Even when shrunk in a time of drought the Pecca Falls always look beautiful, but more especially in the Autumn season when the changing colour of the trees, and the clusters of scarlet berries of the mountain-ash, along with patches of projecting heather and decaying fern, encompass the scene. In a time of flood the whole ravine is choked with foam, and the thundering waters seem to shake the very foundations on which you stand.* Here, as stated, are the slate rocks, coarser than the Cumberland roofing slates, but somewhat the same in colour. They are of Silurian age—the oldest known strata in our county— and are visible eastward at the base of Ingleborough and across Ribblesdale as far as Gordale Scar. In the bed of the stream, notably near the large fault which brings the Scar Limestone against the Silurian rocks, are some remarkable **eruptive dykes,** or ancient lava-flows, visible at the point named for three or four yards above the middle of the bend of the stream, which here runs south-east. In several other places in the Ingleton area these volcanic rocks may be seen too.

Ascending now by the side of the sounding ravine you come to the second fall, from the rocky top of which, near three small holly-

---

* The floods here are sometimes very sudden and prodigious. A year or two ago a large cow belonging to the Manor House farm, Twisleton, happening to be in the glen bottom was swum bodily down a quarter-of-a-mile, and rescued with difficulty.

trees, a lady visitor (Mrs. Parker, wife of the Low Bentham postmaster) in 1885 slipped and fell into the deep pool beneath and was drowned. From the abruptness of the strata and the depth of water in the bottom immediate rescue was impossible, and when a rope had been fetched a man was let down and after considerable difficulty (there being no foothold) the body of the unfortunate woman was secured. The path here has been widened and improved, and there is no danger if you keep to it. Seats have been placed at intervals along the road, which you may be glad of, as the ups and downs of this rough track will be calculated to thoroughly try your staying power ; indeed as a medicament for rheumatic joints or for the test of supple limbs, this route would be hard to beat !

Now we pass the **Cuckoo Island,** the early haunt we are told of the " blithe new-comer," and where in summer days the spongy banks glisten with the rare floral stars of the beautiful Grass of Parnassus. Just beyond, at a curvature of the river, is **Thornton Force,** one of the finest and most interesting waterfalls in the district. Geologically it is perhaps unique, as we see here in admirable sections the base of the Mountain-limestone resting on a conglomerate of Silurian pebbles, which again overlies an exposure of highly-inclined slates. The perpendicular height is 63 feet, but the rocks on the left are fully 30 feet higher. It is a fine sight when there is a good rush of water, and the cascade may be passed from behind as it arches over the face of the cliff. In winter when the hollies and other few trees about are feathered with hoar-rime, and the half-frozen waterfall is hung round with long silvery bars, fleecy curtains, and dependent fringes of translucent ice, it is a perfect fairy-scene. We however, often thought the place rather bare in summer, and that some judicious planting would add considerably to the situation and effect of this fine fall.

Tourists may now retrace their steps up the brow of the hill and return through the fields to the high road near **Thornton Hall** for Ingleton (1 m.), or they may, a little above Thornton Force, cross the foot-bridge and ascend the pasture to the right until the lane is entered. Hence by still keeping to the right you reach the **Twisleton farm-house** (refreshments) in proximity to the Beasley Falls in the Dale Glen. The foot-paths will be found defined on the annexed map.

Above Thornton Force, some 200 yards, is **Raven Ray,** a rocky pass in the scars through which the stream from lonely Kingsdale flows, and which the tourist traverses if he wish to reach **Yordas Cave** (3 m.) or Dent (8½ m.).

Twisleton Hall is identified with the manor of Twisleton from an early period. The present building is of no great antiquity, but preserved here are some relics of its past history. One of these is the pedestal of a font bearing the initials TW and date 1619. There has been a **pre-Reformation Chapel** on or near the site of a barn erected below the front entrance to the hall. It is mentioned in the writs of remission of taxation issued by King Edward II. after the battle of Bannockburn in 1314, when this district was ravaged by

the Scots. During the process of building about fifty years ago,
portions of an old pulpit were found, along with several grave-slabs,
but the latter being much worn no record of them was kept. Some,
we are told, were used for flooring the farm-mistals.

Passing behind the Hall you descend to the head of the ravine
where are the **Beasley Falls**. The approach to the uppermost is

BACKSTONE GILL.

highly romantic, being hemmed in by rock and wood, and the water
comes down in flood time close to the path at its base. Descending
high above the rushing stream which courses down the throat of the
narrow glen, the scenery at every turn reveals some spectacle of rare
beauty or grandeur. The water forms a succession of spouts, leaps,

rapids, strids, and eddying pools,—in one place called the **Child's Leap**, the passage is barely twenty inches wide,—and anon it comes splashing and rising and leaping, then sinking and creeping, deserving indeed all the epithets which Southey has heaped on Lodore. For a great part of its way the torrent runs through a rugged channel of upheaved or pillared band of dark Silurian slates, being a prolongation of the slate-bed already noticed at Pecca and Thornton Force. Here and there a wooden bridge spans the chasm high above the surging waters, and from which the spectator can with perfect safety look up and down the wonderful tree-shaded abyss.

The boisterous and confined waters now enter the romantic gorge known as **Backstone Gill**, or Baxen Gill, a lofty straight-walled alley extending nearly 100 yards, through which the darkened stream is ploughed into a double fall. The solid flanks of upreared rock are beautifully bronzed and tinted with various mosses and lichens, and the whole being shrouded in the gloom of impending forest trees, make this indeed one of the grandest and most singular water-passes in the district. Below it is another fine fall and the **Yew Tree Gorge**, which may be viewed by descending a flight of steps on to a grassy promontory, where the valley opens. The view is now expanded to the vision is exceedingly grand,—a vast swell of ancient forest rising skyward from the declivities of the glen opposite, dense, beautiful, and majestic,—a scene, forsooth, that

> "Speaks to man in one eternal hymn,
> Unfading beauty and unyielding power."

A little further on we descend round the lofty old slate-quarries, and close by observe a deep pool where the rocks rise to a great height, a spot associated with a sad and fatal accident that happened in the summer of 1884. A boy was climbing the cliff for wild flowers when he slipped and fell into the deep water, and was drowned in the presence of his young sister who stood helpless on the brink of the pool. The melancholy incident reminds us of Story's pathetic narrative of the boy at Malham Crags, who met with a similar fate—

> She led them to the fatal spot,
> Where still and cold her brother lay,
> And there they found the violet-knot
> That lured his heedless foot astray.

Our path hence leaves the slates and crosses the Craven Fault by the limestone quarries and the rocky Storrs Common. The extensive quarries, worked by the Craven Lime Co., have been the scene of some big blasts. The most notable was that which took place in July, 1875, when 2 tons 4 cwts. of blasting-powder was placed in a chamber worked 27 yards into the solid limestone. The terrific explosion shattered the stupendous cliff into countless fragments, and it is estimated that 40,000 tons of rock were removed. The blast was witnessed by a large number of people, including several gentlemen from a distance.

Ascent of Ingleborough (2373 ft.). We have already described the ascent from Clapham and Newby Cote (*see* p. 156) but the most popular route is that from Ingleton. From here it is three miles to the top, and about three hours should be allowed for the ascent and descent. Our limited space forbids us making more than the briefest allusions to the scenic, scientific, and historic aspects of this the noblest and most renowned of the Yorkshire hills. " Every mountain," says Ruskin, " is a world and may be in itself a living text-book of the sciences." Such, in truth, is Ingleborough, but for full particulars of it we must, for reasons stated, refer the reader to the ten pages devoted to it in our larger work, *The Craven and North-West Yorkshire Highlands.*

Passing through the village you follow the Hawes or Chapel-le-Dale road for about a ¼ m. when the open common is reached. Ascend this a short distance to a walled lane in the corner on the right, which leads direct to the lonely farm-house at Crina Bottom (1100 ft.), whence the summit is seen. The mountain is a familiar landmark to mariners from the Irish Sea ; its high, flat summit and prominent scar rendering its recognition from a distance easy. Snow often lies on some parts of the mountain when many of the trees and shrubs at its foot are in full leaf and flower, in which respect it is no feeble reminder of Moore's apt description of sky-aspiring Lebanon,—

> Its head in wintry grandeur towers,
> And whitens with eternal sleet ;
> While Summer, in a vale of flowers,
> Is sleeping rosy at its feet.

Perhaps the most notable plant that grows on Ingleborough is the beautiful little purple-saxifrage, which fringes the limestone scar near its western summit for a considerable distance. Its small, densely-clustered leaves and delicate purple flowers may often be seen bursting into life and beauty while the snows of winter still linger about the hoary head of the mountain. It is a typical plant of the Swiss mountains, and is found in but few spots in England.

Some years ago a tourist in one of the local inn books put the following amusing query :

> Stupendous mountain, my hi, my hi,
> I never see'd anything half so high ;
> Was it contracted for ? or did it grow ?
> Or was it made out of a volcanoh ?

Geologically there is nothing volcanic about the mountain ; it is built up of strata of purely aqueous origin, ranging through various formations from the Lower Silurian slates and grits upwards to the Millstone Grits of the summit, each separate deposit or series indicating an incalculable era of time. The Great Scar Limestone, which overlies unconformably the Silurian floor, has an average thickness here of about 600 feet, and above this comes the Hardraw Scar Limestone, the Middle Limestone, and the Main Limestone, with intervening shaly bands belonging to the Yoredale series of rocks. Above these is the summit-cap of Millstone Grit.

The **summit** of the mountain is a bare, or grass-covered plateau nearly a mile in circumference, where in former times horse-races were held, being singularly enough the only suitable extent of level ground in the district for many miles round. It has been a prominent beacon-ground from time immemorial, and is particularly mentioned in the writs of instruction issued during the time of the Spanish Armada.   Traces of ancient fortifications were until very recently conspicuous on the summit. One of these consisted of a stout gritstone wall, about 20 feet long, 4 feet wide, and perhaps 12 feet high, ascended by a stone stair, and which no doubt had been used for the purposes of a beacon-fire.   There was also a strong gritstone wall enclosing an area about 15 acres in extent, and containing the foundations of 19 huts, each about 30 feet in diameter. From their shape resembling a horse-shoe they would appear to date from the original Celtic possessors of Ingleborough, for that peculiar form in building was, according to the superstitions of the ancient Britons, intended to secure their inhabitants from the attacks and depredations of enemies. After the conquest of the country by the Romans, the latter would no doubt secure this useful look-out post, as did the Anglo-Saxons and the tribes that succeeded them, such being the importance and strategical value of this isolated and commanding peak.

The **View** is one of the finest to be had in the north of England. It cannot be described as beautiful, for the objects are too scattered and too distant to admit of any high degree of beauty or picturesqueness in situation and arrangement. But in point of extent and romantic interest the view is almost incomparable. Westward the eye compasses a wide expanse of sun-lighted sea, reaching from High Heysham on the south to Cartmel Fells northwards.   The Isle of Man may sometimes be descried. To the north-west the Howgill Fells, above Sedbergh, and the Lake Mountains are visible. Eastwards is Fountains Fell and the whole of Penyghent, while to the south there is a vast extent of country open, including many familiar hills and fells of Lancashire, from the mammoth bulk of Pendle westward to the estuary of the Ribble. Some old authorities maintain that the Flintshire Hills and the Great Ormes Head, on the coast of Wales, are visible, but this must have been in days before the air of South Lancashire became so clouded with smoke.

On the night of Her Majesty's Jubilee (June 21st, 1887) a huge bonfire was kindled on Ingleborough, the illumination of which the writer was able to descry from Rawdon Billing, west of Leeds, a visual distance of 40 miles. Upwards of 60 fires were visible from the tabular summit, ranging chiefly on the south and west from Pendle to Skiddaw.

Ingleton through Chapel-le-Dale to Ribblehead, 6 m. The direct carriage-road to Ribblehead, which may be continued by the mountain-road into Wensleydale, runs between ranges of limestone scars, terraced on either side of the valley at an altitude above the river of 600—1000 feet ; those on the left being called Twisleton Scars, and those on the right, under Ingleborough, Raven Scars,—at one time a well-known haunt of these now rare birds.

Passing **Storrs Hall** there are in its vicinity a couple of recently opened **Caves**. They cannot however be penetrated very far and contain no stalactites. Next we come in sight of the "**Granite Quarries**," as the peculiarly composite stone here is locally called. In the valley deep below courses the mountain Doe or Dale Beck, which nearer Ingleton leaps with snowy breast down the rugged and picturesque ravine described in the preceding route. The lonely **Dale House** is observed down on our left, and some little distance above is **God's Bridge,** so called because it was not fashioned by human hands. It is a long natural bridge of Carboniferous limestone, overlaid with turf, and concealing for a distance of about 200 yards the waters of the Dale Beck. Up the scars on the right, about ½-m. south-east of the mile-stone opposite God's Bridge, and on the low or south side of the long wall which comes straight down this side of Ingleborough, is an immense and fearful-looking rift in the limestone called **Mere Gill**. The gap is about 80 yards long and its depth about 100 feet, nearly half of which is ordinarily in water. A torrent flows through it which is supposed to emerge at the foot of the hill near God's Bridge. South of this chasm is another called **Tatham Wife Hole**. It is 120 yards in circumference and some 50 feet deep, displaying the whole thickness of the Hardraw Scar Limestone situate at an elevation of about 1400 feet above the sea.

Four miles from Ingleton we arrive at the little hamlet of **Chapel-le-Dale**, which like a little Bethoron, walled in by the mountains, is the chief holy-place and "capital" of the chapelry of Ingleton Fells, comprising an area of over 10,000 acres. The retired little house of prayer here, which is the subject of a picturesque description by Southey in *The Doctor*, is a foundation of great antiquity, but the present building is not very old :—

> "God's lowly temple ! place of many prayers !
> Grey is thy roof, and mossy are thy walls,
> And over old green graves thy shadow falls,
> To bless the spot where end all human cares !

> The humble-hearted, and the meek and pure
> Have, by the holy worship of long years,
> Made thee a hallowed place, and many tears,
> Shed in repentance deep, have blessed thy floor.

> Lowly thou art ; but yet when time is set,
> Will He who loved what wicked men despise—
> Who hears the orphan's voice, that up doth rise
> In deep sincerity—not thee forget !"

In 1869 the little building was restored and beautified at a cost of £500. There are some remarkable caves and chasms within a short distance of the chapel. About 80 yards to the north of it is **Hurtle Pot,** a deep, oval opening, which may be descended by a series of steps to the pool which fills the bottom ordinarily to a depth of 25 to 30 feet. When stones are thrown in or during a rapid accession of water, it *hurtles* or rattles against the choked fissures of the limestone, and produces a curious throb-like noise called by the dalesfolk the "Hurtle Pot Boggart." When the clashing waters beneath the impending rocks and trees are viewed in the gloom of evening we are sensibly reminded of the poet Gray's use of the word :

> "Iron sleet of arrowy shower
> Hurtles in the darkened air."

A short distance higher up the glen is **Gingle Pot,** a narrow rift about 80 feet long and on the north side about 50 feet deep. Stones thrown into it produce a peculiar *gingling* sound, as they rattle down its sloping side, hence the name of the Pot. But the most noted, and by many persons regarded as the most singular and picturesque of all the Yorkshire ground-chasms is **Weathercote Cave.** Though not large it is wonderfully formed and quite unique in its way. If in Clapham Cave you have got the "oyster," you have certainly here got the "pearl." It is the gem of the Dale. As it is situated in private property and judiciously protected, a charge of 6d. is made to see it. Immediately on entering the visitor is struck with the strange and forbidding aspects of the grim scene, which are sensibly increased by the deep-toned roar and swirl of the everlasting cataract as it plunges wildly into the contracted abyss below. A descent is made by a rude stair, passing on the right a bridge of two arches. and on the left at the base of the fall, a tremendous rift or chamber about 10 yards in width and 25 yards in length. A further descent of about 60 steps brings the tourist to an angle of the chasm and to the foot of the fall. The water is now seen leaping from a large cavity 33 feet below the surface, and expanding into a misty sheet of bright dissolving particles, drops 75 feet sheer into a stony whirlpool below with deafening noise. Below the point of effluence of the fall is a curiously-suspended rock, shaped somewhat like a sarcophagus. and on this account is called Mahomet's Coffin. When the sun is shining into the chasm towards mid-day, a beautiful iris is formed by the ascending sunlit spray, and it was under such an aspect that the celebrated artists, J. M. W. Turner and W. Westall, painted the striking scene. The water ordinarily escapes by a low, tunnel-shaped cave at the foot of the fall and reappears in the Dale below. In times of heavy flood the chasm has been known to fill to the brim.

Upon emerging from the gloom and uproar of the deep torrent-lashed hole, what a contrast the bright, tranquil scene of the surrounding landscape presents ! Says the poet Story :

> "What calmer, what holier emotions prevail
> In the breast that beholds thee. sweet Chapel-le-Dale !
> And oh ! when I think on the struggle, the strife,
> The pomp, and the pride, and the nonsense of life,
> And know that all ends, when the turmoil is past,
> In the quiet and calm of the churchyard at last,—
> The toils of the learned, and the feats of the brave,
> Seem the vain noise of waters in Weathercote Cave ! "

On the right or west side of the Dale, about half-a-mile from the road is the **Great Douk Cave**, a remarkable subterranean passage of great extent. The entrance lies in a hollow in the third pasture south of the *Hill* inn, and may be discovered by a conspicuous bend in the wall. The explorer enters a long and immense funnel-shaped depression, about 100 feet wide, and enclosed with perpendicular cliffs 60 to 70 feet high. A mountain torrent descends into the cave at its upper end, which is now open over part of its course, as the rocks have fallen in, and issues at the small cascade, near which an entrance may be effected. A small fault is observable in the strata, having a downthrow north of three to four feet, and coinciding with the present stream-bed. On clambering into the cave the tourist encounters an accumulation of water, which soon intercepts the forward path, but this may be avoided by passing through an opening on the right, and proceeding along the rock-strewn gallery, a distance of 70 to 80 yards, a deep, natural shaft will be entered, into which weird, shadow-making daylight streams down from an opening high above. This is **Little Douk Cave.** Beyond, the cavern may be explored for several hundred yards ; in some places it is wide and lofty. reaching a height of 40 to 50 feet, in others it is narrow, long, and water-logged, rendering progress difficult. The explorer should be well equipped with lights, and with shoes and garments that will stand wetting. Towards its upper end the cavern branches into several contracted fissures that run into the desert heart of Ingleborough, at an altitude of about 1700 feet.

A short distance to the south is **Far Douk Cave,** a deep, narrow cavity. too steep and slippery however to be descended with safety. A few hundred yards to the south of this, again, is another huge, dry opening called **Barefoot Wives' Hole** It is 170 yards round and 25 yards deep, exhibiting to a depth of 20 feet below the surface, glacial drift, composed of clay and gravel, and on the south-east side of the Pot are glacial striæ, indicating ice-movement in a south-westerly direction.

The whole of this romantic dale is honeycombed with pot-holes and caverns in great variety, and many of surprising extent. We will now speak of those on the left or east side of the valley. The tourist is recommended to take the cart-road from a gate on the left, about midway between the Chapel-le-Dale Post Office and the *Hill* inn. **Gatekirk Cave** is the first of the series come to, and it may be reached by following the usually dry bed of the river up to its debouchure. The tunnel-shaped entrance is in a wooded gill, and is about 7 feet high, but rapidly increases in area as you proceed. After a freshet the floor of the passage is choked with water, and at all times there are places where the stream spreads or collects into falls and pools, which require adroit stepping. The cavern has several extensive branches (which have never been explored) and the subdued and sullen roar of, doubtless, large cascades may be heard far up in the heart of Whernside. After proceeding about 80 to 100 yards the cave-hunter may conveniently emerge by a circular cleft in the rock to the outer world. Now crossing the pastures in the direction of Whernside you will reach in a few minutes **Bruntscar House**, a pleasant old building, once the home of the Proctor family, whose initials and date, 1689, appear over the doorway. Against the back wall of the house is the entrance to a remarkable **Cave**, a most unusual position it will be thought for the site of a dwelling, but the fact is the existence of the cavern was not known until 1865, or more than two centuries after the house was built. Permission having been obtained you enter the cave by an iron gate, which is kept fastened for the preservation of the stalactites, and you are soon made aware of a copious supply of water running through the cave, and must be prepared for a wetting. Some little distance in there is a fine double cascade, and the roof and walls of the spacious cavern glisten with a variety of large and beautiful encrustations. On reaching the second waterfall the long gallery expands into a fine lofty chamber, appropriately termed the church. Here there is a so-called "organ," which when gently tapped produces a variety of harmonious sounds ; a " belfry " with lengthy suspended " bell-ropes ;" and a " font " brimming over with crystal water ! There are also a variety of other curious resemblances in this large chamber, which may be advantageously lit up with a piece of magnesium wire.

On emerging into daylight the next points of greatest interest are the **Boggart Holes** at Ivescar House, one mile distant. A path along the enclosed fell side leads by Broadrake farm-house to Ivescar. Close to the house, in the face of a picturesque limestone scar, are two entrances, but that on the left, a few yards in, has got dammed up with flood wreck, so that only a small volume of water now emerges from it ; the main stream coming from the opening on the right. On no account should this cave be entered in very wet or unsettled weather, as the increase of water that flows through it is sometimes sudden and prodigious. There are several branch passages, but the main gallery extends about 200 yards. Many years ago a number of silver coins of the reign of Edward I. were washed out of this cave, being in all probability portions of treasure concealed by the natives during the Scottish raids after Bannockburn (A.D. 1314), when the inhabitants of Ingleton, and in fact the whole district, suffered much from these predatory attacks.

Only about a stone's throw above Ivescar is another extensive opening partially concealed by shrubs, called **Browside Cave**. It occupies a depression excavated by a stream flowing down eastwards to the cave. It is not very easy of access and winds about a good deal, yet the seeker after adventure may find some interest tending, perhaps, to develop his bump of discovery, and if not careful his cranium too, by tracing the rapid sinuosities of the cavern.

The tourist at this point has ascended half the height of Whernside, and may reach the summit (2414 feet), or return to the high-road by taking the path through the pastures to Ribblehead (*see* p. 135).

Ingleton to Ease Gill, 1½ m. On the old Clapham road past the cemetery which, by the way, is situate on a thick bed of glacial drift, deeper than the graves. Hence it is a nice walk as far as Jenkin

Beck bridge (1 m). The stream is followed up half-a-mile when the
waterfall is reached. The sloping pastures on the way are strewn
with the pretty, bird's-eye primrose, with its small, mealy leaves
and tiny pink blossoms, likewise the fragrant orchis, the star-like
sandwort, little milkwort, blue-flowered butterwort (one of the few
carnivorous plants found in Britain) with its pale, sticky leaves, and
many another floral gem. The geology of this locality is also
extremely interesting. The **Tow Scar fault,** which originates on
the south-west side of Gragarth, and crosses the Twiss and Doe, just
above the Catleap Fall, continues in a south-easterly direction by
Ease Gill and Slatingber, bringing up the Mountain Limestone
against the shales overlying the Coniston Limestone. In ascending
the beck we approach on the west side a mass of crumbly shale, and
near it a bed of sandstone (apparently of the Yoredale series
occurring high on Ingleborough), while on the opposite or east
side are the Silurian rocks, indicating a total downthrow of at
least 600 feet. **Ease Gill Force** is formed by this great dislocation,
and occupies a secluded angle of the stream, where the wet rocks,
bowered in luxuriant foliage, rise to a height of nearly 50 feet, and
as completely environ the area of the fall as the walls of a hermit's
cell. The water plunges from a height of 27 feet, under a natural
bridge of rock, having a span of 12 feet, and falls with tumultuous
roar into a confined pool beneath. There is another Ease Gill (where
is a waterfall) on the Leck Beck, a few miles north-west of Ingleton,
likewise an Aisgill Force, near Hawes, and Aysgarth Force on the
Yore. This word Ease or Ais is derived from the Gaelic-Celtic *eas,*
ais, meaning a waterfall, names that the above places must have
borne for at least 2000 years.

The tourist who desires to ascend **Ingleborough** from the Ease
Gill waterfall may do so by following the beck upwards, which is a
good guide to the farm-house at Crina Bottom (1 m.) whence the
summit is gained.

On the south-east side of Ease Gill Wood, or about 600 yards
north-east of the present house at **Yarlsber,** there is a circular
Camp, about 90 yards in diameter, and surrounded with the remains
of a foss and vallum, which measures at the top nine yards across.
It is marked on the ordnance maps as "supposed Roman," but it
was in all probability constructed during the Norse invasion, as
explained in the next route.

Ingleton through Kingsdale to Dent, 10 m. To get into
Kingsdale there are several ways. (1) By Broadwood and through
the grand Pecca Falls glen to Thornton Force, whence keeping the
stream on the right, enter the dale road ½ m. above. (2) By the
main road to Dent (9½ m.) from Thornton Church. (3) From
Broadwood there is a path ascends the plantation behind a photo-
studio, and leading through the fields comes out on the main road at
Thornton Hall (*see* Map on p. 167). There are some extraordinary
rifts in the limestone on Gragarth a little above the highway that
traverses the lonely valley. These are **Little Pot,** 12 yards deep ;
Marble Steps Pot, where a small torrent descends a "marble"

staircase for about 50 feet and then plunges into darkness nearly 30 yards further of vertical depth. **Kale Pot** is a large orifice 33 feet deep, with a peculiar cavity in the north corner descending 20 feet further. Higher up the beck course is **Swinto Hole** and Cave, not very easy of access, but it contains a large chamber and waterfall.

Passing through a gate on the turbary road, and close to it on the right is the most awful open fissure on this side of the dale. Indeed we have heard it affirmed that it is the deepest " pot " or ground-chasm in England. It is known as **Rowten** or **Rowantree Hole and Cave,** and is about 30 yards long at the surface, 12 yards at its greatest width, and barely 4 yards at its narrowest. It is densely hung with trees and shrubs, while many ferns and mosses, moistened with continuous vapours that rise from the gloomy vaults below, clothe the rifted walls. At the north end a short ladder enables you to descend the mouth to a narrow platform, from which a further drop lands you among the thick shrubby undergrowth at the brink of the chasm. It is however impossible to explore this cavern without the aid of ropes. The fissure has been descended to an estimated depth of 600 feet, but the party did not reach the bottom ! They came to the verge of a lofty precipice, where in the fitful glare of torch-light a torrent of water was seen to pour with echoing din into the dark and profound abyss.

Following the road into the next allotment we come to **Gingle Pot** (another of this name), which is 30 feet long, 6 feet across the centre, and greatest ascertained depth 146 feet. On going through the gate and proceeding about 200 yards, the road descends and crosses the rocky bed of a mountain burn, which just below disappears in another chasm of some depth. This is **Bull Pot,** the visible depth of which is not more than 40 feet. About ¼ m. beyond, at the foot of the pine plantation, is the famous Yordas Cave, to be presently mentioned.

To return to the dale road, coming from Ingleton about 100 yards beyond the sheep-wash, and the bridgeless beck at the foot of Twisleton Lane, you pass on the right, close under the wall, the **Keld Head,** (Norse, *Keld,* a spring) whence issues the main volume of the Twiss, which forms Thornton Force and the Pecca Falls. The spring comes from under a low breast of limestone, after a subterranean and somewhat precipitous flight of nearly two miles from above Yordas Cave. The pebbly river-bed above the spring is ordinarily dry to near its junction with the Buck and Gaze Gill Becks, two miles higher up the valley. The long flanks of Whernside hem in the valley on the right.

You are now in the old Vikings dale, or **Kingsdale** as it is now called, for this dale and Dent dale, and the country to the west of Whernside, was peopled with piratical Norsemen, who had entered England from the western sea-board and marching inland gradually established themselves among the fells and dales they loved so well. A bold and dauntless race they were, fighting and pillaging in the day-time, and by night gathering round the blazing logs, they sang and quaffed the foaming bowl, honouring their gods by land and by sea, but most their great god Jordas,* who was the genius of the soil they won, and who had guided them through many a difficulty and danger into ultimate possession of this new land.

> They drank to the grand old Jordas,
> Who had lived from days of yore,
> And as soon as the horn was empty
> They remembered one god more !

Our knowledge of this Norse invasion leads us to a probable solution of the oft-discussed name of **Whernside**, which, with the southern prolongation of the Twisleton Scars, formed the original limit or boundary of the Norse settlement. "Twistle," we may observe is a Scandinavian word for "boundary," and Twisleton is the *town*, on the *border* or *boundary ;* it always having been distinct from Ingleton and a separate manor. East of the Whernside range the country had been long in possession of the Anglians, and some might conclude that in the name of Ingleton we have the *town* of the *Angles*. At anyrate such Anglo-Saxon suffixes as *ham, ton, wick,* &c., are pretty thick in the place-names east of Whernside, and lead us to suppose that the Norse irruption created no little alarm to the Anglian possessors of this country, including Ingleborough, always as before explained. an important vantage-ground and look-out post. Whernside would be a kind of " buffer " ridge between the opposing clans, a " warning " or dangerous ground, and would possess some name characteristic of this belonging. Such an identification we find in the Anglo-Saxon word *werian*, to defend, check, or to beware, while *sid*, in the language of the same people, means spacious, broad, great. Thus Whernside, sometimes pronounced Warnside, Wairnside, Wernset. &c., would be the " great warning," or perhaps " great defence," an apt enough name, bearing as we have ventured to surmise an historical rather than a physical meaning. At other times the Danes seem to have encroached on this territory, from the east, and to have maintained their position by the construction of large and strong camps, as elsewhere pointed out, and doubtless amalgamated with the Anglo-Saxons at a later period. Dr. Whitaker tells us in his chapter on Giggleswick, in the *History of Craven*, that " within living memory," fires were lit on the Craven hills every 9th of August (St. Laurence's Eve) as a memorial of the beacon fires (of which Ingleborough was a chief) kindled by the Saxons to alarm their countrymen on the approach of the Danes.

Passing **Braida Garth**, a lonely farm-house (where the guide to Yordas Cave lives) occupying the site of a steading as old as the Norse conquest, you may see a large cairn, locally known as the "**Apronful of Stones,**" but no doubt commemorating or marking the site of burial of some Norse chieftain who fell during a reprisal or fight for possession of this dale. Near the road, some little distance above, is the entrance to **Yordas Cave**, which the Norse

---

* Jordas (pron. Yordas) is the Earth-god of the Norse Sagas, from the Icelandic *jord*, earth.

warriors named in honour of their earth-god, Jordas, as above explained. It is $4\frac{1}{2}$ m. from Ingleton. A descent is made down 13 constructed steps into a level porch-like opening, 7 feet high, and proceeding along an ample passage, a vast and magnificent chamber, of at first unseen proportions, is then entered, the like of which is certainly unrivalled in England. This is the great Hall of Yordas, and the guide mounts a rock, and holding up a bevy of candles at the end of a fifteen-feet pole, reveals something of its grand dimensions. Stone on stone, wall on wall, it rises up to a height of nearly 80 feet, extending westward 190 feet, with an average width of 50 feet. At the north-east corner is a wonderfully-fashioned canopy, supported by wreathed and fluted pillars of pure stalactite, appropriately called the Bishop's Throne. Other resemblances are the Organ and Keyboard, the Belfry, Eagle with outspread wings, Ram's Head, Brown Bear, White Bear crouched on an iceberg, the Gauntlet, Escutcheon, the Ghost, (beware !) and the dead, old genius of the cave,—grim Yordas, in his coat of mail, with mighty frozen arm and clenched fist, raised in seeming defiance of anyone who dared to dispute his sovereignty of these priceless gem-studded halls !

A narrow opening on the left conducts to another smaller apartment called the Chapter House, having a dome-like roof, about 40 feet high, supported with slender, spiral columns, and decorated with exquisite tracery, and numerous depending stalactites. There is a waterfall at the north end which is absorbed by a natural "sink," and rises "never again," or according to a local tradition, "nowhere in this nation."

On the opposite side of the dale, on the scar south-east of Braida Garth, are several minor chasms in the limestone, known respectively as the **Pin Hole**, **Bread Pot**, and **Dungeon Hole**.

The pass is now ascended by the Kingsdale Head House to the summit (1500 ft.), whence the prospect Dentwards is very grand and wild, the Howgill Fells standing out particularly bold on the county border to the north-west. A descent is now made into secluded Deepdale and by the dobbie-haunted **Yallas Gill** to Dent. This is a grand walk or drive from Ingleton at any season of the year.

N

BENTHAM.

FROM Ingleton to Bentham (four miles) there is a good drivable road. "Bonnie Bentham," as the villagers delight to call the picturesque old place, is beginning to compete with other favourite resorts in the Yorkshire Highlands as a summer sojourn for visitors. "Progress" is evidently the watchword of Bentham. To those who do not care for the greater bustle of Ingleton it may well be recommended as a pleasant and most convenient stopping-place. It is on the Leeds and Lancaster main line, is eight miles from Kirkby Lonsdale, and accessible by good drivable roads in every direction. There are several inns, besides two temperance hotels, and a number of private houses where accommodation can be obtained. To the lover of the "gentle craft" we may state there is free fishing in the Wenning and its tributaries.

The place consists in reality of two villages (about a mile apart), viz. : High and Low Bentham, and about midway on the right of the road going from High to Low Bentham, close by the gate which opens into a plot of land called Maryfield, is an old **Plague Stone**. It is an interesting relic of the time when pestilences of a more or less virulent type were much too prevalent in England. In case of any infection breaking out in one or other of the villages of Bentham, isolation was imperative, and persons were forbidden to pass beyond the Plague Stone. The greatest calamities which befel this district and Craven generally, appear to have been in the years 1597 and 1598, and during the great plague of 1665. In the former period the plague would appear to have originated about 1587-8 and to have been lurking more or less virulently about the West Riding for some ten years afterwards. At Dewsbury, for instance, it was so bad in 1593 that it was not considered safe to remove the bodies for ordinary burial for fear of extending the contagion, and people were actually buried in their own houses! (*See* p. 101.)

Passing through the village of Low Bentham you arrive at the substantial **Wenning Bridge** (inn), near the picturesque Rectory and the historic **Parish Church,** one of the handsomest and most interesting old edifices in the district. Founded before the Norman Conquest it is mentioned as a taxable property in the Domesday survey of A.D. 1086. Of the original structure nothing has been saved but a fragment of a Saxon Crucifixion, which for some centuries was concealed beneath a thick coat of plaster in the east wall of the tower. The stone is about 18 inches square, and bears a crude representation of Our Saviour, with a crown of thorns upon His head, and with long, meagre arms and limbs characteristic of the Anglo-Saxon figures of Christ. When the church was restored in 1878 there was found beneath the chancel floor an ancient coffin, with inscribed lid, the tomb, evidently, of the founder of the chancel. Unfortunately the name is missing, and all that remains of the inscription (which is in Latin and in an alphabet of the early part of the 14th century) translated reads : " —— Who made this chancel, on whose soul God have pity." It would appear as if the church had been burned by the Scots after their success at Bannockburn in A.D. 1314, and the chancel rebuilt some little time afterwards.

The church, as stated, was restored in 1878, under direction of Mr. Norman Shaw, R.A., and, thanks to the interest and care of the then rector, the Rev. F. W. Joy, M.A., F.S.A., the above and other relics have been judiciously preserved and arranged. In the east wall of the chancel aisle is a stone corbel of pre-Reformation age, bearing the initials I.B., and which has evidently held a statue of the patron saint, John the Baptist, now lost. An old tombstone bears the arms of the Masons' Company,—a chevron between three castles,—and the motto : " In the Lord is our trust." Another stone, taken out of the river, bears an inscription in raised letters of the middle of the 17th century. The large and beautiful font is especially noteworthy, and is referred to in an article on " Architecture at the Academy " in the *Spectator* of June 7th, 1890. The base is a square supporting a Greek cross, with small half-steps at the angles. The bowl is alabaster of great natural beauty, but quite plain as to

ornament, with the exception of a foliated band slightly
tinged with green near its upper rim. The canopy is of
walnut to match the organ-case and choir-stalls, and consists
of a circular base overhanging the bowl, upon this are planted
six supports, each terminating in a gilded pomegranate, and
very delicately carved with lilies and roses, typical of Purity
and Perfection, which are met within a few inches of their
top by a slab with moulded cornice, which binds all together,
and which forms the groundwork of another tier, composed
of six pinnacles connected by arcading, and also carrying

BENTHAM.

gilded pomegranates. The height of the rim of the font
from the floor level is 4 feet 7 inches, and the total height to
the top of the canopy is 11½ feet.

There are some beautiful stain-glass windows in the
church. The large east window, of five lights, contains scenes
drawn from the life of John the Baptist, the patron saint of
the church. There are various memorial tablets and brasses ;
one of the tablets erected to the memory of the Rev. George
Holden, LL.D., who died in 1793, is interesting as recording

the connection with this parish of a very able divine and scholar. Dr. Holden was a man of varied attainments, and was one of the first who understood the rotations of sea-tides, and by his calculations produced the once popular *Holden's Liverpool Tide Tables.*

In 1872 High Bentham was made a separate ecclesiastical parish, but the Church of St. Margaret here dates from 1837. It is a beautiful edifice in the Early English style and has sittings for 450 persons. There are also in High Bentham a Roman Catholic Chapel and School, a Wesleyan Methodist Chapel and School, and a Meeting House for the Society of Friends. The Day School, rebuilt in 1830, was originally free, being a foundation of William Collingwood in 1726, who also built and endowed the Almshouses. Over the doorway of the school is an old sun-dial, bearing a Latin motto : " Pereunt et Imputantur," which means " They [the hours] perish, and are placed to our account."

Many pleasant walks, drives, and short railway excursions may be had from Bentham. Crossing the Wenning Bridge and following the Wray road a ¼-m., a cart-road on *r.* leads up to **Robert Hall,** now a large farm, but in the days of the Stuart Kings it was a mansion house of considerable note. Here lived the ancient family of Cantsfield, of Cantsfield, in the parish of Tunstall, the last of whom, Mary, daughter and sole heiress of Sir John Cantsfield, was married to Sir Wm. Gerard, Bart. He died in 1721, and the Hall and estate are now the property of the 15th Baronet of this descent. It is traditionally stated that Catherine Parr, the last and surviving wife of King Henry VIII., was a frequent visitor at the old Hall. This is not improbable as her kinsfolk lived in the neighbourhood ; Sir John Neville, Baron Latimer, a member of the noble house of Neville of Raby, Hornby Castle. &c., being Catherine's first husband. Hornby Castle is at no great distance, and neither is Kendal Castle, the old seat of Sir Thomas Parr, where Catherine, his daughter, was born. From Robert Hall it is a nice breezy walk over the moor down to **Wennington,** whence the return to Bentham may be made by the train. Ingleborough and the Westmorland mountains stand out prominently from this high ground.

On a fine day it is a good " tonic " to climb Burn Moor, 2 m. south of Bentham, for a sight of the great boulder known as **Four Stones,** so called because there was once that number. The remaining stone, a huge weather-stained object left by denudation of the encompassing strata, measures 20 yards round, and 12 feet high. From it there is a magnificent view reaching as far as Morecambe Bay and the Lake Mountains. Another delightful walk is to **Waterscale Wood** (1½ miles), where is a curious cave in the sandstone which can be traversed a distance of 160 feet.

INGLETON TO KIRKBY LONSDALE.

IT is a pleasant walk or drive to Kirkby Lonsdale either from Ingleton (seven miles) or Settle, (sixteen miles). On leaving Ingleton the road runs by **Thornton Church,** close to which sacred fane is a very old hostelry, with an elaborately designed stone above the door, bearing the initials and date M.T.W., 1679. The inn formerly bore the name of the *Church Stile,* and being, as its name suggests, but a step from the church, its proximity seems an apt illustration of Byron's well-known lines—

> There's nought, no doubt, so much the spirit calms
> As rum and true religion !

The Church, dedicated to St. Oswald, was with the exception of the 15th century tower, re-built in 1869-70. At the west end of the north arcade three of the original Norman arches, with contemporary embellishments, have been preserved. There are several ancient memorial tablets within the church, one of these to the memory of Ralph Redmayne, Esq., (ob. 1703) bears a somewhat fulsome inscription, beginning—

> Speak Tomb ! can Brass, can Marble die?
> They may, my sweaty Fears reply—
> What then endures ? Goodness alone
> Survives the Brass, the Marble stone.

Under the church-yard wall are the old-time **Stocks** and the **Whipping-Post,** with its rusty wrist-iron, recalling events of unjoyous memory, when felons and other evil-doers were brought hither and publicly flogged.

About two-and-a-half miles from Ingleton, and reached by a lane from Westhouse, is the quiet little village of **Masongill,** which stands high up, just within the Yorkshire border. The old Hall here was the home of the ancient and distinguished family of Waller, long seated in

Buckinghamshire. One of its members was the celebrated court-poet, Edmund Waller, who was born at Colshill in 1605, and at the age of 17 was sent to Parliament. The descent of the Yorkshire branch is through the second son of the poet, also named Edmund, and the Masongill estate, which is but a remnant of the old family possessions, came by inheritance to the late Mr. Nicholas Procter from his great-uncle, Bryan Waller, on condition that he assumed the name and arms of Waller only, which he did by royal warrant in 1816. Mr. Nicholas Waller's only brother was the late eminent and versatile poet, Bryan Waller Procter, better known as " Barry Cornwall,"—the friend and school-companion of Lord Byron,—who died in 1874, aged 85. Minstrelsy appears to have been long hereditary in this family, and the present owner of Masongill, Bryan Charles Waller, Esq., who is a nephew of " Barry Cornwall," and a native of Masongill is himself a poet of excellent repute, and author of several volumes.

A short walk from Masongill is the equally retired little village of **Ireby,** where is Ireby Hall, now called Over Hall, built by the Tathams, a very old genteel family in these parts, whose name occurs in the earliest local records. The last of the Tathams of Over Hall, who was a High Sheriff of Lancashire, lies buried under the south wall of the chancel of the parish church at Thornton. The hall is a sturdy and picturesque-looking mansion, with walls in some places six feet thick, and has a square tower, with open battlements at its north end. On passing through the ancient stone porch, with its heavy oaken door, the Justice Hall is entered. This was once a court-room, and some old oak benches and the justice's table are still preserved here. Anciently it was the great dining hall and had a low ceiling, but many years ago it was thrown open to the rooms above, and has now a railed balcony connecting the same on each side. Col. G. H. Blucher Marton, D.L., of Capernwray Hall, is the present owner of the property.

We now descend by a delightful open road, passing Leck Hill and Leck Villa and then **Leck Hall,** the old seat of the Welch family, whence an umbrageous lane leads by the Leck Schools and the handsome Cowan Bridge Church, built

in 1881. A turn to the left brings us to the pleasant little
village of **Cowan Bridge**, with its memories of the
Brontës. The house where the distinguished novelists were
at school has long been used as a Reading-room and Savings
Bank. Formerly the school-house was used as a bobbin-mill,
and during the construction of the railway here in 1860-1 it
was temporarily converted into a " public," rejoicing in the
sober-suggestive title of the *Cow* inn. But in 1863 it was
again transformed into a private abode. Cowan Bridge is
the " Lowood " of *Jane Eyre*, and readers should consult the
pages of that stirring novel if they would reap the fullest
interest that surrounds this quiet little spot.

High up on Leck Fell are a number of caves and "pots,"
the principal of which lies in a pasture called Fenwick's
Allotment, about a half-mile south of Leck Fell House.
This is **Lost John's Cave**, which can be penetrated
for a considerable distance, but the cave-hunter should take
the precaution to paper-chase his route, or at all events
leave some indication of the passage followed, as several
lateral alleys strike the depths of the mountain on either
hand. The cave has been known for very many years by
the name stated from the fact of two men, both named
John, having been lost the best part of a day (some say
a week) in the cave. They carried candles which were
extinguished simultaneously by a drip from the roof, and
their only box of matches they let fall into a pool of water
while "fumbling" to relight them, and were thus left in
darkness in a remote and unknown part of the cave to pick
their difficult way out !

From Cowan Bridge to Kirkby Lonsdale town it is a
pleasant run of two-and-a-half miles, but the somewhat
distantly-situated railway station is passed in about a mile.
The Lune is crossed by the famous old **Devil's Bridge**
up into the town. The bridge which is built of a very
durable fine-grained sandstone consists of three lofty semi-
circular arches, the span of the outer two being 55 feet each,
and of the central one 28 feet. The apex of the latter rises
4 feet higher than the others, and from the foundations in
the river-bed to the central parapet it is 52 feet. As to who
built the bridge, or concerning the date of its erection, we

have no record.   Legend and tradition, however, (always
acceptable stop-gaps) supply the place of history, and we are
accordingly told of a certain poor woman who wished to
recover her cow, which had strayed at low water to the

DEVIL'S BRIDGE.

opposite side of the then unbridged river.   The King of Evil,
conveniently appearing at the moment she was calling to her
cow, agreed to span the river with a handsome viaduct on
condition that he should have the first living thing that

crossed it.   He knew very well of her husband's coming
home from market and hoped to make good booty.   But the
cunning woman was equal to the occasion, for upon seeing
the approach of her husband on the opposite hill, she ran for
her scraggy, half-starved dog, and letting it sniff a bone,
suddenly tossed the latter over the fine new bridge.   The
dog at once bounding after it, she stepped back, and raising
her fingers in a very vindictive and certainly most un-
becoming manner,—as the story runs,—lustily exclaimed :

> " Now, crafty Sir, the bargain was
> That you should have what first did pass
> Across the bridge,—so now, alas !
> The dog's your right."
> The cheater, cheated, struck with shame,
> Squinted and grinned, then in a flame
> He vanished quite*—

The probability is that the bridge is co-eval with the erection
or re-erection of the church at

KIRKBY LONSDALE

about the time of Henry I., although the first notice of it
appears in a grant of pontage for its repair in the year 1275.
The church was given early in the 12th century to the
monastery of St. Mary's, York, and the monks, as we well
know were famous bridge builders.   In a recess at the east
end of the bridge is a stone pillar, originally a dial-post,
inscribed in front : " Feare God and Honour the King,—
1673," and on the left hand side appears " W . . . N . . .
Constable of Lonsdale Ward."

The Church at Kirkby Lonsdale, dedicated to St. Mary,
is an interesting structure, and it is mentioned in *Domesday*.

---

* The above version reminds us of a somewhat similar story that
attaches to the old castle of Rheingrafstein, on the Nahe.   In this
case the castle is said to have been built by the Devil on condition
that he should have the first person who looked out of the window.
Whereupon a donkey was disguised in priest's vestments and its
cowled and partially concealed head pushed out of the window.
Satan at once jumped at the " catch." but on discovering the
imposture furiously hurled the animal into the river and vanished
in a flame !

It is partly Norman and partly Early English, and was restored in 1866 at the sole cost of the late Earl of Bective. It has a spacious and lofty interior, and contains numerous monuments and exquisite examples of stain-glass.

At the north-east corner of the church-yard a gate opens on to an elevated natural terrace, whence there is a View of surprising beauty. A long sweep of shapely swelling hills, extending as far as the Howgills and Ingleborough, forms a noble panorama, while deep below, in the bosom of a park-like vale flows the gentle Lune, passing the imposing Underley Hall, the seat of Lord Henry Cavendish Bentinck, the rare and extensive scene being, as is aptly described by Mr. Ruskin, "one of the loveliest in England and therefore in the world."

The environs of Kirkby Lonsdale are eminently pictur-esque, and woodland, river-side, and moorland walks invite the visitor on every hand.

INGLETON TO SEDBERGH.

HE road described in the preceding route may be followed as far as Kirkby Lonsdale station (6 m.), whence it runs above Casterton (7½ m.),— on the old Roman thoroughfare from Overborough to Appleby and Carlisle,—the village being almost hidden from view in a lovely dell formed by the murmuring rivulet which courses through its midst. Here is the Clergy Daughters' School, founded originally at Cowan Bridge in 1823 by the Rev. W. Carus Wilson (who is the prototype of the Rev. Mr. Brocklehurst in Charlotte Bronte's novel of *Jane Eyre*), for the education of the daughters of clergy of limited income. There is also a Preparatory Clergy School for orphan children principally. The Church, which dates from 1838, is a beautiful little edifice, and contains some exquisite mural sculptures in marble and Caen-stone. It was restored in 1891.

Barbon (nine miles) is the next place reached, whence a mountain road strikes off to the right in the direction of the romantically-situated Manor House (Sir U. Kay-Shuttleworth, Bart., M.P.) to Dent (seven miles). There is nothing particularly noteworthy for the visitor at Barbon. The village, which has many good houses, possesses a look of general prosperity, though the appearance of the place is somewhat straggling. East of the village rise open rocky fells and easily-accessible heathery moors, laden with ozone and life-giving breezes, and hence we should think capital ground for convalescents and those who need the tonic of unobstructed sunshine and pure air. There are wide and grand views too from these sunny slopes. The round top of Whinfell Beacon is a conspicuous object northwards, 16 miles off, and when sufficiently clear is well seen from the platform of Barbon railway station. There are two churches (the old and the new) standing, curiously, side by side near the station.

The older building dates from 1815, and occupies the site of a church said to have been founded in the 13th century. The new fabric was erected two years ago chiefly through a bequest left for the purpose by Mrs. Eastham and a munificent donation from Sir U. Kay-Shuttleworth, who is lord of the manor. Some fragments of 13th century stonework, from the original church, may be seen in the vestry wall.

Still keeping to the highway we pass **Hawkin Hall,** a characteristic old Stuart mansion built by Dr. Christopher Bainbridge, a native of the place. He was a great scholar and for some time Master of Christ's College, Cambridge. The immortal author of *Paradise Lost*, John Milton, is said to have been one of his pupils, but little significance, we opine, did the worthy Doctor attach to that distinction in his days, for

> Verse in the finest mould of fancy cast
> Was lumber in an age devoid of taste.

Upon a tree-shaded knoll just above the house, and near to the road, is preserved a fine and rare **Roman mile-stone.** It was dug up not far from its present position about fifty years ago. The interesting relic is in the form of a cylinder $5\frac{1}{2}$ feet high and 4 feet in circumference. It is of fine sandstone, ornamented with a diamond pattern on the back, and on the front is incised M P LIII., that is, 53 "Mille Passus," or Roman miles to Carlisle (presumably). Beneath the inscription was added the following by Dr. Lingard, the historian : "Solo Erutum Restitut. Gul. Moore, A.D. MDCCCXXXVI." Mile-stones of such antiquity are now but seldom met with ; most of them having been broken up in ignorance, in past times, for the repair of the roads.

A little further on and we come to **Middleton Church,** a neat edifice erected in 1879 on the site of an older church founded in 1634. Then we pass the beautiful seat of the Moore family, Grimes Hill, which is now the manor-house of the parish of Middleton, and beyond it, close to the railway is the original manor-house **Middleton Hall,** now a farm-house. It has been a large and grand homestead at one time, but it was much battered and reduced during the troublous strife of the Civil Wars, in which the

Middletons, who were then the manorial owners and loyal Catholics, were great sufferers. The large deer park, too, which once surrounded the old house, was during the same stormy period made a complete wreck. But sufficient of the building remains to tell of the former extent and strength of the place. The walls in some parts are nearly seven feet thick, and to the front have been machiolated and the doorway protected with a portcullis. A fine oak-panelled room (now used as a sitting-room) on the south side of the great hall, has an old Latin inscription cut into the oak above the doorway. It reads, VENTURUM EXHORESCO DIEM, [I dread the coming day,] a warning note which one might think needed only the outlined visage of the grim Puritan, Cromwell, to complete its import. On one of the outside stones is inscribed I.M., 1647, doubtless indicating the time when parts of the hall were restored after Cromwell's destructive visit to the neighbourhood. The pastures round about the house nourish some good cattle, and in the Spring-time it is a treat to see one of these fields golden over with daffodils, a sight that would have rejoiced the heart of the poet Keats, who we know wrote his memorable line : " A thing of beauty is a joy for ever," at the sight of a crowd of beautiful daffodils.

About a mile north of Middleton Hall is **Beckside Hall,** notable as the birthplace in 1620 of Sir John Otway, Vice-Chancellor of the Duchy of Lancaster, a great Royalist, and an eminent counsellor during the unsettled times of the Civil War. He died at Ingmire Hall in 1693 and was buried at Sedbergh Church, where a memorial of him may be seen.

Two miles from Sedbergh the picturesque road turns over the Rawthey Bridge. and we quit Westmorland for Yorkshire again. Presently a short lane leads off to the right where we may obtain a peep at the secluded but famous little Friends' Meeting House at **Brigg Flatts,** which is said to be, with one exception, the oldest Quaker establishment in England. It was built in 1675 ; John Ayrey being the prime mover in the matter, and there is a now almost illegible stone bearing his initials and the date 1712, let into the burial-yard wall.

The highway now skirts the beautiful and well-kept park in front of **Ingmire Hall,** the seat of Mrs. Upton-Cottrell-Dormer, who is a descendant of Sir John Otway,

On the Rawthey.

above mentioned. The handsome, castellated mansion occupies a charming site, partly enclosed with fine woods, backed by the lofty, purple heights of Winder, and the more distant, gloom-shrouded precipices of the Howgills.

SEDBERGH

is now at hand, lying within Yorkshire but at the extreme
north-west angle of the county, and at the northernmost point
of the extensive Archdeaconry of Craven, which stretching
from Bradford southwards, includes an area of nearly
600,000 acres.   The little town stands about a mile from
the railway station.   Romantically situated at the outlet of
three main valleys, amid charmingly diversified lowland and
highland scenery, it is one of the best known and most
attractive inland places of resort in our many-acred shire.
Its remoteness from the great centres of industry render it
however not so much visited by day-excursionists as it
otherwise would be.

Sedbergh was included in the great barony of the
Mowbrays, whose chief stronghold in these parts was at
Burton-in-Lonsdale.   The Church, (St. Andrew's) which
underwent a thorough restoration in 1885, was probably
founded by one of the Mowbrays early in the 12th century.
In A.D. 1330 it was appropriated, through the gift of Sir Ralph
Scrope, to Coverham Abbey, and continued to form part of
the endowments of that house until the Dissolution.   The
main constructive design of the church is in Perpendicular
of the 16th century, with some Norman evidences in the
arches and inner doorway at the west end ; Early Pointed
in the south aisle, and Decorated in the west window, with
later additions,—these various successive orders exhibiting
in a remarkable manner an architectural history of fully
five centuries.   The head of the large east window has been
built with a slight but obvious inclination to the north,
designed apparently to symbolise the leaning of the Head
upon the Cross.   There are various monuments of interest
in the interior ; the font and several of them being of the local
Dentdale marble.   One of the tablets is to the memory of
John Dawson, who was born of humble parents at Raygill,
in Garsdale, in 1734, and died in 1820, aged 86.   He was a
shepherd in his youth, but being of a studious turn he applied
himself diligently to mathematics, and ultimately became a
celebrated tutor and trainer of eleven senior wranglers.

The old **Grammar School** at Sedbergh, well-known as one of the best schools in the country, was founded in 1528 by Dr. Roger Lupton, Provost of Eton and Canon of Windsor, whom the great Roger Ascham praised as "a man of pious memory." Among an earlier generation of men of note who have been educated at this school, may be mentioned, Dr. John Barwick (1612-1664), Dean of St. Paul's; Sir John Otway (1620-1693), mentioned above ; Dr. George Mason, Bishop of Sodor and Man ; Dr. Walker King, Bishop of Rochester ; Dr. Wm. Craven, Master of St. John's College, Cambridge ; Dr. Anthony Fothergill, F.R.S. ; Sir Alan Chambre, Kt. (1740-1823), Judge of the Court of Common Pleas ; Prof. Adam Sedgwick, LL.D., F.R.S., the eminent geologist, &c.

Sedbergh was constituted a market-town by royal charter in A.D. 1250. The grant was made by King Henry III. in the 35th year of his reign to Alice, daughter and heiress of Adam de Staveley, who died in 1225. She became the wife of the wealthy lord of Ravensworth, Henry Fitz Ranulph, from whom the Parrs and the Earls of Pembroke and Montgomery are descended. The following is a copy of the original charter, which has not before been printed :

Grant of Market to Sedbergh.
For Alice de Stavel'

The King to the Archbishops &c. greeting. Know ye that we have granted and by this Our charter have confirmed to our beloved Alice de Stavel' that she and her heirs may have for ever a Market every week on Tuesday at her manor of Sedberg in the County of York. And that they may have there a fair every year lasting two days to wit on the vigil and the day of the Nativity of Blessed Mary with all liberties &c. Unless such markets and fairs be to the damage of neighbouring markets and fairs. Wherefore we will &c. Witnesses John Mansell Reeve of Beverley John son of G. Justice of Ireland Ralph son of Nicholas Master W. de Kilkenny Archdeacon of Coventry John de Lexinton Robert de Mustegros Robert Walery Robert de Norreis Walter de Thurkelby and others. Given by Our hand at Windsor XXI. day of May.

An ancient Market Cross, probably as old as the date of this charter, which stood on the north side of the church-yard, was taken down along with the stone steps forming the base, now a good many years since. This is to be regretted, as it was a quaint and characteristic object of interest well worth retaining. The markets are now held every Wednesday. There are no fine "tourist hotels" in the town, but several good inns of the old-fashioned type.

Castle Haw, at the east end of the town, is a large green hill or mound of glacial debris, bearing on its summit evidences of ancient fortifications, and was doubtless the site of the first Celtic possessors of Sedbergh. The Norsemen subsequently held this place and the whole of the valley Dentwards, as previously explained in our account of Dent and Kingsdale (pp. 178—181).

Around Sedbergh the scenery is exceptionally attractive ; from its geological character partaking more of the typical hills and fells of Westmorland than of the Craven Scar country. Approached in every direction by ample and good roads it is within convenient driving distance of the Lake District, Kirkby Lonsdale, Ingleton, and the romantic reaches of Dentdale, Garsdale, and upper Wensleydale. To the pedestrian the rugged uplands of the Howgills and the surrounding fells afford many delightful tramps. One is to **Black Foss**, (4½ miles), near Beck-Houses, a wild waterfall in a deep and gloomy ravine ; another is by the Rawthey side to the well-known **Cautley Spout,** (5 miles), where the water comes down from a height of 800 feet by a series of leaping cascades, and when there is a sufficient volume the scene among the dark weathered crags is sublime. Many uncommon wild plants luxuriate in this locality, amongst them the pretty Alpine Lady's-mantle (its only station in Yorkshire.)

From the Spout there is a rough but practicable route on to the **Calf** (2200 ft.), the highest of the **Howgill Fells,** which we exhort you to climb, in order that you may in the words of Adam Sedgwick, " warm your hearts by gazing over a noble cluster of dales." Northwards, eastwards, and south-wards range the giant tops of the Yorkshire Highlands, with Ingleborough and the Wensleydale heights conspicuous, and many a winsome valley intervening ; westwards are grouped the whole array of the Lake Mountains, with Windermere shining like a mirror in amethystine frame. Many times have we gained the crown of this lofty hill, sometimes in the early morning when the mists still hung low in the valley, at others in the clear evening of summer to behold the sun go down in rosy splendour beyond the towering majesty of Scafell. Standing upon such a spot and viewing these wondrous creations of the Master we cannot but remember that beautiful sentiment of the poet Browning,—

> O ! solemn-beating heart
> Of Nature, I have knowledge that thou art
> Bound unto Man's by cords he cannot sever !

But as we have referred a few pages back to Milton's association with Dr. Bainbridge, of Hawkin Hall, we may fittingly conclude our contemplations of the noble scene from this solitary height by a quotation of the poet's sublime invocation to the great Architect of Nature—

> These are Thy glorious works, Parent of good,
> Almighty, Thine this universal frame,
> Thus wondrous fair ; Thyself how wondrous then !
> Unspeakable, who sitt'st above these Heav'ns
> To us invisible, or dimly seen
> In these Thy lowliest works ; yet these declare
> Thy goodness beyond thought, and pow'r divine.

*　　*　　*　　*

> Ye Mists and Exhalations, that now rise
> From hill or streaming lake, dusky or grey,
> Till the sun paint your fleecy skirts with gold,
> In honour to the world's great Author rise,
> Whether to deck with clouds th' uncoloured sky,
> Or wet the thirsty earth with falling showers,
> Rising or falling, still advance His praise—
> His praise, ye Winds that from four quarters blow,
> Breathe soft or loud ; and wave your tops, ye Pines,
> With every plant, in sign of worship wave.
> Fountains, and ye that warble as ye flow,
> Melodious murmurs, warbling tune His praise.

THE END.

LIST OF DRIVES.

From SKIPTON

To Draughton (3 m.), Addingham (6 m.), Ilkley (9 m.).

To Skibeden (2 m.), Bolton Abbey (6½ m.), Barden Tower (9 m.), Burnsall (12 m.), Rylston (17 m.). Skipton (22 m.).

To Embsay (1½ m.), Barden Tower (6 m.), Bolton Abbey (8½ m.), Skipton (15 m.).

To Gargrave (4 m.), Eshton (5½ m.), Airton (8½ m.), Malham (11 m.).

To Rylston (5 m.), Hetton (6 m.), Flasby (8 m.), Gargrave (10 m.), Skipton (14 m.).

To Rylston (5 m), Grassington (10 m.), Kilnsey Crag (13 m.), Kettlewell (16 m.), Buckden (19 m.).

To Broughton (3 m.), East Marton (5 m.), West Marton (6 m.), Gisburn (10 m.), Sawley Abbey (13½ m.), Gisburn by News-holme to Long Preston (7 m.).

To Broughton (3 m.), Thornton (6 m.), Earby (7 m.), Colne (11 m.).

To Gargrave (4 m.), Cold Coniston (6 m.), Hellifield (9 m.), Long Preston (11 m.).

To Bolton Bridge (6 m.), Blubberhouses (12 m.), Harrogate (21 m.).

From MALHAM

To Bell Busk (5 m.), Gargrave (7½ m.), Skipton (11½ m.).

To Airton (2½ m.), Winterburn (5 m.), Hetton (7 m.), Skipton (13 m.).

To Kirkby Malham (1½ m.), Scaleber Bridge (5½ m.), Settle (7 m.).

To Gordale Bridge (1 m.), Bordley Moor (4 m.), Kilnsey (7 m.), Grassington (10 m.), or Kettlewell (10 m.)

To Streets, Malham Tarn (2½ m.), Stainforth (7½ m.), Settle (10 m.).

From LONG PRESTON or HELLIFIELD

(The distances are given from Long Preston.)

To Otterburn (3½ m.), Airton (5 m.), Malham (7½ m.).

To Otterburn (3½ m.), Airton (5 m.), Winterburn (7½ m.), Hetton (9 m.), Gargrave (13 m.), Hellifield (18 m.), Long Preston (19½ m.).

To Wigglesworth (2 m.), Paythorne (6½ m.), Newsholme (7½ m.), Long Preston (13 m.).

To Wigglesworth (2 m.), Rathmell (4 m.), Giggleswick (7 m.), Settle (8 m.).

To Settle (4¼ m.).

From SETTLE or GIGGLESWICK

(The distances are given from Settle.)

To Ebbing and Flowing Well (2 m.), Austwick (6 m.), Helwith Bridge (9½ m.), Stainforth (11½ m.), Settle (14 m.).

To Stackhouse (1½ m.), Stainforth Force (3 m.), Langcliffe (4½ m.), Settle (6 m.).

To Stainforth (2½ m.), Malham Moor (7 m.), Malham (10 m.), Airton (12¼ m.), Otterburn (14 m.), Long Preston (18 m.), Settle (22½ m.).

To Lawkland (4 m.), Cross Streets (5 m.), and back by the Ebbing and Flowing Well to Settle (9½ m.).

To Stainforth (2½ m.), by the Silverdale Road between Penyghent and Fountains Fell to Litton (12½ m.), Arncliffe (14½ m.), Kilnsey (19 m.), or Kettlewell (20½ m.).

To Horton-in-Ribblesdale (6 m.), Ribblehead (12 m.), Ingleton (18 m.), Clapham (22 m.), and back by the Scars to Settle (28 m.).

To Stainforth (2½ m.), Helwith Bridge (4 m.), Feizor (6 m.), Settle (10 m.).

To Rathmell (4 m.), Wigglesworth (6 m.), Long Preston (8 m.), Settle (12¼ m.).

To Clapham (6 m.), Ingleton (10 m.), Kirkby Lonsdale (17 m.).

To Clapham (6 m.), Bentham (12 m.), Hornby (17 m.), Lancaster (26 m.).

From INGLETON.

To Ribblehead (6 m.), Newby Head (10 m.), Hawes (16 m.).

To Burton (3 m.), Tunstall (6 m.), Kirkby Lonsdale (9½ m.).

To Thornton (1 m.), Cowan Bridge (5 m.), Kirkby Lonsdale (7 m.).

To Cowan Bridge (5 m.), Barbon (9 m.), Sedbergh (16 m.).

To Thornton (1 m.), Yordas Cave (4½ m.), Dent (10 m.)

To Ribblehead (6 m.), Horton-in-Ribblesdale (12 m.), Helwith Bridge (14 m.), Austwick (17½ m.), Clapham (19½ m.), Ingleton (23½ m.).

To Low Bentham (4 m.), Wennington (7 m.), Cantsfield (9 m.), Burton (11 m.), Ingleton (14 m.).

To Burton (3 m.), Melling Station (7 m.), Hornby (9 m.), Lancaster (18 m.).

From SEDBERGH

To Barbon (7 m.), Kirkby Lonsdale (10 m.).

To Dent (5½ m.), Yordas Cave (11 m.), Ingleton (15½ m.).

Through Garsdale to Garsdale Head (Hawes Junction) (9 m.), Hawes (14½ m.).

Through Ravenstonedale to Kirkby Stephen (12 m.).

To Kendal (10 m.), Bowness (18 m.), Ambleside (24 m.).

To Tebay (10 m.), Orton (13 m.), Appleby (22 m.).

APPENDIX.

SOME WILD FLOWERS OF SETTLE AND DISTRICT.

" Better to rove in fields for health unbought
Than fee the doctor for a nasty draught."

Botanical Name.	Common Name.	Where found.

Flowers in January.

Senecio vulgaris . . .	Groundsel . . .	Giggleswick*
Peziza coccinea	Jew's Ear . . .	Ebbing and Flowing Well

February.

Tussilago farfara . . .	Colt's Foot . . .	Clapham Road
Stellaria media	Chickweed . . .	Castlebergh
Saxifraga tridactylites . .	Rue-leaved Saxifrage . . .	Giggleswick
Eriphila vulgaris . . .	Common Whitlow-grass . . .	Riverside, Settle
Galanthus nivalis . . .	Snowdrop . . .	Little Stainforth

March.

Petasites vulgaris . . .	Butterbur . . .	Locks
Potentilla fragariastrum .	Barren Strawberry.	,,
Primula vulgaris . . .	Primrose	Stainforth
Adoxa moschatellina . .	Moschatel . . .	Stackhouse Lane
Ranunculus ficaria . . .	Lesser celandine .	Locks
Caltha palustris	Marsh Marigold .	Oustry Bank
Mercurialis perennis . .	Dog-Mercury . .	,,
Chrysosplenium alternifolium	Golden Saxifrage .	Stainforth
Anemone nemorosa . . .	Wood anemone .	Oustry Bank
Cochlearia officinalis . .	Scurvy-grass . .	Catterick
Alchemilla vulgaris . . .	Lady's mantle . .	Winskill
Oxalis acetosella . . .	Wood-sorrel . .	Watery Lane, Settle

* Only one locality for each plant is given, although it may occur in several.

Botanical Name.	Common Name.	Where found.
April.		
Viola sylvatica	Dog Violet	Stackhouse Woods
Primula Veris	Cowslip	,,
Cardamine hirsuta . . .	Bittercress . . .	Giggleswick
Capsella bursa-pastoris .	Shepherd's purse .	,,
Cardamine pratensis . .	Cuckoo flower . .	,,
Prunus communis . . .	Black thorn . . .	Stackhouse Lane
Ribes Rubrum	Red currants . .	Stackhouse Scars
Ribes Grossularia . . .	Gooseberry . . .	Stackhouse
Equisetum arvense . . .	Horse tail . . .	Locks
Geum rivale	Water avens . .	Stackhouse Lane
Convallaria majalis . .	Lily of the Valley .	Scars, near Settle
Viola Lutea	Mountain Pansy .	Stackhouse Scars
Vinca minor	Periwinkle . . .	Scars, near Settle
Ranunculus acris . . .	Buttercup . . .	Buck Ha' Brow
Ranunculus Auricomus .	Goldielocks . . .	Clapham Road
Scilla Nutans	Hyacinth . . .	Ebbing and Flowing Well
Primula hybrida . . .	Hybrid Oxlip . .	Oustry Bank Wood
Lotus corniculatus . . .	Fingers & thumbs	Clapham Road
Chrysosplenium oppositi-folium	Golden Saxifrage .	Stackhouse Scars
Arabis Hirsuta	Rock cress . . .	Giggleswick
Fragaria Vesca	Wild Strawberry .	,,
Orchis Mascula	Early purple orchis	Ebbing and Flowing Well
Plantaga lanceolata . . .	Ribwort plantain .	Giggleswick
Arum maculatum . . .	Lords and Ladies .	Cave Hole Wood
Allium ursinum	Garlic	,,
Lathrœa Squamaria . .	Great tooth-wort .	,,
Lychnis diurna	Red Campion . .	,,
Sisymbrium Alliaria . .	"Jack by the edge"	,,
Nepeta Glechoma . .	Ground Ivy . .	Feizor
Lamium purpureum . .	Red Deadnettle .	,,
Anthriscus Sylvestris . .	Beaked parsley . .	,,
Myrrhis odorata	Sweet Cicely . .	Giggleswick
Paris quadrifolia . .	Herb-Paris . . .	Oustry Bank Wood
Galium cruciatum . . .	Mugwort . . .	,,
Asperula odorata . .	Woodruff . . .	,,
Valeriana dioica . . .	Marsh Valerian .	,,
Cheiranthus cheiri (rare) .	Wallflower . . .	Castlebergh
Geranium lucidum . . .	Shining Crane's bill	Settle
Symphytum Tuberosum .	Comfrey	Giggleswick
Panicula Europæa . .	Wood Sanicle . .	Oustry Wood Bank
Antennaria dioica . . .	Everlasting . . .	Huntworth
Primula farinosa	Bird's eye primrose	,,

Botanical Name.	Common Name.	Where found.

April—*continued*.

Potentilla tormentilla . .	Tormentil . . .	Huntworth
Stellaria Holostea . . .	Stitchwort . . .	Stackhouse Lane
Polygala vulgaris . .	Milkwort . . .	Clapham Road
Poterium Sanguisorba . .	Salad Burnet . .	Huntworth
Pedicularis sylvatica . .	Lousewort . . .	
Veronica Montana . . .	Mountain speedwell	Cave Hole Wood
Polygonatum multiflorum	Solomon's Seal . .	Near Settle
Trollius Europœus . . .	Globe Flower . .	Oustry Bank
Hippocrepis comosa. . .	Horse shoe Vetch .	Giggleswick

May.

Cratægus oxyacantha .	Hawthorn . . .	Settle
Sisymbrium thaliana . .	Thalecress . . .	Giggleswick
Geranium Robertianum .	Herb Robert . .	Clapham Road
Veronica Chamædrys . .	Speedwell . . .	,,
Hieracium murorum. . .	Wall-hawkweed . .	,,
Myosotis arvensis . . .	Field Scorpion-grass	Mill Hill
Myosotis palustris . . .	True Forget-me-not	,,
Rumex acestosa	Sorrel	Giggleswick
Sinapis nigra	Common Mustard.	Settle
Chenopodium Bonus-Henricus.	Good King Henry.	,,
Ulex Europæus	Gorse	,,
Myosotis Sylvatica . . .	Wood Scorpion-grass	Mill Hill
Cytisus scoparius . . .	Common Broom . .	Settle
Aquilegia vulgaris . . .	Columbine . . .	Near Clapham
Helianthemum Vulgare .	Rock Rose . . .	Clapham Road
Hieracium Pilosella. . .	Mouse - ear Hawk-weed	,,
Lamium purpureum . .	Red dead-nettle .	Mill Hill
Lamium album	White dead-nettle .	,,
Pyrus malus	Crab Apple . . .	Bond Lane
Anchusa Sempervirens. .	Alkanet	Lawkland
Lysimachia nemorum . .	Yellow Pimpernel.	Helwith
Potentilla anserina . . .	Silver Weed . . .	Giggleswick
Polygonum Bistorta. . .	Snake-root . . .	Stackhouse
Trifolium procumbens . .	Hop Trefoil . . .	High Rigg
Linaria Cymbalaria . . .	Ivy-leaved Toad flax	Settle
Vicia sepium	Bush Vetch . . .	High Rigg
Lathyrus macrorrhizus .	Bitter Vetch. . .	,,

Botanical Name.	Common Name.	Where found.

May—*continued.*

Rubus Idæus . . , .	Raspberry , .	Oustry Bank
Pinguicula Vulgaris. . .	Butter Wort . . .	Huntworth
Hieracium Vulgatum . .	Hawkweed . .	Giggleswick
Pyrus Acuparia	Mountain Ash . .	Lawkland
Conopodium denundatum.	Earth nut. . . .	Giggleswick Scars
Chrysanthemum Leucan- themum	Ox-eye.	,,
Orchis Maculata . . .	Spotted orchis .	Oustry Bank
Trifolium minus	Lesser trefoil . .	Giggleswick
Geum urbanum	Wood Avens . .	Oustry Bank
Geum intermedium . . .	Hybrid Geum . .	,,
Chelidonium majus . .	Celandine. . .	Giggleswick
Achillea millefolium . .	Yarrow . . .	,,
Cardamine Amara . .	Large flowered bitter cress . .	Oustry Bank
Meconopsis Cambrica .	Welsh poppy . .	Locks
Ribes nigrum	Black Currant . .	Helwith Moss
Andromeda polifolia .	Marsh andromeda .	,,
Menyanthes trifoliata .	Buckbean . . .	,,
Euphrasia officinale . .	Eyebright . . .	Giggleswick
Geranium pratense . .	Blue crane's bill .	Stainforth
Nasturtium officinale .	Water-cress . . .	Clapham Road
Saxifraga granulata .	Meadow saxifrage .	Malham Cove
Saxifraga hypnoides .	Mossy saxifrage .	,,
Draba incana	Whitlow-grass . .	,,
Draba muralis	Whitlow-grass . .	,,
Lychnis Flos-cuculi . .	Ragged Robin . .	Stackhouse
Listera ovata	Twayblade . . .	Oustry Bank
Galium saxatile	Smooth heath Bed- straw	Giggleswick
Thymus serpyllum . .	Thyme	High Rigg
Stachys sylvatica . .	Hedge Woundwort	,,
Hydrocotyle vulgaris .	Marsh pennywort .	Huntworth
Linum Catharticum .	Purging flax. . .	High Rigg

June.

Barbarea præcox . .	Early winter-cress .	Lawkland
Myrica gale	Bog Myrtle . . .	Lawkland Moss
Vaccinium myrtillus .	Bilberry	High Rigg
Habenaria albida. . .	Small Habenaria .	Giggleswick
Urtica dioica	Great Nettle . .	Stainforth
Veronica Beccabunga .	Brooklime . . .	,,
Rumex acetosa . . .	Sorrel	,,
Rumex acetosella . . .	Sheep's sorrel . .	,,

Botanical Name.	Common Name.	Where found.
	June—*continued.*	
Rhinanthus Christa-galli .	Yellow Rattle . .	Stainforth
Epilobium montanum . .	Willow-herb . .	,,
Conium maculatum . .	Hemlock	,,
Geranium sylvaticum . .	Wood Crane'sbill .	,,
Plantago major	Greater Plantain .	Riverside, Settle
Plantago media	Hoary Plantain .	,,
Cochlearia armoracia .	Horse-radish. . .	Mill Hill
Habenaria conopsea .	Fragrant orchis .	Huntworth
Iris Pseud-acorus . . .	Yellow Flag . . .	Locks
Orchis latifolia	Marsh orchis . .	Helwith Moss
Lathyrus pratensis . . .	Meadow Vetch . .	High Rigg
Trifolium repens	Dutch clover . .	Gildersleets
Rosa canina	Dog-rose	Horton
Sambucus nigra	Elder	Giggleswick
Heracleum sphondylium .	Cow-parsnip . .	Giggleswick Scars
Lotus pilosus	Bird's foot Trefoil.	,,
Genista tinctoria . . .	Dyer's green weed	,,
Melampyrum sylvaticum .	Wood cow-wheat .	,,
Geranium dissectum . .	Jagged-leaved Crane's bill . .	Mill Hill
Saxifraga geum	London-pride . .	Giggleswick Scars
Stachys Betonica . .	Wood-betony . .	,,
Anthyllis vulneraria .	Kidney Vetch . .	,,
Geranium sanguineum . .	Bloody Crane's bill	,,
Arenaria trinervis . .	Three-nerved Sandwort . . .	,,
Viola tricolor	Pansy	Stackhouse
Actæa spicata . , . .	Baneberry . . .	Malham Cove
Urtica urens	Small nettle . . .	Settle
Spirea ulmaria . . .	Meadow-sweet . .	,,
Arenaria serpyllifolia .	Thyme-leaved Sandwort . . .	Giggleswick
Habenaria bifolia . .	Butterfly orchid .	Helwith Moss
Pyrola minor	Lesser winter-green	,,
Pedicularis palustris . .	Marsh Lousewort .	,,
Prunella vulgaris . .	Self-heal	,,
Achillea ptarmica . .	Sneeze-wort. . .	,,
Cnicus palustris . . .	Marsh thistle . .	,,
Campanula rotundifolia .	Hare-bell . . .	Sherwood Brow
Vaccinium oxycoccus . .	Cranberry . . .	Helwith Moss
Potentilla comarum . .	Marsh potentil . .	,,
Erica tetralix	Cross-leaved Heath	,,
Hippuris vulgaris . .	Mare's tail . . .	,,
Lactuca muralis . . .	Ivy-leaved lettuce .	Giggleswick Scars
Ranunculus hederaceus .	,, Crowfoot	Watery Lane

Botanical Name.	Common Name.	Where found.

June—continued.

Botanical Name.	Common Name.	Where found.
Crepis paludosa	Marsh hawks-beard	Watery Lane
Sedum villosum	Hairy stone-crop .	Swarthmoor
Lapsana communis . . .	Nipplewort . . .	Clapham Road
Hieracium murorum . .	Wall-hawkweed .	,,
Hieracium caesium . . .	Wall hawkweed .	Attermire
Ilex aquifolium	Common holly . .	Merebeck
Ranunculus flammula . .	Lesser Spearwort .	Lodge Dingle
Hypochœris radicata . .	Cat's ear	Settle
Scrophularia nodosa . .	Fig-wort	Giggleswick
Epipactis Atro-rubens . .	Helleborine . . .	Glggleswick Scars
Montia fontana	Water-blinks . .	Near Catterick
Symphytum officinale . .	Comfrey	Riverside, Settle
Leontodon hispidus . .	Rough hawk-bit .	High Rigg
Rubus cæsius	Dewberry . . .	Bishop's Weir
Tragopogon pratensis . .	Goat's-beard . .	Long Preston Road
Vicia sativa	Common Vetch .	,,
Viburnum opulus . . .	Guelder-rose . .	High Rigg
Papaver dubium. . . .	Poppy	Settle
Galium aparine	Cleavers	Anley Road
Galium sylvestre . . .	Mountain bed-straw	Giggleswick Scars
Digitalis purpurea . . .	Fox-glove . . .	Lawkland
Thlaspi alpestre	Alpine penny-cress	Attermire
Sagina procumbens . .	Procumbent pearl-wort	Scars
Carduus lanceolatus . .	Spear thistle . .	Attermire
Hieracium Gibsoni . . .	Hawkweed . . .	,,
Polemonium ceruleum .	Jacob's ladder . .	Malham Cove
Orchis incarnata . . .	Marsh orchid . .	Malham Tarn
Centaurea nigra	Black Knapweed .	Clapham Road
Scabiosa columbaria. . .	Small Scabious .	Buck Ha' Brow
Sonchus oleraceus . . .	Sow-thistle . . .	Mill Hill
Thalictrum minus . . .	Lesser meadow-rue	Smearside
Thalictrum saxatile . .	Meadow-rue . . .	,,
Hypericum perforatum .	St. John's wort . .	,,
Rhamnus catharticus . .	Buckthorn . . .	Giggleswick Scars
Potentilla Verna . . .	Spring cinquefoil .	Gordale
Sedum acre	Biting stone-crop .	Malham
Tamus communis . . .	Black Bryony . .	High Rigg
Galium palustre	Water bed-straw .	Lawkland Moss
Valeriana officinalis . .	Great wild valerian	,,
Vicia Cracca	Tufted Vetch . .	Lawkland
Sagina nodosa.	Knotted pearlwort	Huntworth
Epipactis palustris . . .	Marsh Helleborine	,,
Stellaria uliginosa . . .	Bog stitchwort . .	,,
Rubus Fruticosus . . .	Bramble	Lawkland

Botanical Name.	Common Name.	Where found.

July.

Fumaria officinalis . . .	Common Fumitory	Birkbeck Weir
Galium verum	Yellow Bed-straw .	Banks, Settle
Galium mollugo	Great Hedge Bed-straw	Scaleber Road
Carduus crispus	Welted Thistle . .	Birkbeck Weir
Scabiosa arvensis. . . .	Field Scabious . .	Smearset
Potentilla reptans . . .	Creeping Cinque-foil	Feizor
Lonicera Periclymenum .	Honeysuckle . .	Lodge Dingle
Scabiosa succisa	Devil's bit Scabious	,,
Senecio aquaticus . . .	Marsh Ragwort .	,,
Stellaria aquatica . . .	Water Stitchwort .	Watery Lane
Hypericum pulchrum . .	Small St. John's Wort	Lodge Dingle
Alchemilla arvensis. . .	Parsley-Piert . .	Feizor
Achillea Ptarmica . . .	Sneeze-wort . . .	Helwith Moss
Erica cinerea	Fine-leaved Heath	,,
Sonchus arvensis. . . .	Corn Sow-thistle .	Ingleborough
Solanum Dulcamara . .	Bittersweet . . .	Runley Bridge
Narthecium ossifragum .	Bog-Asphodel . .	Helwith Moss
Silene maritima	Sea Campion . .	Moughton
Senecio Jacobœa	Ragwort	Scaleber Road
Hypericum quadrangulum	St. John's Wort .	Watery Lane
Teucrium Scorodonia . .	Wood Germander .	High Rigg
Malva sylvestris	Common Mallow .	Mill Hill
Pyrus Aria	White Beam-tree .	Lawkland
Epilobium palustre . . .	Narrow-leaved Willow Herb . .	High Rigg
Hypericum hirsutum . .	Hairy St. John's Wort	Airton
Circœa lutetiana	Enchanter's night-shade	,,
Carduus nutans	Musk Thistle . .	,,
Aconitum napellus . . .	Monkshood . . .	Malham
Epilobium angustifolium .	Rose-bay Willow Herb	Catterick
Carlina vulgaris	Carline Thistle . .	Winskill
Angelica sylvestris . . .	Wild Angelica . .	Airton
Epilobium hirsutum . .	Great Hairy Willow Herb . . .	Settle
Papaver Rhœas	Common Red Poppy	Hellifield Station
Scophularia aquatica . .	Water Fig-wort. .	Horton
Atriplex patula	Orache	,,

Botanical Name.	Common Name.	Where found.

July—*continued.*

Ligustrum vulgare . . .	Privet	Near Airton
Ægopodium Podagraria .	Gout-weed . . .	Gisburn Road
Saxifraga aizoides . .	Yellow Mountain Saxifrage	Ingleborough
Centaurea Scabiosa . . .	Great Knapweed .	Gordale
Geranium columbinum. .	Long-stalked Crane's-bill	Mill Hill
Melilotus officinalis . . .	Melilot	„
Caucalis Anthriscus. . .		Malham
Arctium minus	Burdock	„
Calamintha Clinopodium .	Wild Basil . . .	Long Preston Road
Origanum vulgare . . .	Marjoram . . .	„
Hypericum montanum. .	Mountain St.John's Wort	Gordale
Æthus cynapium. . .	Fool's Parsley . .	Rathmell Road
Pimpinella Saxifraga . .	Burnet Saxifrage .	Smearset
Sagina nodosa	Knotted Pearlwort	High Rigg
Ononis repens	Rest-Harrow . .	„
Gentiana campestris . .	Field Gentian . .	„
Crepis virens	Smooth Hawk's-beard	„

August.

Sedum Telephium . . .	Orpine Live-long .	Helwith Moss
Drosera rotundifolia . .	Sun-dew	„
Epilobium parviflorum .	Small-flowered Willow Herb	„
Calluna vulgaris	Common Ling . .	„
Galeopsis Tetrahit . . .	Common Hemp-nettle . . .	„
Polygonum Persicaria . .	Spotted persicaria .	„
Arctium majus	Burdock	Sherwood Brow
Apium nodiflorum . . .	Procumbent Apium	Giggleswick
Hieracium boreale . .	Savoy Hawkweed .	Ribble Banks
Stachys palustris. . . .	Marsh Woundwort	Lawkland Moss
Serratula tinctoria . . .	Saw-wort . . .	„
Senecio viscosus . . .	Stinking Groundsel	„
Bartsia odontitis	Red Bartsia . . .	Gildersleets

INDEX.

The figures in heavy type indicate the page where the place is specially described.

A

Aire, source of, 57
Airton, 34, 45
Alum Pot, *see* " Caves "
Animals, Wild, 53, 85, 99, 108, 115, 125, 130, 138, 160
Anley, 90
" Apronful of Stones," 107, 180
Armitstead, 124
Arncliffe, 128
Arten Gill, 141
Attermire Scars, 117
Austwick, 109, 131, 156, **157**
Avalanches, 142
Ayrton, 15, 24

B

Bainbridge, 131
Baines, 16
Bank Newton, 78
Barbon, 192
Barden, 8, 21
Barrows, 73, 85, 128
Barwick, 197
Beacon Coppy, 88
Beasley Falls, 170
Beckside Hall, 194
Becks, smoking, 125
Beecroft, 131
Bell Busk, 39, 41
Bentham, 169, **182**
Bentinck, 191
Birkbeck, 98, 129
Birkwith, 130
Birds, 61, 116, 124, 145
Blake Gill, 141
Blea Moor, 134, 142
Bolton Abbey, 14, 19, 22, 52, 53, 81
Bookilber Farm, 88
Boss Moor, 67

Botany, 13. 25, 29, 44, 62, 101, 127, 130, 136, 138, **172**, Appendix
Bradford, 14, 33, 81, 109, 122, 129, 166, 196
Brayshaw, 97, 105
Brigg Flatts, 194
Bright, 75
Brontë, 188
Broughton, 15
Buckhaw Brow, 109
Burton-in-Lonsdale, 163
Buttertubs, 139
Byles, 109
Byron, 90, 122, 187

C

Calton, 37, 46
Camps, ancient, 36, 70, 77, 88, 108, 112, 128, 178
Cam End, 140
Capelside, 85
Capon Hall, 67
Carr, 96, 98, 105
Casterton, 192
Castleberg, 92
Cat Steps, 111
Catterick Force, 111
Cautley Spout, 198
Caves and Pot Holes:
    Alum Pot, 113, **128**, 130, 157
    Attermire Cave, 88, 116
    Barefoot Wives Hole, 176
    Batty Wife Hole, 136
    Birkwith Cave, 131
    Boggart Holes, 177
    Bread Pot, 181
    Browgill Cave, **139**
    Browside Cave, 177
    Bruntscar Cave, 177
    Bull Pot, 179
    Cave Ha', 119
    Clapham Cave, 151, 153

Caves and Pot Hole s:—*Con.*
Dangerous Cave, 103
Diccan Pot, 129
Douk Gill Cave, 125
Douk Cave, 176
Dove Cote Gill Cave, 146
Dungeon Hole, 181
Elbolton Cave, 25
Far Douk Cave, 176
Gaping Gill, 155, 156
Gatekirk Cave, 176
Gingle Pot, 175, 179
Hackergill Cave, 144
Hellen Pot, 128
Horse-shoe Caves, 88, 116
Hull Pot, 125, 126
Hunt Pot, 125, 127
Hurtle Pot, 174
Ingleborough Cave, 151, 153
Ivescar, Caves, 135
Janet's Cave, 64
Jackdaw Hole, 119, 130
Jingling Hole, 67
Juniper Gulf, 157
Kale Pot, 179
Katnot Hole, 137
Kelcowe Scar Cave, 109
King Scar Cave, 116
Little Pot, 178
Long Kin Holes, 156
Long Churn, 129
Long Close Cave, 68
Lost Johns' Cave, 188
Marble Pot, 157, 178
Mere Gill, 174
Moughton Scar Cave, 132
Nanny Carr Hole, 131
Pin Hole, 181
Rainscar Caves, 136
Rowten Cave, 179
Sel Gill Cave, 130
Skirethorns Cave, 68
Staircase Cave, 103
Storrs Hall Caves, 174
Swinto Hole, 179
Tatham Wife Hole, 174
Thirl Pot, 125, 126
Thund Pot, 125, 127
Turn Dub, 130
Victoria Cave, 99, **113,** 151

Caves and Pot Holes :—*Con.*
Weathercote Cave, 130, 134, 135, 175
Yordas Cave, 169, 180
Celtic Walls, 108, 110
Chapel-le-Dale, 130, 160, 174
Churches, smallest in England, 118
Civil War, 9, 33, 194
Clapdale Hall, 153
Clapham, 147
Clapham family, 79, **99,** 109, 153, 158
Cleatop, 85, 90
Clifford, 7, 8, 23, 48
Coniston Cold, 40
Coulthurst, 32, 39, 90
Coverham Abbey, 196
Cowan Bridge, 188, 192
Cowgill, 142
Cracoe, 16, 25
Craven :
Baths, 14
Cattle, 7, 28
Celts in, 52, 73, 85, 108, 124, 173
Customs, 6, 7, 23, 26, 46, 64, 91, 97, 102, 160, 165
Danes in, 36, 52, 70, 80, 141, 145, 179
Faults, 88, 101, 111, 120, 171
Harriers, 30, 37, 78
Inns, 67, 75, 92, 133, 153
Fish, 59, 125, 146
Mines, 54
Markets, 5, 80, 91, 97, 148, 197
Plagues, 101, 182
Quakers, 119, 142, 194
Romans in, 29, 73, 99, 108, 113, 118, 173
Seven Wonders of, 113, 129
Tales, 16, 67, 75, 79, 87, 99, 103, 158, 189
Turnpikes, 75, 79, 103, 118, 131, 137, 151
Wells, 20, 22, 49, 58, 85, 95
Craven family, 105, 197
Cromwell, 38, 49
Cross streets, 118
Crummack, 118, 132

D

Dawson, 105
Dee Side, 141
Deepdale, 134, 144
Dent, 134, 145
Dent Head, 134, 139, 140
Devil's Bridge, 188
Devonshire, Duke of, 12, 26
Dewhurst, 28
Douk Gill, 125
Dove Cote Gill, 146
Draughton, 20
Druid's Circle, 68, 85,

E

Ease Gill Force, 178
Ebbing and Flowing Well, 95,
    102, 109, 113, 118
Elbolton Cave, 25
Eldroth, 119
Elslack, 15
Embsay, 21
Eshton, 34

F

Fair Rosamond, 7, 11
Faraday, 150
Farrer, 140, 148, 149, 151, 152,
    157
Feizor, 76, **109**, 121, 132, 157
Finchale Priory, 95
Flasby, 19, 30
Flasby Fell, 29, 78
Flintergill, 146
Floods, 142, 168
Foster, 123, 124, 128
Fothergill, 197
Fountains Abbey, 43, 46, 53,
    123, 131
Fountains Fell, 66, 173
Four Stones, 185
Frankland, 87
Friar's Head, 35
Furness Abbey, 35, 37, 103, 131,
    138

G

Gaping Gill, 113, 153
Gargrave, 28, **30**, 64
Gearstones, 131, 134, **136**, 139
Giants' Graves, 128

Geology

Geology, 20, 21, 120, 121, 127,
    132, 135, 139, 159, 166, 172,
    178
Giggleswick, 90, **93**, 112,
    117
— Scars, 100, 118
— Tarn, 90, 103
Gisburn, 17
Gledstone, 18
God's Bridge, 174
Gomersall, 43, 70, 78
Gordale Scar, 52, **59**, 113
Grassington, 14, 23, 67
Gray, 62, 164
Green Haw Moor, 139
Greensett Moss, 136

H

Hamerton, 75, 82, 84
Hanlith, 46
Hanlith Gill, 65
Hardraw Scar, 139
Harrogate, 49
Hartley, 95
Hawes, 131, 139, 178
Hawkin Hall, 193
Heber, 17, 18, 38
Helen Gill, 146
Hellifield, 34, 70, **74**
Hell's Cauldron, 144
Helwith Bridge, 121
Hetton, 26
High Gale, 140
High Gill, 146
Holden, 124, 184
Horton-in-Craven, 14, 18
Horton - in - Ribblesdale,
    89, 112, 120, **122**, 157
Horton Tarn, 130
Howgill Fells, 173, 191, 194,
    198
Howitt, 144
Howson, 98, 99, 123, 128, 196

I

Ibby Peril, 144
Ingleborough, 55, 71, 122, 130,
    133, 155, **172**, 178
— Cave, see "Caves"
Ingleton, 55, 101, 144, **161**

Ingleby, 118, 148, 149, 153
Ingman Lodge, 139
Ingmire Hall, 194
Ireby, 187,

J

Janet's Cave, 64, 67
Jerusalem, Knights of, 41, 75
Jervaulx Abbey, 123, 131
Joy, 183
Jubilee, Her Majesty's, 173

K

Keasden, 148
Kendal, 75, 80, 87, 165
Kettlewell, 128
Kilnsey, 14, 68, 113
King, 47, 197
Kingsdale, 179
Kirkby Fell. 66, 69
Kirkby Lonsdale, 132, 163,
Kirkby Malham, 37, 47

L

Lambert, 28, 37, 38, 49
Langcliffe, 90, 91, **105,** 111
Lawkland, **118,** 148, 158
Lea Gate, 141, 142
Leck, 187
Leeds, 14. 75, 122, 165, 166
Lettsom, 98
Ling Gill, 113, 130, 131, **137**
Linton, 25
Littondale, 128
Locks, 105
Lodore, 61, 168
Long Preston, 44, 76, 79
— Peggy, 83
Long Streams, 87
Lowther, 163
Lunesdale, 160

M

Malham, 26, 46, **50**
— Cove, 55, 63, 113, 125, 155
— Tarn, 58, 63
Manchester Anglers, 125, 130
Marsden, 33
Marton, 17, 49
Masongill, 186

Mauleverer, 52
Metcalfe, 46, 129
Mickle Fell, 133
Middleton, 39, 193
Milton, 193, 198
Montague. 35, 153
Moore, 193
Moorhouse, 16, 20, 24
Morrison, 48, 59. 99
Moughton Fell, 121, 131
Mowbray, 130, 148, 153, 163

N

Nether Lodge, 138
Nevison's Nick, 103
Newby, 137
— Cote, 156
— Head, 135,139
New Houses, 130
New Inn, 126, 130
Newton, Sir Isaac, 25, 105
Nidd Valley, 118
Norber Boulders, 159
Norton Tower, 23

O

Oliver, Gill, 139, 146
Otterburn, 42, **43,** 70
Otley, 37
Otway, 194, 197

P

Paley, 93, 105
Paley Green, 118
Paradise. 78
Parker, 35, 163, 164
Park Fell, 134
Parson's Pulpit, 68
Peake, 116. 124
Pecca Waterfalls, 168
Penyghent, 85, 89, 93, 112, 122,
        125, 138, 160
— Beagles, 127
Percy, 52, 53, 81, 95, 130
Piked Haw, 50, 54
" Pot," meaning of, 128
Preston, 19, 87
Prior Rakes, 53
Proctor, 98, 124

P

R

Railways, highest in England, 120
Rathmell, 85
Raven Ray, 169
Raven Scars, 173
Redmayne, 186
Ribblehead, 131, 133
Rickards, 40, 43, 54
Robert Hall, 185
Robin Proctor's Scar, 160
Roman Mile-stone, 193
Romille, 5, 7, 21
Ruskin, 57, 172, 191
Ryeloaf, 49, 65, 69, 71, 78
Rylstone, 23, **24,** 37, 148

S

Sallay Abbey, 53, 77, 109, 130, 164
Samson's Toe, 113
Scaleber Force, 44, 69, 87, 117
Scarnber Hill, 36
Scosthrop, 45
Scrope, 123
Sedbergh, 143, 196
Sedbusk, 149
Sedgwick, 143, 144, 146, 197
Selside, 128, 135, 157
Semon, 15
Settle, 43, 68, **89,** 158
—and Carlisle Railway, 120, 134
—Plants—*see* APPENDIX.
Seven Wonders of Craven, 113, 129
Sherburne, 84, 85
Shute, 98
Shuttleworth, 157, 192
Simon Fell, 130, 156
Skipton, 5, 165
— Buses, 14
— Castle Woods, 12
— Rock, 13
Skirethorns, 67
Smearside, 108, 110, 128
Snowdon, 55, 133
Spofforth, 81
Stackhouse, 103

Stainford, 96
Stainforth, 109, 110, **112,** 120
— Force, 105, 111
Stainton, 78
Story, 34
Studfold, 121
Sutcliffe, 98
Swaledale, 139
Swinden, 75, 77

T

Tarn Thwaite, 160
Tatham, 187
Tempest, 15, 48, 76, 96
Thorns Gill, 137
Thornton, 186
— Force, 169
Threapland Gill, 25
Trow Gill, 153, 154
Twisleton, 111, 112

V

Victoria Cave, *see* "Caves"

W

Waller, 186
Waterscales Wood, 185
Weathercote Cave, *see* "Caves"
Weatherhead, 139
Weets, 65
Wenning Bridge, 183
Wharfe, 132, 157
Whelpstone Crag, 77
Whernside, 122, **135,** 180
Whitaker, 30, 82, 94, 164
Whittington, 163
Wigglesworth, 76, 84
Wild Share, 87
Wilson, 32, 34, 131
Winshaw, 139, 140
Winskill, 111, 120
Winterburn, 35, 36
Wordsworth, 23, 69

Y

Yallas Gill, 181
Yarlsber, 178
York, 81, 97, 149, 190
Yorke, 157

NEW BOOKS! NEW BOOKS!

. . . . AT THE . . . .

Craven Printing & Stationery Co. Ltd.

DUKE ST. & NEW ST., SETTLE,

Will always be found an attractive

ASSORTMENT OF BOOKS

Suitable for persons of all classes and ages.

Bibles, Prayers, and Church Services in calf, Morocco, and other bindings.

A choice selection of Recherché Books, suitable for Birthday, Wedding, or Christmas Gifts, always in stock.

The Poets, in attractive bindings, at various prices.

Circulating Library, well supplied with New Books for the season.

✤ FANCY GOODS IN GREAT VARIETY, ✤

Including a choice selection of the newest designs in

Fire Screens,
Flower Pot Covers,
Plaques for painting,
Views of Settle and the surrounding district, framed & unmounted
Albums,

Ladies' and Gentlemen's Purses,
Card Cases,
Tourist Cases,
Writing Desks,
Work Baskets & Boxes
Ladies' Companions,

Dressing Cases, &c.
Fancy Note,
Birthday Cards,
Wedding & Congratulation Cards,
Playing Cards,

And a good assortment of New Games.

⊱ BLEAZARD'S ⊰

FAMILY AND

COMMERCIAL HOTEL

And Boarding House,

BANK VIEW, INGLETON,

(One minute's walk from Station).

Pic=nic Parties and Schools

Accommodated on Reasonable Terms.

Two Large Rooms for the accommodation of Large or Small Parties.

CLEAN AND COMFORTABLE APARTMENTS. ✱ ✱

✱ ✱ THREE SITTING AND SEVEN BEDROOMS.

COMMANDS CHARMING PROSPECTS OF DALE SCENERY.

THE CROWN HOTEL, HAWES,

offers good accommodation for Anglers, Tourists, and others visiting the beautiful valley of Wensleydale. Tickets to be had at the above Hotel for the Upper Yore Fishing. For terms, apply to James Fawcett, Proprietor.

SHIP HOTEL,

(NEAR THE POST OFFICE)

SKIPTON.

Proprietor - - M. ACKERNLEY.

Good Commercial & Family Hotel & Posting House.

❦

'BUS TO AND FROM THE STATION.

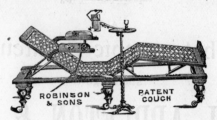

ҺELLIFIELD.

JOHN HOAR,

The People's Warehouse,

GROCER, DRAPER,

— AND —

CORN DEALER.

A Large Stock of Prime Home=fed Bacon and Hams always on hand.

Craven Butter direct from the Farmers, Fresh Eggs, etc.

THE BEST AND CHEAPEST WAREHOUSE IN THE DISTRICT.

♣ **Draught and Bottled Ale and Porter.** ♣

CASKS SUPPLIED.

Orders by post promptly attended to.

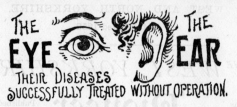

❧ APARTMENTS. ❧

MRS. JOHN HUNT,
> 11, Craven Terrace, SETTLE.

MRS. PARKER,
> 6, Halstead Terrace, SETTLE.

MRS. JAMES BULCOCK,
> 4, Halstead Terrace, SETTLE.

MRS. JOHN RALPH,
> 2, Halstead Terrace, SETTLE.

MRS. JACKSON,
> Croft House, Main Street, High Bentham.

MRS. SWINBANK,
> Ingleborough View, BENTHAM.

MRS. BENTHAM,
> Scar View, INGLETON.

MRS. PARKER,
> Ingleborough View, INGLETON.

MRS. T. BRISCOE,
> New Road, INGLETON.

HELLIFIELD.

CRAVEN HOUSE

Temperance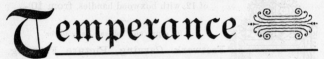

Hotel,

NEAR TO RAILWAY STATION.

The above Hotel is well furnished, and
replete with every comfort.

Tourists and Cyclists will find in this Hotel a

. . *"Home from Home"* . .

for a short or prolonged stay.

Accommodation provided for Horses and Vehicles.

Terms on application to the Proprietors,

J. & E. FELL.

Demy 8vo, cloth, 470 pp. By post, 10s. 6d.
Demy 4to, half roxburgh, superior paper, gilt tops extra, Frontispiece
Plate, 30s. Out of print.

The Craven and North-West Yorkshire Highlands,

BEING A COMPLETE ACCOUNT OF THE

HISTORY, SCENERY, AND ANTIQUITIES

OF THAT ROMANTIC DISTRICT.

BY

HARRY SPEIGHT,

Author of "Nidderdale and the Garden of the Nidd;" "Through Airedale
from Goole to Malham," etc.

WITH ILLUSTRATIONS AND MAP.

SOME PRESS NOTICES.

TIMES.—The title-page is very fully justified by the contents of the
book. With the exception of Whitaker's *History of Craven*, published early in the century, the district has never had a competent
historian, though Sedgwick and his biographers have done not a little
for the local history of Dent. Mr. Speight now supplies the deficiency
in an admirably competent manner.

LEEDS MERCURY —Since Dr. Whitaker's great book we have had
nothing so painstaking and instructive relating to Craven and the
North-West Yorkshire Highlands as is the volume for which we are
indebted to Mr. Speight. It deals with every aspect of the life and
conditions of the country it describes.

BRADFORD OBSERVER.—The work is distinguished by the same
attention to details, and the same grasp of the general theme, which
stamped his *Airedale* as the work of a writer thoroughly imbued
with conscientiousness and literary ability. In neither of these
books will be found that hashing-up of old material which too
frequently characterises the publications of some modern book-makers.

CRAVEN HERALD.—It is no flattery to say that Dr. Whitaker at
the beginning and Mr. Speight at the close of the present century
stand out as the ablest authorities on a district claiming, without fear
of rivalry, to be one of the most romantic in England.

WEST YORKSHIRE PIONEER.—Mr. Speight's researches have supplemented by much new historical matter the writings of Dr. Whitaker,
and we have no hesitation in saying that it is the most complete
account of the history. scenery, and antiquities of the area comprised
which has been published.

LONDON : ELLIOT STOCK, 62, PATERNOSTER ROW, E.C.

MIDLAND RAILWAY.

TOURIST TICKETS

will be issued from May 1st, to October 31st, available for Return on any day up to December 31st, to

INGLETON, APPLEBY, &C.,

From the following Stations:—

STATIONS	Bell Busk for Malham 1 cl*	3 cl*	Settle 1 cl	3 cl	Ingleton, Bentham 1 cl	3 cl	Horton-in-Ribblesdale 1 cl	3 cl	Dent 1 cl	3 cl	Appleby 1 cl	3 cl
FROM												
London (St. Pancras)			61 8	32 3	63 6	33 6	63 4	33 0	66 6	34 6	72 6	38 3
Barnsley	10 6	5 6	15 2	8 0	18 6	9 3	17 8	8 9	21 2	11 3	26 9	14 0
Bath			64 6	31 9	61 10	31 0	66 2	32 9	70 0	37 0	75 4	37 9
Bedford			48 10	25 9	50 9	28 6	51 0	28 0	53 2	29 3	59 8	31 9
Birmingham			38 6	19 3	37 4	19 0	40 2	20 3	44 0	22 9	49 4	25 0
Blackburn			8 7	4 6	11 3	5 9	10 3	5 6			19 7	10 3
Bolton			12 7	6 6	15 3	7 9	14 3	7 6	17 1	9 0	23 7	12 3
Bradford	5 0	2 6	9 0	5 0	11 6	6 3	10 8	5 9	13 4	7 3	19 10	10 9
Bristol			62 0	30 3	60 3	30 0	64 10	32 6	68 8	36 3	74 0	37 9
Burton	20 0	10 0	30 0	15 0	32 0	16 6	35 6	18 3	36 8	19 6	40 10	22 0
Cambridge			52 8	27 0	55 8	28 6	54 4	27 9	60 4	30 3	63 6	32 6
Carlisle			19 0	10 6			17 4	9 0	14 6	8 0	8 2	4 6
Cheltenham			51 8	25 6	50 6	25 0	53 4	26 0	58 10	30 9	62 6	31 6
Chesterfield	16 0	8 0	23 8	13 3	26 8	14 6	25 10	13 3	28 0	15 0	34 6	18 6
Derby	20 0	10 0	30 0	15 0	32 0	16 6	31 8	16 3	34 4	18 3	40 10	22 0
Evesham			50 4	27 0	46 0	23 9	52 0	27 9	54 4	26 8	58 4	30 3
Gloucester			52 8	25 6	50 6	25 0	54 4	26 0	58 10	30 9	63 6	31 6
Godmanchester			50 4	24 0	50 10	25 9	52 2	25 0	54 4	26 8	60 0	30 3
Great Malvern			49 2	24 3	46 9	22 9	50 10	25 0	54 4	26 8	60 0	30 3
Hereford			55 3	28 0	47 0	22 0	56 11	28 6	61 10	31 0	64 6	30 0
Kettering			43 2	23 0	45 0	25 0	45 4	24 0	47 6	26 0	54 0	29 0
Lynn			47 2	24 0	50 2	26 0	48 10	25 0	54 8	28 6	58 8	30 0
Leeds	6 6	3 6	10 6	5 9	13 6	7 3	12 9	6 9	14 10	8 3	21 4	12 0
Leicester	20 0	10 0	36 0	19 0	38 0	21 0	38 0	20 0	40 0	22 0	46 10	25 3
Liverpool			18 4	9 6	21 0	10 6	20 0	10 6			29 4	15 3
Loughboro'	20 0	10 0	33 10	17 3	36 0	19 6	35 6	18 3	37 4	20 3	43 10	23 6
Luton			54 2	29 0	56 0	30 0	56 4	30 0	57 0	31 0	65 0	35 0
Manchester			15 7	8 0	17 2	9 3	17 3	9 0	19 0	10 0	25 6	14 0
Market Harboro'			40 2	21 0	42 0	23 0	42 0	23 0	44 0	24 0	51 0	27 3
Masboro'	13 0	6 6	19 2	10 6	22 6	12 3	21 8	11 0	23 10	13 0	30 4	16 9
Melton Mowbray	20 0	10 0	37 0	19 6	39 6	21 0	38 8	20 6	40 10	22 0	46 10	25 3
Newark			29 6	15 0	35 0	18 0	31 2	16 0	36 2	19 0	42 10	21 6
Normanton	9 6	4 6	16 6	8 7	16 8	8 9	15 2	7 9	17 10	9 0	23 6	13 0
Northampton			45 0	24 0	45 0	25 0	48 6	25 0	49 4	27 0	55 10	28 9
Nottingham	20 0	10 0	31 4	16 0	34 10	17 6	33 0	17 0	36 0	19 0	42 2	22 3
Peterboro'			43 2	22 0	45 0	23 0	46 8	22 9	48 10	24 0	54 0	27 0
Rugby			41 4	21 0	42 0	22 0	43 6	23 0	45 8	25 0	52 2	27 3
St. Albans			56 10	30 0	58 6	31 6	59 0	32 0	61 2	33 0	67 8	36 9
Sheffield	13 0	6 6	20 2	10 0	24 0	12 0	21 10	11 0	24 10	13 9	31 0	16 9
Stamford			41 6	20 0	43 6	22 0	41 10	20 0	47 2	22 9	52 4	26 0
Tamworth			37 10	19 0	33 4	17 0	39 6	20 0	34 0	18 0	44 4	23 9
Walsall, W'hampt'n			38 2	19 6	34 0	16 6	39 10	20 0	41 6	21 3	48 8	24 6
Wellingboro'			45 0	24 0	45 0	25 0	47 2	25 0	49 4	27 0	55 10	29 0
Worcester			45 10	22 9	44 8	21 6	47 6	23 9	51 4	26 9	56 8	29 0

And from other principal Stations, for complete list of which, and full particulars as to break of journey, &c., see **Tourist Programme** inserted in the **Company's Time Tables**, or to be obtained at their **Stations** and **Parcels Receiving Offices** during the period when the Tickets are issued.

* Tickets at these fares are issued on Fridays and Saturdays available for returning on the following Sunday, Monday or Tuesday, for particulars see bills to be obtained at the stations.

Derby, 1895.

GEO. H. TURNER, General Manager.